Wilson's Ghost

Wilson's Ghost

Reducing the Risk of Conflict, Killing, and
Catastrophe in the 21st Century

Robert S. McNamara and
James G. Blight

PublicAffairs

NEW YORK

PublicAffairs books are available at special discounts for bulk purchases in the U.S. by cor-porations, institutions, and other organizations. For more information, please contact the Special Markets Department at The Perseus Books Group, 11 Cambridge Center, Cam-bridge MA 02142, or call (617) 252-5298.

Excerpt from "Little Gidding" in FOUR QUARTETS, copyright 1942 by T.S. Eliot and renewed 1970 by Esme Valerie Eliot, reprinted by permission of Harcourt, Inc. *Faces of the Enemy: Reflections of the Hostile Imagination*, by Sam Keen. Published by Harper & Row (San Francisco) 1986. Reprinted with permission of the author. "Young Dead Soldiers" by Archibald MacLeish originally appeared in the collection *Act Five and Other Poems*, pub-lished in 1948 by Random House.

Book Design by Jenny Dossin.

Library of Congress Cataloging-in-Publication data
McNamara, Robert S., 1916-
Wilson's Ghost: reducing the risk of conflict, killing, and catastrophe in the 21st century / by Robert S. McNamara and James G. Blight
p. cm.
Includes bibliographical references and index.
ISBN 1–891620–89–4
1. Peaceful change (International relations) 2. Security, International. 3. Pacific settlement of international disputes. 4. Disarmament. 5. United States—Foreign relations—1989-
I. Blight, James G. II. Title.
JZ5538 .M36 2001
327.1'7—dc21
2001019182

First Edition
10 9 8 7 6 5 4 3 2 1

. . . This is the use of memory:
For liberation—not less of love but expanding
Of love beyond desire, and so liberation
From the future as well as the past.

T. S. Eliot, "Little Gidding"

Liberalism must be more liberal than ever before, it must even be *radical,* if civilization is to escape the typhoon. . . . I do not hesitate to say that the war we have just been through, though it was shot through with terror of every kind, is not to be compared with the war we would have to face the next time.

Woodrow Wilson, January 1919[1]

Wilsonianism's . . . image of the world was utterly terrifying. . . . Wilson was . . . the first statesman to understand the self-destructive side of modern international relations and to formulate a comprehensive new approach that promised to salvage society's progressive machinery. According to his grim diagnosis, only a radical experimental treatment promised any hope at all for a cure.

Frank Ninkovich, 1999[2]

CONTENTS

I WAS BORN IN 1916 and grew up in San Francisco with the living
memory of the end of the First World War and of President Woodrow
Wilson's pledge that it would be the "war to end all war." Serving on a
U.S. merchant marine ship anchored in Shanghai in 1937, I was an eye-
witness to the outbreak of the Pacific war when the Japanese began their
bombing campaign against China. After three years as a Harvard professor (1940–1943), I served in the Army Air Corps during the Second
World War, moving to the Ford Motor Company in 1946. I resigned as
president of the company in 1960 to accept President Kennedy's request
that I become his secretary of defense. During my seven years in that
office, war between the U.S. and the Soviet Union was a constant threat.
I participated in the agonizing decisions leading to the escalation of the
war in Vietnam. And from 1968 to 1981, while serving as president of the
World Bank, I was personally involved in many areas of the world in
which communal violence and killing threaten to destabilize entire
regions. I saw these and other events "from the inside," as a participant,
and that experience has caused me to reflect on what went wrong in the
20th century that led to such wholesale killing of human beings by other
human beings, and what might be done to prevent its recurrence.

I retired from the World Bank in 1981, having reached age 65. Since
my retirement, I have participated in dozens of research projects involving both academic specialists and practitioners in the issues that have
continued to concern me: reduction of poverty across the globe; and the
three principal issues addressed in *Wilson's Ghost*—risk of Great Power
conflict, communal violence and killing, and risk of nuclear catastrophe.
Among the most important of these research projects have been those
that have been organized by my co-author, James G. Blight. These have

included a five-year investigation of the Cuban missile crisis, involving not only Americans, but also Russians and Cubans, that has yielded important findings leading to the conclusion that the world came within a hair's breadth of nuclear catastrophe in October 1962. In another project, which is still ongoing and has already extended over six years, American and former North Vietnamese officials have held seven meetings, the chief outcome of which has been to identify opportunities that both sides missed to avoid the Vietnam war entirely, or to end it much earlier than was the case, and to draw lessons that apply to the future.

I have for some time wanted to try to draw on my experience to formulate a set of policies to be followed by the United States and other nations across the globe, which would have the objective of avoiding in the 21st century the terrible carnage caused by war in the 20th century.

However, while I have been a practitioner in international affairs, I am by no means a scholar of international relations. I began to realize that my lack of formal training and, to a certain extent, my lack of familiarity with the writing of specialists in the field, would inevitably constrain both the quality of what I wished to write and its reception. I saw this clearly two or three years ago, as I began to draft and redraft an outline of this book. The range of topics, the obviously vast literatures on each of them, and the necessity of connecting the lessons of the past, via the present, to the uncertain future—these began to seem like very daunting tasks for a man in his eighties who hadn't taught full-time at a university since before the Second World War!

With these thoughts in mind, I asked Jim Blight, a research professor at Brown University's Watson Institute for International Studies, and a former colleague of Joseph Nye's at Harvard's Kennedy School of Government, if he would consider working with me on the book. Jim agreed to join me.

We then discussed matters with Peter Osnos, who had previously published my memoir of Vietnam, *In Retrospect: The Tragedy and Lessons of Vietnam,* in 1995, and a subsequent book on which Jim and I had collaborated (with Robert Brigham) as principal authors, *Argument Without End: In Search of Answers to the Vietnam Tragedy,* in 1999. Peter said he was interested in having his firm PublicAffairs publish it. Jim and I, therefore, began to pull together our thoughts and to meet regularly to discuss them. We also hired a very capable research assistant, Dr. Svetlana Savranskaya, an international relations specialist from Emory University, who deployed her considerable research skills to inundate Jim and me regularly with up-to-date material, from a wide variety of sources, on the topics we wished to consider.

A word about the format. This is a jointly written book in every sense, with the exception of occasional passages for which I alone am responsible, and which are clearly marked as such. These insertions derive from my personal experience. I hope they enrich the text by giving our projections of events in the 21st century the benefit of some of my involvement in the 20th with matters of peace and war.

The thoughts Jim Blight and I express in *Wilson's Ghost* are by no means all original with us. Some are very controversial. But it is my hope, and Jim's, that by putting them together in a multipronged program, we will stimulate a debate not only in the United States but in many other parts of the world as well—a debate that can contribute to a more peaceful world for generations to come.

ROBERT S. MCNAMARA

January 2001

Washington, D.C.

A 21st-Century Manifesto

Choose Life over Death

THE 20TH CENTURY WAS, in important respects, a century of tremendous advancement for the human race. In developed countries, life expectancy increased dramatically; literacy became virtually universal; productivity—both industrial and agricultural—reached levels undreamed of previously; and income per capita grew to similarly stunning and unprecedented levels. Even in underdeveloped countries, people's lives began to improve. Despite a tripling of population in underdeveloped countries, income per capita (in 1999 dollars) rose from $200 to $1,240; literacy increased from 25 percent to 74 percent; and average life expectancy rose from 40 to 65 years. In addition, potable drinking water, improved sanitation, better housing, and other infrastructure improvements were introduced in poor areas across the globe. Although much remains to be done to advance the poorest of the poor, in these and other ways, the human race advanced dramatically during the 20th century in its capacity for dealing with many of the causes that brought untold suffering, impairment and early death to human beings throughout all of recorded history.

Yet the 20th century also produced a bloodbath of war and destruction that dwarfed earlier periods, as approximately 160 million human beings were killed in violent conflict. We enter the 21st century, moreover, with the capability of destroying all the gains of the 20th. We are demonstrating radically increased efficiency in killing our fellow human beings in cross-border wars, and in civil and communal conflicts. And there continues to hang over us the risk that whole nations will be destroyed in wars in which weapons of mass destruction are used.

This paradox of the 20th century—our success at saving, lengthening, and improving lives, coexisting with our incapacity to prevent mass slaughter—is epitomized in the life of one of the century's most admired figures, Albert Schweitzer, winner of the 1952 Nobel Peace Prize, physician in rural Africa, musician, scholar, and crusader for saving and improving the lives of his fellow human beings. His philosophy of "reverence for life," which he practiced in Africa, contrasts vividly with the catastrophic events in Schweitzer's native Alsace, on the French-German border. Twice in his lifetime, in the world wars, it became a killing field in which human beings slaughtered one another by the tens of thousands with weapons whose development derived from the same scientific method as the medicine that allowed Schweitzer to save and improve lives in west Africa.

Woodrow Wilson, whose presidency encompassed the whole of the First World War and its immediate aftermath, was one of the first leaders of the 20th century to sense that without radical political changes, the human race might destroy itself in ever greater numbers in what he called metaphorically the "typhoon"—catastrophic wars of ever greater destructiveness. The key requirements to avoid the catastrophe, he believed, were to make a moral priority of reducing the killing, and to take a thoroughly multilateral approach to issues of international security. He failed utterly, however, to implement these objectives. Thereafter, Wilson's ghost haunted the 20th century: in the Second World War, in which 50 million people were killed; in the Cold War, with its nuclear fear and destructive "proxy" wars; and in the countless post–Cold War conflicts that threaten anarchy, death, and destruction.

Why this anomaly? Why has the killing of human beings by other human beings been immune from the overall trend toward achieving longer, more fulfilling lives that characterized so much of the 20th century? We argue that fundamentally, the human race—in particular foreign and defense policy makers of the Great Powers—has not made the prevention of human carnage a central priority. In *Wilson's Ghost*, we describe the basis and implications of making a reduction in carnage a priority—not the only priority, and at times perhaps not even the most important one—but a central priority nonetheless.

In the Old Testament book of Deuteronomy we are told, "I set before you life or death, a blessing or a curse. Choose life then." It has never been more important to reduce the curse of human killing, so that the blessings of life can be enjoyed now, and in the generations to come.

Wilson's Ghost

Armed force is in the background in this program. If the moral force of the world will not suffice, the physical force of the world shall. But that is the last resort, because this is intended as a constitution of peace, not as a League of War. . . . This document [the Covenant of the League of Nations] is a definite guarantee of peace. It is a definite guarantee by word against aggression. It is a definite guarantee against the things which have just come near bringing the whole structure of civilization into ruin.

Woodrow Wilson, address to the Paris Peace Conference, February 14, 1919[1]

Woodrow Wilson's ordeal . . . was a Greek tragedy, not on the stage of imagination, but in the lives of nations.

Herbert Hoover, The Ordeal of Woodrow Wilson, *1958*[2]

Wilson's Tragedy, and Ours

Wilson's Ghost and Our Future

Just as the ghost of Jacob Marley haunted Ebenezer Scrooge in Charles Dickens's *A Christmas Carol*, the ghost of Woodrow Wilson, whose presidency encompassed the whole of the First World War and its immediate aftermath, has haunted world leaders from his day to ours. The message of Wilson's ghost is this: Beware of the blindness and folly that led Europe's leaders into the First World War, a disaster theretofore without compare in world history; and beware of the temptation to believe that sustainable peace will be maintained simply by plotting to achieve an alleged "balance of power" without a strong international organization to enforce it. That message has gone unheeded. Not only did the 20th century become the bloodiest century by far in all of human history, but we enter the 21st century with conflicts breaking out around the globe—so far, largely within states—and with the capacity utterly to destroy ourselves in a nuclear holocaust. In this book, we hold up the Wilsonian tragedy as a historical mirror in order to illuminate our own security risks, and as a stimulus to finding ways to lower those risks.

Paradoxically, the post–First World War era began for Americans with a feeling of supreme optimism, moral conviction, and idealism. Some Americans can still recall vividly the excitement of the moment when, on November 11, 1918—Armistice Day—the combatants in the First World War agreed to lay down their arms and go to Paris to work out a peace treaty. Of course, many were celebrating simply because loved ones could now return home at war's end. But the celebrations all over America were about more than the prospect of family reunions and the return to normal life. For President Wilson had convinced many Americans that Armistice Day represented not merely the end of the most devastating war in world history, but also, in the phrase Wilson made famous, "the war to end all war."

In the ensuing peace conference in Paris, Wilson sought to lay the institutional groundwork for accomplishing what he believed were the two principal prerequisites for enduring peace in the 20th century: "peace without victory," a nonpunitive peace treaty devoted to reconciliation between Germany and its European enemies, England, France, and Italy; and a League of Nations that would have the power to enforce the peace thereafter. Leadership of the League of Nations, he believed, would fall naturally to the Americans because they were relatively disinterested and lacked the cynicism the war engendered in many Europeans. "America," said Wilson, "is the only idealistic nation in the world."[3]

Wilson failed to accomplish these objectives. In the end, Germany was humiliated and embittered by the terms of the Treaty of Versailles, which required not only the ceding of vast tracts of land but also the payment of exorbitant reparations to Germany's European enemies. Wilson's League of Nations, moreover, was rendered nearly irrelevant by America's absence from it, due to Wilson's failure to persuade the U.S. Senate to ratify the treaty creating it. During a cross-country speaking tour in the summer of 1919 on behalf of the treaty, Wilson suffered a stroke, from which he never recovered. The Senate voted down the League shortly thereafter. Thus did his personal tragedy reflect that of his country and the world.

Were this a work of history, it would not only delve into the details of Wilson's failures but would also endeavor to trace the causal links between them and the present moment.[4] But this is not a history, not a book about Woodrow Wilson, not a biography. It is a book about Wilson's ghost or, if you prefer, a book in which Wilson's travail is used as a metaphor for our own. This is a book about the future that takes account of some important lessons of the past century—lessons that, we believe, are most forcefully and relevantly articulated with the assistance of our dark muse, whom we choose to call "Wilson's ghost."

The Imperatives: Moral and Multilateral

The conflicts of the past 100 years have two fundamental messages for us now, as we confront the first century of the new millennium, both of which are derived from the tragedy associated with the First World War and its aftermath, including the Second World War, the Cold War (including the Korean and Vietnam wars), and the brief post–Cold War era. These messages are best conveyed in the form of two "imperatives" that should shape U.S. foreign policy and defense policy in the 21st century. They are:

- The Moral Imperative:
Establish as a major goal of U.S. foreign policy, and indeed of foreign policies across the globe, the avoidance in this century of the carnage—160 million dead—caused by conflict in the 20th century.[5]

- The Multilateral Imperative:
Recognize that the United States must provide leadership to achieve the objective of reduced carnage but, in doing so, it will not apply its economic, political, or military power unilaterally, other than in the unlikely circumstances of a defense of the continental United States, Hawaii, and Alaska.

Wilson, facing the immediate aftermath of the First World War, believed that acting on each of these imperatives was a necessary condition for preventing the world from sliding into ever greater catastrophes. The subsequent bloody history of the 20th century shows that Wilson was right to believe this.

These two imperatives provided the core of his radical program. Updated, they provide the core of our own program. They were so controversial in Wilson's day, however, that he was unable to enact either of them, a failure leading to even greater tragedy later on in the 20th century. We hope to encourage a debate on these imperatives, and related measures—a debate that may lead to success where Wilson failed.

It will be far from easy. Because he sought to establish his postwar foreign policy on a moral imperative—reduction of carnage—Wilson was accused of being a naïve idealist. Senator Frank Brandegee (R-Conn.), for example, said after a meeting with Wilson regarding the peace treaty that he felt "as if I had been wandering with Alice in Wonderland and had tea with the Mad Hatter."[6] David Lloyd George, Great Britain's prime minister and the head of the British delegation to the Paris Peace Conference, wrote in his memoirs: "I really think that at first the idealistic president regarded himself as a missionary whose function it was to rescue the poor European heathen from their age-long worship of false and fiery gods. He was apt to address us in that vein."[7] No doubt Wilson's manner could appear to be naïve and self-righteous. Yet the tragic history of the 20th century that followed strongly suggests that Lloyd George and the other Europeans—self-styled "realists"—might with considerable profit have listened more closely to the "idealist" from America.

Wilson's insistence on multilateral authorization for the application of military force was the most important factor in the Senate's rejection of the League of Nations and, ultimately, of America's failure to join the organization. The multilateral imperative lay at the heart of Wilson's plan to act in accord with the moral imperative of reducing carnage.

In Wilson's day, the principle was this: that the United States, and indeed all members of the League of Nations, must relinquish a significant portion of their sovereignty to the League, which would deal with decisions to apply external military force. Wilson believed that until the power to make war was given over in large part to an international body such as the League, there could be no insurance against the kind of miscalculation, paranoia, suspicion, and error-ridden decision making that had led to the First World War. The security of the members of the League would thus be *collective*. If all of the world's countries joined the League and accepted this condition, then the League would become something like the mother of all alliances, with all protected from all, by all.

Wilson's multilateral imperative was embodied in Article X of the Covenant of the League, which Wilson personally drafted, and which reads as follows:

The members of the League undertake to respect and preserve as against external aggression the territorial integrity and existing political independence of all members of the League. In case of any such aggression, or in case of any threat or danger of such aggression the Council shall advise upon the means by which this obligation shall be fulfilled.[8]

Wilson refused all attempts to delete, or even to amend, this portion of the League of Nations charter. As he told the Senate Foreign Relations Committee on August 19, 1919, "Article X seems to me to constitute the very backbone of the whole covenant. Without it the League would be hardly more than an influential debating society."[9]

Wilson was absolutely convinced that only by means of Article X could decision making on matters of war and peace be democratized. And only by means of Article X would it become clear that seeking unilateral advantage at the expense of others would not be tolerated and would thus, Wilson believed, be significantly deterred. Had Article X been in place in 1914, Wilson believed, the First World War would never have broken out, because Germany, as well as the other powers, could have seen in advance the adverse consequences to themselves of the kind of attack that the Germans ultimately carried out in their invasion of neutral Belgium. Without Article X, he believed, nations and leaders were bound to waver in moments of crisis, when "the will to war is everything," as it had been during the July crisis of 1914.[10] Thus, there must be no unilateral application of military force by any member of the League of Nations against any other member, under penalty of a guaranteed and proportionate military response by the forces of some or all of the other members.

Opposition to the League focused on Article X of its Covenant and was led by Senator Henry Cabot Lodge (R-Mass.), chairman of the Senate Foreign Relations Committee, who believed, correctly, that Article X required an important dilution of American sovereignty. Lodge saw Article X as therefore both unconstitutional and un-American, and he proposed redrafting it as follows:

The United States assumes no obligation to preserve the territorial integrity or political independence of any country or to interfere in controversies between nations . . . under the provisions of Article X . . . unless in any particular case the Congress, which, under the Constitution, has the sole power to declare war or authorize the employment of the military or naval forces of the United States, shall by act or joint resolution so provide.[11]

In other words, the United States would retain its traditional *unilateral imperative*—the preservation of its independence in deciding when, where, and why it would initiate the use of force. Wilson, realizing this, rejected Lodge's version out of hand.

Wilson thus found himself at loggerheads over what he believed was the one absolutely essential feature of the League: its multilateral imperative, embodied in Article X of the Covenant. Without it, Wilson foresaw more catastrophes such as had just concluded in Europe. Feeling his back was to the wall, Wilson embarked on his ill-fated speaking tour of America, as he sought to bring pressure on the Senate by going directly to the American people.

Despite exhaustion and ill health, Wilson was often eloquent in defending the necessity of Article X. "I do not hesitate to say," he declared, "that the war we have just been through, though it was shot through with terror of every kind, is not to be compared with the war we would have to face next time."[12] In St. Louis, Wilson told his listeners that without Article X of the League covenant, and without America's leadership of the organization, "there will come some time, in the vengeful Providence of God, another war in which not a few hundred thousand men from America will have to die, but . . . many millions."[13]

On this crusade, Wilson suffered a stroke, on September 25, 1919, following a speech in Pueblo, Colorado. Neither he, nor Article X of the League Covenant, ever recovered. On November 19, the Senate voted 55–39 not to ratify the treaty without reservations. Wilson would accept no reservations to Article X and the treaty died.

No one can say whether American leadership of the League of Nations could have prevented World War II. Yet surely it would have lowered the likelihood of that bloodbath. But Wilson failed to prevent the punitive actions against Germany that provided the breeding ground for a vengeful Adolf Hitler, while the failure to implement Article X led to exactly the sort of waffling and fudging with the Nazis in the 1930s that forever gave a bad name to the term "appeasement."[14]

Why Wilson? Why Now?

We are far from alone in feeling that as the 21st century dawns, we are being pursued by Wilson's ghost: by Wilson's failure to convince the European allies to base their foreign policy upon the moral imperative of preventing carnage; and by his failure to convince the U.S. Senate to ratify Article X, the embodiment of his multilateral imperative. George Kennan, an early and strident "realist" critic of the "idealist" Wilson, recently recognized, as have others, that the times may have at last caught up with Woodrow Wilson. "I now view Wilson," he wrote in 1991, "as a man who like so many other people of broad vision and acute sensitivities, was ahead of his time and did not live long enough to know that great and commanding relevance many of his ideas would acquire before this century was out."[15] Many other recent observers have also noticed the sudden reemergence to prominence of "Wilsonianism" since the end of the Cold War. Their views are taken up in Chapter One.

Why now, after the Cold War, does Wilson seem so relevant, in important respects almost our contemporary? Fundamentally because Wilson, almost alone in his own day, focused on the all-consuming character of the First World War, on the enormous loss of life it caused, and on the consequent necessity for a comprehensive and radical program to prevent another such catastrophe. This has been called Wilson's "crisis internationalism."[16] The First World War was, for Wilson, what the Cuban missile crisis became for President John F. Kennedy: a clear-eyed look into the abyss of human destructiveness, leading to a steely determination to "make it our business never to pass this way again."[17] With the Cold War over, yet with the fear associated with it still vivid and alarming in our memories, now is the time for a radical approach to reducing the risk of human carnage such as Wilson saw in the First World War, a war that was but the harbinger of history's bloodiest century. This was Wilson's essential message and it is our own.

There are other similarities between Wilson's world and ours. Like Wilson nearly a century ago, we look toward the future after a major transformation of the world political system—for Wilson, the disastrous First World War and the collapse of many of the governments and empires of the Great Powers; for us, the surprisingly quick and nearly bloodless end of the fifty-year Cold War between East and West, the collapse of the Soviet Union and of its empire. Like Wilson, we seek a postwar world built on what we regard as a moral imperative: radically to reduce the carnage of the previous period. For Wilson, again, the objective was to avoid a repetition of the carnage during the four years of the First World War. We, on the other hand, wish to avoid a repetition of the deaths of the tens of millions who were killed in all the wars of the 20th century. Thus we, like Wilson before us, seek to learn the lessons of a tragic history in order to avoid repeating in the future the mistakes made in the past.

Lessons of Wilson's Failure

But can we succeed in the 21st century where Wilson failed in the 20th? We believe we must. But first, we must ask: *Why* did Wilson fail? If we can identify the reasons for his inability to implement his program, then it may be possible to learn from his mistakes, raising the odds of success this time. In the list that follows, we have focused on Wilson's mistakes, or what seem to us to be mistakes, that are especially relevant to the emerging world of the 21st century.

A Moral Imperative Versus Moralism

Wilson was driven powerfully by a moral vision that he had acquired as a young boy, living in Augusta, Georgia, during the Civil War and its aftermath, and which was reinforced by the terrible suffering of the First World War.[18] The vision was this: Create a new system of international relations that would radically reduce the risk of the recurrence of the carnage that occurred in the two epic tragedies of his lifetime. His Presbyterian background got the best of him, however, as he appeared to many to become a condescending and rigid moralizer at the Paris Peace Conference, and in his dealings with the Senate over Article X. He often preferred to preach, not negotiate. He rejected compromise. He belittled those one might classify as "realists"—those consumed by the search for a "balance of power"—rather than engaging them. In this way, he became his own worst enemy, and the opponent of those like his associate, Herbert Hoover, who preferred American participation in a League without Article X, rather than no participation at all.

The lesson: Do not allow attempts to implement a morality-based foreign policy to be frustrated by moralistic self-righteousness. Our own concept of a radical, morality-based foreign policy for the 21st century is analyzed in Chapter One, along with the views of its contemporary skeptics: political "realists," liberals, and isolationists (or minimalists). Its purpose is to stimulate debate rather than to provide the last word on the topic.

A Multilateral Imperative Versus Token Multilateralism

Wilson's League of Nations failed to prevent the Second World War. Why? German expansionism, under the Nazis, was not meaningfully resisted at its outset because of the lack of binding mutual security guarantees between the members of the League. One can speculate whether U.S. participation in the League would have made a difference, given the absence of an enforcement mechanism that Article X of the League Covenant would, in Wilson's view, have provided. As it was, the League became what Wilson feared it might—a debating society of sovereign European unilateralists pretending to be multilateralists. (American unilateralism during the period became isolationist in the absence of any ties to the League.) The Second World War occurred in large part because a way could not be found to convince the major combatants in the First World War to relinquish sovereignty in matters of war and peace, and to commit to a binding collective security arrangement.

The lesson: In the absence of a firm commitment to multilateral decision making, preferably institutionalized in credible international and regional organizations, sustainable peace is illusory. Multilateralism and its skeptics are taken up in Chapters One and Three. We focus on the difficulties with so-called American exceptionalism, and the necessity, as we see it, for radical changes in multilateral security relationships, particularly in the UN Security Council and regional security organizations.

Preventing Versus Risking Great Power Conflict

Despite Herculean efforts, Wilson was unable in Paris to avoid the terribly punitive actions taken against Germany by the European powers, who were intent on revenge, with little or no thought given to the long-term consequences of bringing a Great Power to its knees. The historian John Keegan goes to the heart of the matter:

> The First World War was a tragic and unnecessary conflict. . . . The Second World War, five times more destructive of human life and incalculably more costly in material terms, was the direct outcome of the first. On 18 September 1922, Adolf Hitler, the demobilised front fighter, threw down a challenge to defeated Germany that he would realise seventeen years later: "It cannot be that two million Germans should have fallen in vain. . . . No, we do not pardon, we demand—vengeance!"
>
> The monuments to the vengeance he took stand throughout the continent he devastated.[19]

In a word, Wilson was unable to impart to the leaders of the victorious European powers—France, Britain, and Italy—something he felt strongly: *empathy* for the plight of Germany at war's end, and the possible consequences of treating Germany so punitively, thus raising the risk of another, and even more devastating, Great Power conflict.

The lesson: Empathize with your adversary or risk the kind of miscalculation, misperception, and misjudgment that, among Great Powers, can lead to catastrophic war. We expand on this theme in Chapter Two by considering the possible impact on Russia and China of such issues and events as the war in Kosovo, NATO expansion, U.S. plans to build a national missile defense system, the expansion of the U.S.-Japan Security Treaty, and difficulties regarding Taiwan.

Reducing Versus Inadvertently Encouraging Communal Killing

Wilson was unable to resolve the extraordinarily difficult issues of sovereignty, self-determination, and intervention. Now, at the dawn of the 21st century, these issues have once again come into the foreground, and for much the same reason that they emerged in 1919. An epoch has ended in which many peoples and nations were forced to abide by international borders defined by the Great Powers. Wilson often seemed to promise self-determination wherever it was desired—a view that can easily lead to chaos. Wilson realized, too late, that his eloquent endorsement of the universal right of self-determination was unworkable and dangerous. He did not appreciate the significance of the ethnic diversity, for example, of the territories comprising the former Austro-Hungarian and Ottoman empires. He also did not sufficiently comprehend the depth and historical roots of the suspicion and hatred that many of these national groups felt for one another—factors that would greatly complicate any attempt by outsiders to influence them.

The lesson: The redrawing of national borders, particularly secession and the creation of new states, is likely to be dangerous and destabilizing, and should therefore be attempted only as a last resort, and then only if the new borders do not threaten the neighbors of the states involved. This cluster of problems is taken up in Chapter Three, along with related issues such as what constitutes a war crime, how war crimes can be deterred, and what changes international organizations must make if they hope to reduce communal killing.

The First World War is generally taken to be the first "total war," in the sense that advanced industrial societies used every means at their disposal to annihilate one another. For the first time, air power made a significant difference in war. Tanks were introduced by the British at the battle of the Somme in the summer of 1916 and added, in their way, to the frightful toll of that six-month slaughter. It was not for nothing that Wilson and others often referred to the war as the "Great War for Civilization." So unexpected at its outbreak was the war, so bloody in its execution, so seemingly pointless in its human and material toll, that civilization itself seemed to hang in the balance. At its end, in a cascade of understandable yet blind hopefulness, it became the "war to end all war." Yet the Second World War brought worse devastation and, at its conclusion, the prospect of a future war of even worse, if ever major powers were to engage in a war involving the use of nuclear weapons. It is even possible that the black prophecy of Wilson and his generation could literally come true: Whole nations, even civilization itself, could be destroyed utterly and completely, an eventuality that was never far from the minds of those leaders involved in the Cuban missile crisis of October 1962, the closest the world has come to nuclear war.[20]

A catastrophic nuclear war is indeed possible under present and evolving circumstances, and radical measures are needed to reduce that risk, measures that would allow a rapid and safe return to a nonnuclear world. The problem of avoiding nuclear war, which is the subject of Chapter Four, adds to the urgency of moving in the direction to which Wilson pointed.

Wilson's Tragedy, Again?

Director of postwar food relief in Europe (and later President) Herbert Hoover wrote in 1958 that "Woodrow Wilson's ordeal . . . was a Greek tragedy, not on the stage of imagination, but in the lives of nations."[21] The magnitude of Wilson's tragedy can be measured as the difference between Wilson's aspirations in Paris—to ensure that the conflict just ending was "the war to end all war"—and the horrific history of what historian Robert Conquest has rightly described as "a ravaged century."[22]

We have noted that those who experienced Armistice Day in 1918 were joyful, in part, because they believed they were celebrating the "war to end all war." On that day the American diplomat and historian George Kennan was fourteen years old and witnessed the celebrations in his home city of Milwaukee, Wisconsin. On November 11, 1984, Kennan, at 80 years of age, described decades of having been haunted by Wilson's ghost, when he wrote the following in the pages of the *New York Times*:

> On the 11th of November 1918, there ended that four-year orgy of carnage known at the First World War. When the shooting ceased, some 8.5 million young men lay dead and buried in Flanders Fields or near the other great battlefields of the war. Over 20 million more had been injured—many of them maimed for life. Nearly 8 million were listed as missing or as having been taken prisoner. . . .
>
> And we of this age? How about us? We are now at a distance of sixty-

six years from Armistice Day 1918. We have before us the example not just of that war but of a second one no less destructive and even more unfortunate in its consequences. How fine it would be if it could be said of us that we had pondered these ominous lessons and had set about, in all humility and seriousness, to base our national conduct on a resolve to avoid the bewilderments that drove our fathers and grandfathers to these follies. . . .

If civilization is to survive, these perceptions must come, ultimately, to the governments of all great nations. The question is only: will they come soon enough? The time given to us to make this change is not unlimited. It may be smaller than many of us suppose.[23]

We have written this book in an effort to contribute, in some measure, to raising the odds that civilization will survive in the 21st century, by preventing a repetition of the conflicts of the century just past.

The only question is whether we can refuse the moral leadership that is offered us, whether we shall accept or reject the confidence of the world.

Woodrow Wilson, July 10, 1919[1]

The Wilsonian edifice, its Rooseveltian version of 1945, the Bush coat of fresh paint in 1990, all were undertaken to deal with a world of interstate conflicts. . . . What is now at stake is the very nature of the state. . . . Internationalism thus faces a predicament. First, it needs a set of clear principles to set goals.

Stanley Hoffmann, 1998[2]

1

A Radical Agenda

The U.S. Role in Global Security in the 21st Century

The end of the Cold War ushered in a brief period of optimism about prospects for world peace in the 21st century. Speaking at the United Nations in October 1990, President George Bush welcomed "a partnership whose goals are to increase democracy, increase prosperity, increase the peace, and reduce arms."[3] Three years later President Bill Clinton told the United Nations that "in a new era of peril and opportunity, our overriding purpose must be to expand and strengthen the world's community of market-based democracies."[4] Yet by the beginning of the 21st century, even as America's political, economic, and military power remained unchallenged, such grand pronouncements are seldom made without attached qualifications, ambivalence, and uncertainties. Why? Because throughout the post–Cold War period, brutal war and communal killing on an alarming scale have increased, and the danger of nuclear catastrophe remains ever present. The ghost of Woodrow Wilson, the fear of failing to prevent a postwar catastrophe *again*, has become pervasive. In the following chapters we emphasize that our first responsibility is to reverse these alarming and dangerous global trends. We lay the foundation for a new foreign and defense policy for America and the world based on a moral imperative to reduce deaths from war, and a U.S. commitment to lead the world toward that objective but never to apply its political, economic, or military force unilaterally.

The Great Illusion of the 20th Century

As we look back from the 21st century on the events of the 20th, we cannot help being struck by the enormity of the human carnage, beginning with the First World War. It is in fact difficult to avoid the conclusion that something in the stars must have cursed the 20th century, must have determined that it would be almost uniformly bloody, from beginning to end. And yet, it is useful to recall that at its outset, the 20th century looked to many thoughtful and informed people to hold unlimited promise of peace and prosperity. Witnessing the explosion of technology-driven economic interdependence, some even believed that major war had become obsolete, just as the horse and buggy was becoming obsolete. In retrospect, this belief may have led to a degree of complacency that itself contributed to the onset of the First World War. Dare we, in a subsequent era of burgeoning interdependence, claim that it can't happen again?

By 1910, Europe was enjoying unprecedented growth and prosperity, a circumstance made possible by an equally unprecedented degree of cooperation and integration among the economies of the major nations of Europe, and of the United States. At about this time, many political leaders, intellectuals, industrialists, and ordinary citizens of these countries made what the Oxford historian Niall Ferguson recently called "the greatest *error* of modern history."[5] They reasoned—some consciously, some less so—as follows: First, the new interdependence and cooperation among the Great Powers was necessary for prosperity; second, anything that destroyed these conditions for prosperity would also destroy prosperity itself; third, an outbreak of war involving the Great Powers would certainly disrupt, possibly even destroy, prosperity; fourth, this connection between war and economic disaster was understood by all concerned; therefore, fifth, a major war was unthinkable. The road to the hell that was the First World War was "paved" with this logic: Since war had become economically counterproductive, it would be deterred by awareness of this fact or, in the quite unlikely event of an outbreak of war, hostilities would quickly be terminated, for the same reason.

This line of thinking was formalized in a 1910 best-seller by the British journalist Norman Angell, *The Great Illusion: A Study of the Relation of Military Power to National Advantage*. Angell set out to prove that war had become irrational—not worth the cost—and thus a thing of the past. Angell asked: "What is the real guarantee of the good behavior of one state to another?" His answer: "It is the elaborate interdependence which, not only in the economic sense, but in every sense, makes an unwarrantable aggression of one state upon another react upon the interests of the aggressor."[6] Because war no longer made sense, Angell said, "the day for progress by force has passed; it will be progress by ideas or not at all."[7] Speaking two years after the publication of *The Great Illusion*, Angell drew this conclusion: "Morality after all is not founded on self-sacrifice, but upon enlightened self-interest, a clearer and more complete understanding of all the ties that bind us the one to the other. And such understanding is bound to improve."[8] The Americans were far from immune from this quaint but deadly complacency. David Starr Jordan, the president of Stanford University, said in a 1910 speech at Tufts University that "future war is impossible because the nations cannot afford it."[9]

Not everyone was convinced. In his 1910 essay "The Moral Equivalent of War," the American philosopher William James admitted that "modern war is so expensive that we feel trade to be a better avenue to plunder," but, he added, "modern man inherits all the innate pugnacity and all the love of glory of his ancestors. Showing war's irrationality and horror is of no effect on him. The horrors make the fascination."[10] James's remark is an almost clairvoyant description of events all over the British isles in August 1914, when young men by the hundreds of thousands, laughing and carrying on as if on their way to a sporting event or a picnic, deluged conscription centers in an effort to be among the first to fight.

The "great illusion" Norman Angell set out to debunk in 1910 was the outmoded belief, as he saw it, that any economic or other advantage derives from military conquest. Having proved this to his satisfaction, and to the satisfaction of his many readers, he concluded that war had become an absurdity and *therefore* wildly improbable. This was the great illusion of the 20th century. It would be refuted four years after the appearance of Angell's book by the First World War, and again by the Second World War and the Cold War, which followed in its wake.

The Tragic Reality of the 20th Century

In reality, the 20th century became the bloodiest by far in all of human history. How bloody was it? The available statistics, while helpful in comparative terms, are often wildly erroneous in literal terms. Before listing some of the estimates, therefore, it is necessary to convey the warning given by Dan Smith, director of the International Peace Research Institute in Oslo, Norway (PRIO), whose atlas, *The State of War and Peace,* is a leading reference on war deaths and related issues:

> Data on war deaths are supremely unreliable. Among the reasons for this are the propaganda needs of the contending sides. In most wars, there is no agency whose task it is to count the civilian dead who constitute the vast majority of war fatalities. . . . Estimates are not factual but human and political. The issue is not about statistics. Putting a figure to the number of deaths [is] simply a shorthand from which the horror of what was happening could be easily understood.[11]

Almost anyone who is motivated to count war dead, therefore, and who is in a position to do so, is also likely to be a partisan of one side or another in an ongoing war. The issuance of so-called data on war dead is often little more than carrying on the war by statistical means. That said, it is worthwhile considering some estimates from people who make it their business to sift through the numbers, taking the biases into account as best they can.

What is a war? The PRIO group defines it as: "an open armed conflict about power or territory, involving centrally organized fighters and fighting with continuity between clashes."[12] On the number of such wars in the 20th century (through 1995, the last date for which the data are regarded as reasonably comprehensive), one widely cited estimate identifies, between 1900 and 1995, 83 interstate wars and 135 intrastate wars, for a total of 218 wars. This is compared with 102 interstate wars, 69 intrastate wars, and a total of 171 wars between 1816 and 1899.[13] And war became much more lethal in the 20th century than in previous eras; in fact, it has been estimated that in the 20th century there were "six times as many deaths per war as in the 19th."[14] In total, it appears that something on the order of 110 million people died due to wars between 1900 and 1995. One often-cited source, Ruth Leger Sivard's *World Military and Social Expenditures,* fixes the number of war deaths at (a curiously precise) 109,746,000.[15]

Indicative of the changing nature of war are the rates at which civilians have been victimized. One source breaks down an estimated 105 million killed in 20th-century wars into 43 million military dead and 62 million civilian dead.[16] Another estimates that whereas at the end of the 19th century, approximately 10 percent of war deaths were civilians, 50 percent were civilians in the Second World War, and 75 percent were civilians in the wars fought in the 1990s.[17] From all these estimates, it is clear that in the 20th century, war was a common occurrence, it was increasingly lethal, and its toll fell primarily on civilians—noncombatants, the elderly, women, and children.

The 20th century was not just history's bloodiest century but also the century in which noncombatant immunity—long held in the West to be a requirement of a "just" war—virtually ceased to operate. German journalist and scholar Josef Joffe recently gave this epitaph to the 20th century:

How will we remember the 20th century? First and foremost, it was the century of the Three T's: total war, totalitarianism and terror. . . . In the 18th and 19th centuries, enemies were defeated; in the 20th, they were exterminated in [places like] Auschwitz or in the killing fields of Cambodia.[18]

This applies equally to the roughly 140,000 people who died instantly at Hiroshima on August 6, 1945, and to the victims of the systematic terror inflicted over decades by Stalin and Mao on their own people.[19] No one knows how many died in the Stalinist purges and forced removals of the 1920s and 1930s, or how many died due to famines associated with Mao's Great Leap Forward initiatives and from the chaos of the Cultural

Revolution. (The number usually cited is 20 million in each country.) Suffice it to say that millions died due to Stalinist and Maoist cruelty and mistakes.

It is obvious that whatever one fixes as the number killed in war and domestic conflict in the 20th century, the number must be understood as indicating only the approximate level of magnitude of the tragedy. No matter how the total is broken down, there can be nothing approaching numerical precision regarding any of the constituent numbers.

But if approximately 110 million died in war from 1900 through 1995; and if 20 million each died due to the brutal policies of Stalin and Mao; and if approximately 10 million died in war, or for reasons related to war, between 1995 and 2000 (a figure commonly used), we arrive at the figure of 160 million killed in conflict—including interstate and intrastate conflict. We believe this figure—160 million war and war-related deaths—is a useful approximation that illustrates the level of violence in the century just ended.

As we have indicated, most of these 160 million or so would have been civilians. How many? If we add the 60 million civilians we calculate were killed in war to the estimated 40 million who died due to Stalin's and Mao's ideologically driven internal violence, on the order of 100 million of the 160 million killed due to violence and war in the 20th century were innocent civilians—an appalling statistic. Whatever the actual numbers may have been, there can be no dissent from the assessment of the 1997 report of the Carnegie Commission on Preventing Deadly Conflict: those numbers we can derive, however imperfectly, tell a tale of "mass violence on a scale that dwarfs all previous centuries."[20]

The trend toward civilian victimization due to war is continuing. An illustration of this is reported in a June 2000 epidemiological study of the conflict in the Democratic Republic of the Congo (formerly Zaire). The study estimated that "since January 1, 1999, there have been at least 1.6 million deaths in war-affected areas, over and above the 600,000 deaths that would have occurred in normal times." Approximately 15 percent of the deaths seem directly attributable to the various wars underway. "The rest," according to the report, "resulted from . . . preventable or curable diseases that have proliferated amid the social and economic chaos caused by the war, with most in the latter group being women and small children."[21] The wholesale slaughter of innocents that became the grisly hallmark of the 20th century thus continues into the 21st.

While the numbers permit an appreciation of the scale of the tragedy, they can also be mind-numbing: so many wars, so many millions of dead, so many tragic cases. But numbers of course cover only those aspects of the horror of the 20th century that can be quantified, however roughly and unreliably. Poets, novelists, memoirists, playwrights, painters, photographers, and filmmakers are left to convey as best they can the *human* tragedy as it has occurred, human being by human being. Alongside the numbers, we need to consider individualized records of the colossal tragedy of 20th-century violence and war. We need to think about the Cambodian women who are blind, but who have no known organic defect, and are assumed to have witnessed horrors so unspeakable that physical blindness resulted as a protective mechanism.[22] We need to meditate on the moment in William Styron's novel *Sophie's Choice*, when Sophie arrives at a concentration camp and is forced by a Nazi prison guard to decide, then and there, which of her two children shall live and which shall be killed by the Nazis.[23] We need to stare for a while at the recent photographs taken by James Nachtwey of the victims of torture in the wars in West Africa and elsewhere.[24] We must try to identify with other human beings who have been victimized by war and violence—like the hundreds of children whose arms and legs were brutally chopped in half recently in Sierra Leone—in order to make human sense of the numbers, and in order to be moved by the numbers to take preventive action.

In this way, we can guard against the tendency to treat numbers of this magnitude as if they were *only* numbers. They are not. Attached to every number is the suffering and premature extinction of an individual human being, a person capable of enjoying life, of suffering, and of facing death quite consciously, often courageously—they were all human beings who were, or who should have been, treated as selves, as ends in themselves.[25] Long before the 20th century, the human race became familiar with the perversion of Immanuel Kant's imperative—of treating people as means, rather than ends. What is a soldier but a person willing to fight and sacrifice himself for a cause—to become a means for achieving victory? But in the 20th century, the debasement of Kant's imperative was taken a step further, as human beings' relation to war and violence became, by and large, neither an end nor a means. Most victims of war became something that simply got in the way—to be destroyed and discarded, like rubbish. Thus in the 20th century, dying in war or because of war became, for the first time, largely meaningless or absurd.

What Kind of World for the 21st Century?

The post–Cold War world is in many ways as surprising and as violent as that which confronted Norman Angell and his shocked contemporaries with the outbreak of the First World War. Beginning in late 1989, states, nations, and peoples were suddenly freed from the constraining influence of the two "blocs" headed by the United States and the Soviet Union. Thus liberated, their territorial claims, ethnic rivalries, religious differences, historical grievances, and other sources of tension led to widespread violence and killing. Indeed, by the mid-1990s, war and civil violence arising from such roots had become pervasive and unmanageable in many parts of the world.

In response, the Carnegie Corporation of New York established a high-profile international Commission on Preventing Deadly Conflict, headed by former U.S. Secretary of State Cyrus Vance and Carnegie Corporation president Dr. David Hamburg. The commission's 1997 report is focused squarely on new threats that are likely to be central in the 21st century:

Peace will require understanding and respect for differences within and across national boundaries. We humans do not have the luxury any longer of indulging our prejudices and ethnocentrism. They are anachronisms of our ancient past. The worldwide historical record is full of hateful and destructive behavior based on religious, racial, political, ideological, and other distinctions—holy wars of one sort or another. Will such behavior in the next century be expressed with weapons of mass destruction? If we cannot learn to accommodate each other respectfully in the twenty-first century, we could destroy each other at such a rate that humanity will have little to cherish.[26]

According to the commission, a crisis has arisen due to the convergence of several factors: the "unlocking" of widespread communal violence at the end of the Cold War; unchecked population growth in many areas prone to such violence; and the widespread availability of lethal weapons and high technology (not excluding the knowledge of how to construct weapons of mass destruction). It is not the sort of crisis with which officials in Washington and Moscow were obsessed during the Cold War—a direct confrontation between nuclear-armed Great Powers. Rather, it is a "crisis in slow motion"—violence that escalates slowly at first, then more rapidly until, by the time it gets the attention of high-level officials, the situation may be sufficiently perverse that nonescalatory options seem out of the question.[27] The escalation of the conflict in Vietnam in the 1960s was an example of this.[28]

We see evidence of this on all sides: the Iraqi invasion of Kuwait, the civil wars in the former Yugoslavia, the turmoil in northern Iraq, the tension between India and Pakistan, the unstable relations between North and South Korea and between China and Taiwan, and the conflicts across the face of sub-Saharan Africa in Somalia, Sudan, Ethiopia and Eritrea, Rwanda, Burundi, the Democratic Republic of the Congo, Sierra Leone, and Liberia. These all make clear that the world of the future will not be without conflict—conflict among disparate groups within nations and conflict extending across national borders. Racial, religious, and ethnic tensions will remain. Nationalism will be a powerful force across the globe. Political revolutions will erupt as societies advance. Historical disputes over political boundaries will endure. And economic disparities among and within nations will increase as technology and education spread unevenly around the world. The underlying causes of conflict that existed long before the Cold War began remain now that it has ended. They will be compounded by civil strife among the states of the former Soviet Union and by continuing tensions in the Middle East. It is just such tensions that in the past 50 years have contributed to the deaths of tens of millions of people in war.

When the Carnegie Commission report was issued it was greeted with skepticism in some quarters. The skeptics felt the authors had exaggerated the problem of war and violence in the 21st century. We disagree. Consider the following calculations, which, while speculative, we consider to be conservative:

- Estimates given in the previous section list the number of wars fought in the 20th century as 218.

- Assume no increase in the number of wars in this century versus the last and no increase in their intensity.

- But recognize that the average population of the globe will increase roughly threefold.[29]

Under these circumstances fatalities from war would be substantially higher, at least 300 million. Further, let us assume that the rate of civilian casualties remains constant at approximately 75 percent (which is judged to be the approximate post–Cold War rate in the 1990s). In this case, 75 percent of 300 million yields a projected 225 million civilian war deaths.

We reiterate that these numbers are speculative. The estimation of *past* war deaths is just that—estimation, based on data of often unknown reliability. To the uncertainty attached to estimates of the pattern and number of war deaths in the 20th century we must, in dealing with projections into the 21st century, add additional uncertainties: the rate of technological advance and dissemination; political leadership or its lack; and a host of other essentially unknowable factors. So neither we, nor the Carnegie Commission, nor anyone else can say with any degree of precision how many people will have died in war by December 31, 2100. But our projections—300 million war deaths, 225 million of them civilians—may well be *underestimates!*

We believe strongly, therefore, that the urgency of the Carnegie Commission's call to war prevention in the 21st century is warranted. We simply cannot believe that our increasingly interdependent global village—civilization as we know it—can in this century withstand the killing of anything like 225 million innocent civilians without leading to political, economic, and social instability that would severely penalize most, if not all, nations and all peoples.

And what if—as seems entirely possible—nuclear weapons were to be used in one or more of these conflicts? In that case, our estimates for war deaths would have to be revised significantly upward. For example, just a few nuclear detonations in a border war between India and Pakistan would likely kill millions—perhaps tens of millions—in densely populated South Asia. The same applies to a nuclear conflict in the Middle East between Israel and one or more Arab adversaries. And it is highly probable that the United States would be drawn inexorably into any conflict of this magnitude. Then what of the Russians and Chinese? What form would their probable involvement take? Alas, this worst-case scenario may not be as unlikely as we all hope it is.

Estimates from the period 1990–1995 support the view that "conflicts" are occurring at a rate that could have catastrophic results of the magnitude hypothesized in the preceding paragraphs. Using relatively conservative numbers throughout, PRIO recently published its analysis of war deaths in the half decade following the end of the Cold War. They find that the number of wars each year was fairly constant and that, at a minimum, 5.5 million people were killed between 1990 and 1995 as a *direct* result of war, with an unknown number dying due to chaos, starvation, disease, and other factors associated with war.[30] Other estimates are much higher. As we have said, approximately 8.5 million people are said to have died in the First World War. Those four and a half years of killing led directly to a century of bloodshed and tension among the Great Powers. According to the PRIO estimates, the post–Cold War world contains civilizations, cultures, and nations that are already at, or beyond, the breaking point. These failed or failing states will continue to be a breeding ground of instability, violence, and killing.[31]

No one has made this point more forcefully than the American journalist Robert D. Kaplan, whose now famous 1994 article on sub-Saharan Africa, "The Coming Anarchy," appeared in the *Atlantic Monthly* just months before the genocide in Rwanda.[32] Kaplan reports that wherever he went throughout the region, he carried a letter from a friend, a member of the U.S. foreign service in West Africa. The note said:

The greatest threat to our value system comes from Africa. Can we continue to believe in universal principles as Africa declines to levels better described by Dante than by development economists? Our domestic attitudes on race and ethnicity suffer as Africa becomes a continent-wide "Wreck of the Medusa."[33]

The reference is to an early 19th-century shipwreck whose survivors nearly starved to death, and which is depicted in a horrifying 1819 painting by the French artist Théodore Géricault, *The Raft of the Medusa*. Kaplan returns repeatedly to this letter throughout his journey, and to the macabre warning given him by a woman in Danane, in the western Ivory Coast: "The thieves are very violent here," she said, "they will cut you up if you are not careful."[34]

Leaving ravaged West Africa, Kaplan then traveled to other "ends of the earth": Iran, Afghanistan, and Cambodia among them. He was searching, he says, for "a paradigm for understanding the world in the early decades of the 21st century."[35] He found none. He did, however, reach this conclusion: *"We are not in control."*[36] He notes that the failure of just a few relatively insignificant states in the post–Cold War era has overwhelmed the West's (and the UN's) coping mechanisms. What will happen, he asks himself, when a major regional power implodes and ceases to function? Will it be nuclear-armed Pakistan? Or will it be Iraq, perhaps following another war? Or possibly Russia, collapsing into anarchy? In all such eventualities, he muses, "we would have no answers."[37]

Of course, West Africa of the 21st century is not the whole world, nor are places like Pakistan or even Russia. Some may be reluctant to follow Kaplan all the way to his apocalyptic conclusion: that "the coming anarchy" will soon leave no people, no country untouched—that Dante's West African inferno may impact on all of us at some point in the 21st century, with chaos and anarchy spreading like a communicable disease, or even faster, like a computer virus, throughout the world. Yet we believe the image is a useful one to keep in mind, an impressionistic yet powerful complement to our calculations above regarding war deaths in the century ahead.

Such situations exist. Other human beings, people like ourselves, are already burning in Dantean infernos. Whole nation-states are on the brink of collapse. At a minimum, they deserve our sympathy and whatever assistance we can give. But we must also consider the possibility that their fate and ours may be linked to a greater extent than we suppose.[38] How much chaos, turmoil, and killing can occur before the cool islands of tranquility in which we live begin to burn? The Canadian journalist Michael Ignatieff has written that "most of us persist in the belief that while the fires far away are terrible things, we can keep them from our doors, and that while they may consume the roofs of our neighbors, the sparks will never leap to our own."[39] We suggest that the figurative "sparks"—refugees, ethnic killing, disease, chronic political instability, perhaps leading to major war, even nuclear war—will begin to burn down (or at a minimum, severely damage) our own abode long before 300 million people are killed in war in this century. We propose to confront this danger by action based on a moral imperative.

The Moral Imperative: Reduce Carnage!

This is our moral imperative: Establish as a major goal of U.S. foreign and defense policy, and foreign policies of countries across the globe, the avoidance in the 21st century of the carnage—160 million dead—caused by conflict in the 20th century.

In urging the adoption of a "moral imperative" for reducing human carnage in the 21st century, we mean that a major foreign and defense policy objective of the United States and all other nations should be a radical reduction in the killing of human beings. Because the application of these concepts—both "moral" and "imperative"—to foreign and defense policy is highly controversial, we will first define our terms and give them some context. Then we will turn to what many will see as difficulties with our unorthodox proposal. Indeed, many scholars and practitioners of foreign policy have traditionally believed that considerations of morality have either no place at all in the calculations of statesmen, or at most a role that is subordinate to that of protecting the national interest— which is widely seen as the only "imperative" that statesmen need worry about.

The idea of a "moral imperative" was central to the thinking of the 18th-century German philosopher Immanuel Kant, whose writings on this topic have influenced Western thinking for the past two centuries. There are two principal components to this concept.

First, what is *moral?* To Kant, to act morally is to act in accordance with what he called "the moral law within," that is to treat a human being "as an end in himself, that is never as a means."[40] This injunction at first appears somewhat unrealistic, even otherworldly. In everyday life, let alone the rough-and-tumble affairs of state, we often find it at least advantageous, and sometimes downright necessary, to "use" people in various ways—as means—for our own purposes. But Kant did not presume to issue an inviolable commandment. Coming as he did from the German Lutheran tradition, Kant had unbounded appreciation for human fallibility and the limitations imposed on human action in a world overflowing with evil. He was, instead, clarifying what he thought we ought to mean when we speak of morality—an ideal to keep in mind and against which to measure the moral correctness of our actions as individuals, in dealing with other human beings. His use of the term connotes deep respect for the wishes and interests of others. It is the opposite of selfishness.

Second, what is an *imperative?* Kant's many treatises on this topic have made him one of history's most influential thinkers. According to Kant, "I am never to act otherwise than so *that I could also will that my maxim should become a universal law.*"[41] If we can formulate principles of action that, as best we can determine, apply across the board, to all people in all possible situations that we can imagine, we are acting in accordance with a Kantian *imperative.* To the extent possible, we are to act in such cases, according to Kant, "from duty," not from "apprehension of injurious consequences." Kant recognized clearly that acting in this way, "from duty" to one's moral maxims, can lead to difficult, even agonizing decisions. For "to deviate from the principle of duty," he held, "is beyond all doubt wicked; but to be unfaithful to my maxim may often be very advantageous."[42] It may sometimes cause pain, to ourselves and to others, to act in accordance with a moral imperative.

We call these "moral dilemmas," and statecraft, in Kantian terms, is filled with them from beginning to end. "Thou shalt not kill" may be a maxim that, in our private lives, we adhere to universally. But suppose we are statesmen and our country has been attacked. Citizens to whom, and for whom, we are responsible have been killed. Our advisers tell us that if we do not respond in kind, we can expect another attack. What do we do? We are wicked, according to Kant, if we do not order the retaliatory attack, because we may be putting our own citizens at risk. But we are also wicked if we do order the attack because we have violated a maxim ("Thou shalt not kill") that we formerly held to be universally applicable. Most leaders in this situation will of course override the moral maxim and choose the utilitarian option. Why? Because a leader may come to believe that a counterattack will result in fewer deaths than no counterattack. But of course, he may be wrong about the effects of his decision. The counterattack may only inflame the conflict rather than dampen it down. For leaders with strong personal moral convictions, and also a strong sense of duty to their constituents, these dilemmas can be acute.

Consider the case of Harry Truman's decision to use the atomic bomb in August 1945 during the Second World War.[43] President Truman "excused" himself for ordering the atomic bomb dropped on Japan, saying he did so to save the lives of perhaps a million members of the U.S. armed forces who might be killed in an invasion of Japan. He believed that, in the absence of the atomic bombing, American soldiers would have to subdue the tenacious Japanese island by island, city by city, man by man. Was Truman justified in making that decision? Would he have been justified in making the opposite decision—to withhold the atomic bomb because its probable effects, involving the deaths of 200,000 noncombatants—were too horrible to contemplate? What if, having withheld the atomic bomb, American war deaths in the Pacific had actually reached something like the astronomical levels predicted by some of Truman's advisers? Truman's ultimate decision led him, in effect, to assume responsibility for the deaths of hundreds of thousands of Japanese civilians. But would he not have been equally responsible for the deaths of tens of thousands of American military personnel who were judged to have died in battles that would have been unnecessary if the bomb had been used?

Combining Kant's two principles, "moral" and "imperative," we arrive at a universalization of what is often called "the golden rule": Do unto others as you would have them do unto you—not some people some-time, but all people all the time, no matter what. This is Kant's *moral imperative*, the injunction to treat human beings not as means but as ends in themselves. When moral issues arise, Kant implores us to try *at the outset of our deliberations* to avoid thinking in terms of specific situations involving others. Specificity leads to making exceptions and the more exceptions one admits into the moral calculus, the more meaning-less the moral maxim becomes. Exceptions, in Kant's view, strip the maxim of its universality. In fact, Kant was inclined to view many "exceptions" as mere excuses, the main function of which is to assuage one's conscience when confronted with difficult moral dilemmas.

Here is our outline of the Kantian calculus for resolving moral dilemmas:

- Identify possible courses of action.

- State your moral principle that should guide the action.

- Make the principle a moral imperative by universalizing it.

- Try to act in a way consistent with the moral imperative.

- Or, if necessary, consider the utilitarian consequences of action, and act so as to achieve an acceptable result while deviating minimally from the moral principle.

For foreign policy makers, the "if necessary" is almost always neces-sary. But according to this calculus, they should begin with moral imper-atives, thus lowering the odds that they will lose their moral bearings in the course of making difficult decisions.

The Roman Catholic tradition of the "Just War Doctrine" also requires that decision makers begin their calculations with moral imper-atives—for example, "Thou shall not kill"—but it acknowledges, in the words of St. Augustine, that "Love may require force to protect the inno-cent."[44] Sometimes killing is justified, in order to halt the killing. The Just War Doctrine requires that two kinds of questions be addressed: first, those concerned with the justice of a decision to intervene with force, or *jus ad bellum;* and second, what level and kind of force is justified in the actual application of force, or *jus in bello.* (These categories are taken up in more detail in Chapter Three.)

The key question for students of foreign policy is: Can such utilitarian "excusing" of one's own behavior be avoided *at all?* Is all talk of moral imperatives, whether in the Kantian or Just War traditions, merely window dressing? Some scholars and practitioners of foreign policy have inclined to the view that moral analysis, while perhaps inspiring in its idealism, cannot possibly offer guidance for decision making in a domain as morally ambiguous and complicated as making foreign policy. What is the point, after all, of accusing those in leadership positions in the midst of war of abandoning a moral imperative such as "Thou shalt not kill"? Private citizens, it is true, may declare themselves to be principled pacifists and refuse to fight, sometimes at severe personal cost. They may refuse to pay taxes, or engage in other activities they regard as noncompliance with a national war effort they cannot support in good conscience. But even private citizens who are pacifists are advised to consider what effect their activities may have on the level of fighting to be carried on by the enemy. Pacifism is not necessarily "neutral." If this is true for private citizens, then for public officials, especially those with responsibilities on war and peace issues, all talk of "moral imperatives" not to kill may seem totally out of place, inconsistent with the nature of the situation these people actually face. This is why, to some scholars and practitioners of foreign policy, morality and foreign policy do not mix. In fact, they believe, to dwell excessively on the supposed moral implications of foreign policy decisions only gives the advantage to adversaries who do not feel bound by any moral constraints.

People who hold the view that the moral dimension is, or ought to be, alien from foreign policy making, often call themselves *realists.* They refer to people like ourselves, who believe that moral considerations should play a significant role in the conduct of international affairs, as *idealists.* We seem a little otherworldly to them, while they appear to us to recommend an approach and policies that are unnecessarily cynical, focused on a national self-interest that is too narrowly defined.

Realists believe that the end of the Cold War signals not a need for moral imperatives but its conceptual opposite: a return to the game of pure power politics played by sovereign states. They argue that the disappearance of ideological competition between East and West will soon trigger a reversion to traditional relationships based on territorial and economic imperatives. They believe that the Great Powers—the United States, Russia, Western Europe, China, Japan, and perhaps India—will seek to assert themselves in their own regions while competing for dominance in other areas of the world where conditions are fluid. This view was expressed in December 1989 by the Harvard political theorist Michael Sandel, in the immediate aftermath of the fall of the Berlin Wall. According to Sandel:

> The end of the Cold War does not mean an end of global competition between the superpowers. Once the ideological dimension fades, what you are left with is not peace and harmony, but old-fashioned global politics based on dominant powers competing for influence and pursuing their eternal interests.[45]

Sandel appears to have been at least half right in his predictions. The post–Cold War world has certainly not been one of peace and harmony. As we noted, more than 5.5 million people were killed in wars during the first five years following the fall of the Berlin Wall. But has old-fashioned global politics reasserted itself? Hardly. We are in a new situation, with but one dominant power, the United States, which has no clear objectives and no well-defined plan for pursuing them; and a flurry of activity by influential regional states that bears little resemblance to the back-room diplomacy of the pre–Cold War era.

Perhaps the best-known advocate of looking backward, rather than forward, for clues as to what awaits us in the 21st century is former Secretary of State Henry Kissinger. He brings to the issue not only his experience in the Nixon and Ford administrations but his reputation as an historian—and the world's leading geopolitician—as well. His 1994 book *Diplomacy* is organized around what he calls "the hinge"—the tension in U.S. foreign policy between the "idealism" of Woodrow Wilson, which Kissinger disdains, and the "realism" of Theodore Roosevelt, which

Kissinger respects and believes anticipated his own European-style power politics better than the approach of any U.S. president before his former boss, Richard Nixon.

Kissinger's analysis is almost exactly the opposite of our own:

> The premise of Wilsonianism is becoming less relevant and the dictates of Wilsonian foreign policy—collective security, the conversion of one's competitors to the American way, an international system that adjudicates disputes in a legal fashion—are becoming less practicable. [Therefore] on what principles ought America to base its foreign policy in the coming century? History provides no guidebook, nor even analogies that completely satisfy. Yet history teaches by example and, as America moves into uncharted waters, it would do well to consider the era before Woodrow Wilson and the "American century" for clues about the decades to come.[46]

Kissinger urges us to look backward to earlier centuries for guidance for reasons similar to those of Sandel:

> Victory in the Cold War has propelled America into a world which bears many similarities to the European state system of the eighteenth and nineteenth centuries. . . . The absence of both an overriding ideological or strategic threat frees nations to pursue foreign policies based increasingly on their immediate national interest. In an international system characterized by perhaps five or six major powers and a multiplicity of smaller states, order will have to emerge much as it did in past centuries from a reconciliation and balancing of national interests.[47]

Kissinger appears to sense Wilson's ghost peering over his shoulder, but it is the ghost of a dreaded "idealist" who, because of his excessive attachment to morality and multilateralism, failed to assemble a sustainable peace at the Paris Peace Conference following the First World War. Instead, Kissinger recommends that American leaders pay close attention to *raison d'état*—to reasons of state, to the national interest—and manipulate the "balance of power" according to their view of that interest. He goes on to caution that "America will need partners to preserve equilibrium in several regions of the world, and these partners cannot always be chosen on the basis of moral considerations alone."[48]

In contrast to Sandel and Kissinger, Carl Kaysen, the former director of the Institute for Advanced Study in Princeton, has written:

> The international system that relies on the national use of military force as the ultimate guarantor of security, and the threat of its use as the basis of order, is not the only possible one. To seek a different system . . . is no longer the pursuit of an illusion, but a necessary effort toward a necessary goal.[49]

We agree with Kaysen that the "realist" view expounded by Sandel and Kissinger is in fact based on an imperfect analysis of the world that lies ahead and a failure to recognize the degree to which moral considerations have influenced our foreign policy over past decades, and should do so to an even greater degree (particularly with respect to nuclear weapons) in the future.

Our increasingly interdependent world is wired together via exploding trade and investment, a shared environment, the Internet, jet travel, and the mass media. National borders and sovereign states are no longer the principal obsession of diplomats. And diplomats are no longer the only important players in international politics. National interest now encompasses far more than the defense, and/or expansion, of national borders, or even rights to sea lanes and ports, which were paramount in the 19th century. And no nation, or any alliance of nations, can stand alone in a world that is joined together as is the world of the 21st century—economically, informationally, environmentally, and therefore with regard to security.

Should not moral considerations play a far greater role in shaping foreign policy in such a world?

Surely, in the most basic sense, one can apply a moral judgment to the level of killing that occurred in the 20th century. There can be no justification for it. Nor can there be any justification for its continuation into the 21st century. On moral grounds alone, we should act to prevent such an outcome. As we have said, a first step would be to establish such an objective as the primary foreign policy goal both for our own nation and for the entire human race.

The United States has defined itself in highly idealistic and moral terms throughout our history. We have seen ourselves as defenders of human freedoms across the globe, and our moral vision has had an impact on the world. America's ideals have led to the formation of a score of international institutions in the economic, social, and political fields. But our moral vision remains under attack—both within and outside the United States—by those who question its applicability to foreign policy. And we must admit that many of the most controversial foreign policy debates have found both sides basing their arguments on moral considerations. Supporters of U.S. policy toward Cuba today justify it on moral grounds by saying that it is immoral to support dictators who abuse human rights. And critics attack it on moral grounds saying that it leads to suffering by the mass of the Cuban people. Similarly, a U.S. policy toward China that placed primary emphasis on support of individual civil rights might well weaken the Chinese government's ability to increase the access of the mass of its population to major advances in nutrition, education, and health. Nor do moral considerations offer a clear guide to action in many other foreign policy disputes, for example the recent conflicts in Bosnia and Kosovo.

Moreover, peoples of different religions and different cultures, confronting common problems, often arrive at different moral judgments relating to conflicts between individual and group rights, between group rights and national rights, and between the rights of individual nations. But closer inspection reveals that most great religions have a common belief in what we call "the golden rule." For example, Buddhism: "Hurt not others in ways that you yourself would find hurtful." Christianity: "All things whatsoever you would that men should do to you, you do even so to them." Confucianism: "Do not unto others what you would not have them do unto you." Hinduism: "This is the sum of duty: do not unto others that which would cause you pain if done to you." Islam: "No one of you is a believer until he desires for his brother that which he desires for himself." Judaism: "What is hateful to you, do not do to your fellow man. That is the law; all the rest is commentary."[50]

There is general acceptance in the United States of the proposition that our foreign policy should advance the welfare of peoples across the globe in terms of political freedom, freedom from want, and preservation of the environment. However, those objectives are so general that they often provide little guidance to those who would address the problems that a government confronts each day.

But can we not agree—as we have proposed—that there is one area of foreign policy in which moral principles should prevail and in which they have not? That is in relation to the *settlement of disputes within nations and among nations without resort to violence.*

Happily, in our view, the realist "school" of international relations is no longer the juggernaut it once was in leading the way in discouraging foreign policymakers from integrating moral considerations into their work. We are hardly alone in our belief that sound foreign policy and moral imperatives are not incompatible. The Carnegie Commission's report devoted a good deal of space to the thinking of the contemporary Swiss theologian and philosopher Hans Küng, who is quoted in the report as follows:

> [This is] a fundamental demand: Every human being must be treated humanely. There is a principle which is found and has persisted in many religions and ethical traditions of humankind for thousands of years: What you do not wish done to yourself, do not do to others! Or in positive terms: What you wish done to yourself, do to others! This should be the irrevocable, unconditional norm for all areas of life, for families and communities, for races, nations, and religions.[51]

This is very much what Kant had in mind. It states an imperative based on a moral principle that is held to apply universally: from relations between individuals to relations among nations. It is, or should be, the point of origin for all decision making, including decisions affecting foreign policy—not the end of wisdom for foreign policy makers in a complex and confusing world, but the beginning. What we are urging in this book is the adoption as a major foreign policy objective of the United States, and nations around the world, one particular and, we believe, utterly basic imperative subsumed by the general principles of

Kant and Küng: Settle disputes within and among nations without resort to violence!

Realists will still be skeptical of the applicability of this proposed morality to foreign policy. It is all well and good, they would admit, to act privately, as individuals, according to some version of the biblical commandment: Thou shalt not kill. The problem, they say, lies with our inappropriate application of moral principles that are useful guidelines for *individuals* in domestic societies to the anarchical, dog-eat-dog *international* system. In the world of nation-states, after all, there is no "law" worthy of the term, no higher "authority" to which one can appeal beyond a state's ability to protect its interests, its property, and its people.

In such a situation, a statesman is said by the realists to have a *duty* to do whatever is necessary to uphold and protect the interests of his state and its constituents. This duty may include acts of intimidation, threats of war, or even acts of war, if leaders deem such acts to be in the state's interest.

What exactly is different, according to our realist critics, about the situation of leaders with regard to foreign policy? Alexander Hamilton put it this way: "The rule of morality . . . is not precisely the same between nations as between individuals. . . . Existing millions and future generations are concerned with the present measures of a government while the consequences of the private action of an individual ordinarily terminate with himself."[52] Leaders act on behalf of others, with their authorization. Indeed, the constituents demand that their leaders look after their collective interest, whatever their personal beliefs and scruples may be.

The Bible of this political philosophy is Niccolò Machiavelli's classic handbook of political advice, *The Prince*. His formulation of the situation faced by statesmen is somewhat more explicit than Hamilton's about what is required of foreign policy makers. "Where the safety of the country depends upon the resolution to be taken," according to Machiavelli, "no considerations of justice or injustice, humanity or cruelty, nor of glory or shame, should be allowed to prevail."[53] Machiavelli, we can assume, would have had even fewer moral qualms than did Truman about using the atomic bomb. Committing injustice, being cruel to other human beings, and shameful actions of every description may be required of "princes" in order that they preserve and protect their states' interests. It's all in the line of duty—that duty being, fundamentally, the prevention of the weakening or extermination of the state by its enemies.

This is, in effect, a perfect inversion of Kant's moral imperative. Everything is said to depend on the situation. Those responsible for foreign policy are urged to pay no attention whatever to anything other than the intended outcome—to do whatever is necessary to prevail, moral imperatives be damned. Foreign policy makers are to reserve the application of moral imperatives for their interactions with family and friends, but to leave their moral scruples at home when they deal with the likes of, say, Iraq's Saddam Hussein, North Korea's former leader Kim Il Sung, or Libya's Muammar Qaddafi. To put it another way, the realists believe that the "morality" of a decision or action in the international arena should be judged strictly according to whether foreign policy makers are acting in ways to uphold the state's national interest. The outcome is the only criterion by which to judge an action. Did we win or did we lose—the contract, the argument, the territory, the battle, the war? This outlook has been called Machiavelli's "philosophy of emergency," or his "morality of public safety," and with good reason.[54] It focuses almost exclusively on the anarchy existing in the world of nation-states, where the security of one's nation—even the security of superpowers—may be at risk.

Reinhold Niebuhr, one of the most influential American philosophers and theologians of the 20th century, attempted to synthesize these two approaches: that deriving from Kant, urging that moral imperatives be fundamental and universal; and that associated with Machiavelli, with its exclusive emphasis on utilitarian calculations of the national interest deriving from the particulars of a given situation. Niebuhr was wary of an exclusive reliance on either moral imperatives or utilitarian consequences. He believed that an exclusive reliance on either could lead to *evil.* Niebuhr, whose greatest works were written during and just after the Second World War, was acutely aware of, and not the least bit hesitant to label, what he considered evil. What is evil in the international sphere, he said, is "the assertion of some self-interest without regard to the whole, whether the whole be conceived as the immediate community, or the total community of mankind."[55]

We must, he believed, be especially wary of the counsel given by realists like Machiavelli, whom Niebuhr regarded as "merely the first of a long line of *cynics* in the field of international relations."[56] The rise of the Nazis in Germany demonstrated to Niebuhr the danger of an approach to foreign policy anchored in pure self-interest: it could be twisted perversely to justify the most hideous policies, as Hitler had done, in the name of the "national interest." When this happened, "evil" was the result. This seemed self-evident to both Niebuhr, writing in 1944, and his readers. Those who followed in Machiavelli's footsteps he called "children of darkness," using an image found in the Gospel According to St. Luke.

Opposed to the "children of darkness," Niebuhr placed the "children of light," whom Niebuhr described as "those who seek to bring self-interest under the discipline of a more universal law and in harmony with a more universal good."[57] If the "children of darkness" are capable of justifying great evil, the "children of light" are often guilty of naïveté. America's weakness as a nation and as a people, according to Niebuhr, is that we tend to be "sentimental rather than cynical."[58]

The corrective, he believed, was to combine "the wisdom of the serpent and the harmlessness of the dove," by which he meant that we must hold fast to our moral imperatives, beginning our foreign policy making with them and never losing sight of our basic values.[59] But we must also not delude ourselves into believing that others in the international arena will necessarily follow our example. And we must be prepared for some to interpret behavior based on a moral foundation as weakness. But most of all, we must not, in our efforts to survive as a state, lose our soul in the process—abandoning the universal moral maxims that give meaning to our lives and permit us, as human beings, to rise above the level of the beasts—or the Nazis, for that matter.

Niebuhr was unusually influential. His works were studied by President John F. Kennedy and his inner circle of advisors. And in 1964, Niebuhr was awarded the Medal of Freedom by President Lyndon Johnson.

Robert McNamara: The moral dilemmas just described became especially acute for me during the Vietnam war. As the war escalated, views on the conduct of the war became polarized. I believe the moral tension—the tension between doing what seems right according to the moral imperative which prohibits the killing of other human beings on the one hand and, on the other, doing what seems right according to one's institutional responsibility to preserve and protect our nation—this tension was felt by all of us in the Johnson administration, including the president. We had become involved in Vietnam, we believed, to prevent the spread of Soviet and Chinese-backed communism in Southeast Asia. Had we not become involved, we were convinced, U.S. security interests around the world would have been put at risk. That is what we told ourselves, and we believed it completely, as did the majority of the American people until early 1968, according to polls taken at the time.

But as the war went on, and the killing went on, one event in particular brought the moral tension I was feeling almost to the breaking point. I wrote about it in my 1995 memoir, *In Retrospect: The Tragedy and Lessons of Vietnam,* from which the following account is taken.

"Antiwar protest had been sporadic and limited up to this time and had not compelled attention. Then came the afternoon of November 2, 1965. At twilight that day, a young Quaker named Norman R. Morrison, father of three and an officer in the Stoney Creek Friends Meeting in Baltimore, burned himself to death within forty feet of my Pentagon window. He doused himself with fuel from a gallon jug. When he set himself on fire, he was holding his one-year-old daughter in his arms. Bystanders screamed 'save the child!' and he flung her out of his arms. She survived without injury.

"After Morrison's death, his wife issued a statement:

Norman Morrison [gave] his life to express his concern over the great loss of life and human suffering caused by the war in Vietnam. He was protesting our government's deep military involvement in this war. He felt that all citizens must speak their convictions about our country's action.

"Morrison's death was a tragedy not only for his family but also for me and the country. It was an outcry against the killing that was destroying the lives of so many Vietnamese and American youth."[60]

After presenting more details of the subsequent protests against the war, I quoted a December 3, 1965 column by *Washington Star* columnist Mary McGrory. It read in part as follows:

> The secretary is an admirer of Norman Thomas, the venerable Socialist leader who was the most effective orator at last Saturday's demonstration here. But he takes issue with Thomas' contention that he "would rather see America save her soul than her face in Southeast Asia."
>
> "How do you save your soul," McNamara asks. "Do you save your soul by pulling out of a situation, or do you save it by fulfilling your commitments?"[61]

My own answer to this last question is obvious: I thought then, as did the president and my other colleagues, that we could protect our national interest and "save our soul," to use Norman Thomas's phrase, by one and the same action: fighting in Vietnam until the communist forces were subdued, thus preserving the integrity of our South Vietnamese ally and demonstrating to Russia and China that we would not be intimidated.

But due in part to the impact of Norman Morrison's suicide, I began to experience even more acutely the moral tension we have been discussing. Morrison's action dramatized for me the tremendous discrepancy between the moral imperative—the prohibition on the killing of other human beings that I had subscribed to all my life—and what was occurring daily in Vietnam. The war was escalating and would continue to escalate. The killing would go on and, in fact, increase dramatically. When would it stop? What would it accomplish? Could it have been avoided? What if, in fact, the Vietnamese communists had more staying power than either we or our South Vietnamese allies? How then would we justify—to our military personnel, to our constituents, to ourselves, and to history—what we were doing in Vietnam?

It was with such thoughts as these on my mind that in late 1965 I became much more involved than previously in an aspect of the war that normally is not handled by the secretary of defense: the search for a diplomatic settlement—for peace. At my initiative, a 37-day-long bombing pause began in the month following the Morrison suicide, coupled with intense diplomacy. It failed to draw the Hanoi government to the negotiating table. During the next two years, other bombing pauses and diplomatic initiatives were tried and also failed. My final effort to find a way to stop the killing in a way that was politically feasible was via a secret channel I established in the summer and fall of 1967 with Hanoi via two French scientists and Henry Kissinger, then a Harvard professor.[62] It too failed. I left the government shortly thereafter.

At my farewell ceremony, on February 29, 1968, I found myself choking and unable to reply to the words of praise from President Johnson. Why? In part because of tension brought on by events such as Norman Morrison's suicide in November 1965. But more fundamentally, because by the end of 1967, nearly 16,000 Americans and several hundred thousand Vietnamese had been killed.[63]

Were my colleagues and I guilty of what Reinhold Niebuhr called "the assertion of some self-interest without regard to the whole ... the total community of mankind"? No. We thought we were acting in the interests of mankind, but the cost in lives lost was far greater than we or others had predicted. What should we have done differently? I believe we should have elevated to the same level as other objectives our intention to keep human carnage to a minimum. Had we done so, we would have explored more fully other ways to achieve our goals. If we had, I now believe—and the available evidence strongly suggests—that we could have ended the war as early as 1962, and not later than 1967, without any significant loss in our strategic position worldwide.[64] In that case, we might have "saved our soul," as Norman Thomas said, and protected our interests as well.

◆

It is important to understand that by adding a moral imperative to foreign policy making, one does not thereby merely consult a figurative "handbook" of dos and don'ts and decide accordingly. Such a "handbook" does not exist. This is the straw man of "idealism" attacked by the realists and other cynical students and practitioners of foreign policy— those who, in the felicitous phrasing of the Harvard international relations scholar Stanley Hoffmann, assert that people like ourselves, who wish to insert morality into foreign policy making, require "the statesman to come straight out of the Ten Commandments."[65] Nothing could be further from what is required, which is to enter the moral factor into the calculations, and to give appropriate weight to it as the policies are formed. Calculations do not thereby become simpler or more rigid due to their moral content. They become, if anything, more complex, more nuanced, more attuned to universal values like the sanctity of human life. According to Hoffmann, "the conflict between interest and morality should not be dramatized, and the task of moral politics is to bring the two together."[66]

❖

Robert McNamara: On October 15, 1962, Soviet missile sites were identified on the island of Cuba, thus initiating the Cuban missile crisis, the most intense, frightening, and dangerous experience of my life. As to performance: We in the Kennedy administration were everything in that crisis that we were not with regard to Vietnam—in either the Kennedy or Johnson administrations. In the missile crisis—a brief (thirteen-day), scorchingly intense confrontation with the possibility of escalation to nuclear war—we focused on nothing else until the crisis was resolved, on October 28. It was then that the Soviet leader Nikita Khrushchev signaled his willingness to remove the missiles from Cuba, in exchange for a public pledge from the United States that we would not invade Cuba and overthrow the government of Fidel Castro.[67]

I said we were focused, and we were. I, like many of my colleagues, did not go home for the entire duration of the crisis. I slept in the Pentagon each night on a cot so I could respond immediately to developments. But in addition to being riveted on the problem at hand, we also did not lose our sense of who we were as representatives of the United States, and of what we owed our country and the world. I will illustrate this with two references to the audiotapes President Kennedy secretly made of many—though far from all—of the meetings involving him and his closest advisers. They will show the way moral factors influenced all of us—but particularly President Kennedy and his brother, Attorney General Robert Kennedy—and thereby influenced many of our most important decisions during the crisis.

The problem was this: For all sorts of political reasons, we knew the missiles had to come out of Cuba. There was no question about that. Khrushchev had lied to us repeatedly—the missiles had been introduced into Cuba under a cloak of deceit—and this sort of behavior could not be tolerated between superpowers in the nuclear age. It was believed by many that the "cleanest" way to take them out would have been by a so-called surgical air strike against the missile sites, using the same logic by which NATO decided on an air war against the Milosevic regime in the Balkans in 1999.

However, beginning on the first day of discussion, October 16, and continuing all through our discussions from beginning to end as we endeavored to agree on a response, moral considerations were introduced time and again. We were challenged to define who we were as a people and what were the moral limits of what we should be prepared to do.

For example, here are some excerpts from the transcripts of the tapes, with some of my personal annotations:

October 18, 1962

George Ball: Mr. President . . . if we strike without warning, that's like Pearl Harbor. It's the kind of conduct that one might expect of the Soviet Union. It's not the conduct one expects of the United States.[68]

[Bobby Kennedy picked up on George Ball's point. Pacing back and forth in the meeting room, his remarks were delivered calmly, but passionately.]

Robert Kennedy: I think George Ball has a hell of a good point.

President Kennedy: What?

Robert Kennedy: I think it's the whole question of, you know, assuming you do survive all this, the fact that we're not . . . what kind of a country are we.

Dean Rusk: This business of carrying the mark of Cain on your brow for the rest of your life is something . . .

Robert Kennedy: We did this against Cuba. We've fought for 15 years with Russia to prevent a first strike against us. Now, in the interest of time, we do that to a small country. I think it's a hell of a burden to carry.[69]

October 22, 1962

[The following remarks are from a meeting taking place just hours before the president was to make a televised speech to the nation announcing that missiles had been discovered, and that we were instituting what we called a "quarantine" (essentially a blockade) of Cuba as a first step in getting them removed. I was one of the strongest backers of this strategy because it signaled our resolve but gave Khrushchev room to back down and increased the probability of achieving our objective without catastrophic military action.]

President Kennedy: Now, the second question . . . . : Why not take stronger action now, such as an air strike or air invasion. I think I've already answered that.

Robert Kennedy: It's a Pearl Harbor thing.

President Kennedy: Now, Bobby mentioned Pearl Harbor. Is this action justified, what we're now doing? This is one of the problems which is going to be most troublesome in our discussions with our allies. Inasmuch as Soviet missiles are already pointed at the U.S., and U.S. missiles are pointed at the USSR—particularly those—the most obvious example is in Turkey and Italy. In other words, what is the distinction between these missiles and the missiles which we sent to Turkey and Italy, which the Soviets put up with, which are operational, and have been for 2 to 3 years?[70]

Here you can see the president beginning to understand that no matter how angry he and his advisers may have been about the discovery of the missiles, and no matter how badly they may have wanted to remove them instantly, many people would want him to answer the moral questions: First, how could he, as an American president, justify a sneak attack of the type that the Japanese carried out on Pearl Harbor; and second, how could he justify risking nuclear war over a group of missiles that put the United States under no greater military threat than before? After the crisis, Bobby Kennedy posed the question in these terms: "What, if any, circumstance or justification gives this government or any government the moral right to bring its people and possibly all people under the shadow of nuclear devastation?"[71]

Moreover, throughout six hours of debate on October 27, the most dangerous day of the crisis, some of the president's advisers expressed the view that a "trade" of Turkish missiles for Soviet missiles in Cuba—which had been proposed by Khrushchev—would inflict irreparable harm on the NATO alliance, since the (obsolete) missiles had been committed to Turkey. In response, the president returned over and over again to an essential point: He was not going to take our nation to war over a pile of junk—worthless missiles in Turkey. It was a view I strongly shared.

In fact, at the end of the crisis, we informed Khrushchev that we intended to withdraw the missiles from Turkey, though secretly, and not as part of a deal. A foundation of the President's actions, as the tapes show, was *moral*.

McGeorge Bundy, the national security adviser at the time, once wrote that President Kennedy "was a man of the generation that learned from Reinhold Niebuhr that in the end one must accept the obligation to choose the lesser evil."[72] That he was, as were some of the rest of us. Kennedy acted on the belief that "victory" without the preservation of moral imperatives would be hollow. In the missile crisis, it may have meant a war in Cuba, or perhaps Soviet attacks on our Turkish missile bases, with worse to follow, or both.

❖

Stanley Hoffmann has written that "utilitarianism is better at giving one a good conscience than at providing a moral compass," while "the advantage of imperatives is that they provide at least a sense of direction."[73] Both are needed in the making of foreign policy: a moral compass and deviations from one's moral center, when necessary, to preserve and protect the national interest. The trick, the art, is in finding ways—the Kennedy brothers and some of their associates in the missile crisis provide a good example—to preserve the national interest while also holding fast to the essence of one's moral convictions.

The potential crises we are addressing in this book—a continuation into the 21st century of the unacceptable human carnage of the 20th century—are likely to be more like Vietnam, crises in slow motion, than like the Cuban missile crisis, which was brief and riveting. Our task in the years ahead will be to urge policies we believe will substantially reduce the killing of our fellow human beings by war without unacceptable risks to U.S. national interests.

The Multilateral Imperative:
Collective Decision Making, Collective Security

We believe we must associate the moral imperative with a multilateral imperative.

This is our multilateral imperative: Recognize that while the United States must provide leadership to the world to achieve the objective of reducing the risk of conflict, it will not apply its power—economic, political, or military—other than in a multilateral context, subject to multilateral decision making processes.

In the prologue, we listed the following among the lessons to be learned from Woodrow Wilson's failed attempt to implement his moral and multilateral imperatives: First, stick to basic moral values and avoid moralistic self-righteousness; and second, practice the multilateralism that you preach. Wilson himself tended to be both self-righteous and immune to the counsel of others. As a result, his efforts after the First World War ended in personal, national, and global tragedy. In fact, Wilson was afflicted with what might be called the "American disease," an insensitive unilateralism. Wilson's own case of it was once described as follows:

> Wilson was a great man but he had one basic fault. He was willing to do anything for people except get off their backs and let them live their own lives. He would never let go until they forced him to and then it was too late. He never seemed to understand there's a big difference between trying to save people and trying to help them. With luck you can help them—but they [must] always save themselves.[74]

Friends and foes alike attributed to Wilson this attitude: We Americans know best and the proof is in our success. Americans of Wilson's era believed, not without reason, that the entrance of the United States into the First World War had allowed the Allies to win the war. However, to many Americans—Wilson, perhaps, above all others—this meant that the United States had not just the right but the duty to dictate the terms of peace to others.

A similar sanctimoniousness characterizes the U.S. attitude toward the rest of the world in the wake of the end of the Cold War: We won and therefore we have the right and duty to dictate post–Cold War arrangements to friend and foe alike. Clinton administration Secretary of State Madeleine Albright recently proclaimed that the United States is "the indispensable nation" because "we stand tall and hence see further than other nations."[75] To some, this implies that other nations with whom we might wish to involve ourselves are "dispensable" in some sense. Albright's deputy secretary of state, Strobe Talbott, has provided a more nuanced statement of what America's modus operandi in the post–Cold War era should be, but often is not:

> In a fashion and to an extent that is unique in the history of the Great Powers, the United States defines its strength—indeed its very greatness—not in terms of its ability to achieve or maintain dominance over others, but in terms of its ability to work *with* others in the interests of the international community as a whole.... American foreign policy is consciously intended to advance *universal* values.[76]

As the Harvard political scientist Samuel P. Huntington has said, "American foreign policy is in considerable measure driven by such beliefs."[77] And yet, as he pointed out in a 1999 article in *Foreign Affairs* magazine, we consistently act unilaterally. According to Huntington, among our recent unilateralist actions are the following:

- Pressuring other countries to adopt American-style values and democracy.

- Preventing others from acquiring military capabilities that might challenge U.S. conventional superiority.

- Grading countries according to their adherence to American standards on human rights, drugs, terrorism, military issues, and religious freedom.

- Applying sanctions to countries that get failing "grades" on these issues.

- Promoting American business interests under the slogans of free trade and open markets.

- Promoting American arms sales abroad while trying to prevent similar sales by other countries.

- Forcing out one UN secretary general and dictating the appointment of his successor.

- Categorizing certain countries as "rogue states," excluding them from global institutions because they refuse to kowtow to American wishes.[78]

Many Americans do believe that America is the light of the world. The problem is that only Americans believe this. Others, including allies as well as adversaries, find remarks such as Albright's and the actions listed by Huntington to be self-righteous and arrogant, and as further evidence of U.S. duplicity—pretending to consult, pretending to take the views of others into account, but listening only to the sound of its own voice. It has been said that the United States cannot decide if it wants to be the world's policeman or the world's nanny.[79] This is why, as the *New York Times* recently reported, "At this moment . . . American power is unquestioned, but its authority is anything but."[80] The police and nannies are all-powerful in their respective domains. But authority is not solely, or even mainly, a derivative of power. Huntington has studied this issue carefully, empirically, and his conclusion is sobering:

> While the United States regularly denounces various countries as "rogue states," in the eyes of many countries it is becoming the rogue superpower. . . . The United States is unlikely to become an isolationist

country, withdrawing from the world. But it could become an isolated country, out of step with much of the world . . .

At a 1997 Harvard conference, scholars reported that the elites of countries comprising at least two-thirds of the world's people—Chinese, Russians, Indians, Arabs, Muslims, and Africans—see the United States as the single greatest threat to their societies. They do not regard America as a military threat but as a menace to their integrity, autonomy, prosperity, and freedom of action. They view the United States as intrusive, interventionist, exploitative, unilateralist, hegemonic, hypocritical, and applying double standards, engaging in what they label "financial imperialism" and "intellectual colonialism," with a foreign policy driven overwhelmingly by domestic politics.[81]

In other words, according to Huntington's data, the world as a whole feels policed and nannied by a United States that is unilateralist to its core and thus uninterested in the perspectives and opinions of others. That the United States is also regarded as hypocritical and self-righteous—claiming to consult when it only informs—only adds to the aggravation of the others.

If Huntington is right, it will not be long before America's reputation as hypocritically and arrogantly unilateralist comes back to haunt us. As the 21st century evolves, the United States will find that even its power, which peaked during the so-called unipolar moment of the Gulf War, will steadily diminish. We will not be able to shape the world as we choose. Japan and Western Europe will continue to play a large role on the world scene and are likely to assume greater economic and political responsibility. And by the middle of the 21st century, several of the countries belonging to what we formerly called the Third World will have grown so dramatically in population and economic power as to become major forces in international relations. India is likely to have a population of 1.6 billion; Nigeria, 400 million; Brazil, 300 million. And if China maintains satisfactory but not spectacular economic growth rates for the next 50 years, by midcentury its 1.6 billion people will have the income of Western Europeans in the 1960s. It will indeed be a power to be reckoned with economically, politically, and militarily.

These figures are of course speculative, but they emphasize something of the magnitude and pace of the changes that lie ahead and thus the need to adjust our goals, policies, and institutions to take account of them. This is the significance of the *perceptual* problem—the widespread belief that the United States refuses to decide and act multilaterally. If the U.S. reputation remains intact—as a unilateralist "wolf" poorly disguised as a multilateralist "sheep"—then finding partners to get things done will be difficult. But partners will be necessary, as the relative power of the United States to act unilaterally—effectively and at acceptable cost—will decline steadily throughout the century.

There is also another issue involved, disturbing in its implications. We are not practicing in an international context what we preach, and what we practice domestically—which is *democratic* decision making. We are not omniscient. We say that we believe that better decisions result from a decision-making process that has the comprehensive involvement of representatives of all the affected parties, but here again, the United States is hypocritical. Often we proceed without seeking, or listening to, advice from those with common values and common objectives. If we cannot convince them of the merit of our proposed action, we should question the wisdom of our decision.

Had the United States applied this rule to Vietnam, it would never have been at war in Indochina. Not one of its major allies—not Britain, France, Germany, or Japan—supported the American decision to intervene. The United States should have paid particular attention to the French, who had over 100 years of experience in the region. "Do not get bogged down," they said many times, and in many contexts, "the way we got bogged down in Vietnam." President Charles de Gaulle advocated a "neutral solution" for Vietnam as early as 1963. Vietnam, de Gaulle told George Ball, is a "rotten country."[82] U.S. leaders should have listened. They didn't, and they paid the price of tragically repeating many of the mistakes the French had made earlier.

The historian Arthur Schlesinger, Jr. has written that "a democracy is in bad shape when it keeps two sets of books—when it uses one scale of values for its internal policy and another in foreign affairs."[83] Schlesinger is right: The United States will make better decisions when it applies its democratic processes to foreign policy decision making as comprehensively as it does to domestic actions. It can do so by widening the circle of those who are consulted. As Richard Haass recently wrote in *Foreign Affairs*: "If *negotiations* were at the center of Cold War diplomacy, *consultations* must form the core of post–Cold War foreign policy. The goal is to build or strengthen global institutions that buttress the basic principles of order."[84] The United States did not do this with respect to Vietnam—and Cuba, Iran, Iraq, and elsewhere—and it has paid a double price: decisions leading to less than optimal results (or, in the case of Vietnam, to tragedy); and the reinforcement of its unsavory reputation as a unilateralist policeman-nanny.

Principles of Security and Defense Policy for the 21st Century

The end of the Cold War was a watershed event, ushering in a new international situation, such as occurred following the two world wars. Stanley Hoffmann has identified the conundrum at the heart of this new situation:

> The Wilsonian edifice, its Rooseveltian version of 1945, the Bush coat of fresh paint in 1990, all were undertaken to deal with a world of interstate conflicts. . . . What is now at stake is the very nature of the state. . . . Internationalism thus faces a predicament. First, it needs a set of clear principles to set goals.[85]

The world of more or less sovereign nation-states, inaugurated by the Treaty of Westphalia in 1648, seems to be falling apart.

Threats to the viability of many states can be characterized as "postcolonial," in a sense similar to the postcolonial breakups, chaos, and violence that followed the First and Second World Wars. This time, as before, empires are crumbling. Wars rage off and on in a half-dozen former republics of the Soviet Union. Many of these conflicts can be described as "communal," as ancient claims are brought to bear with regard to peoples, borders, and sovereignty. The same can be said of two nations not previously thought of as "empires," but which are nevertheless in various stages of disintegration: the former Yugoslavia, whose collective disaster in the 1990s was one of the decade's worst; and Indonesia, a vast archipelago in which communal violence has been initiated by various separatist groups in attempts to apply pressure on Jakarta for their independence. And in Africa, deadly conflicts have cost millions of lives in Rwanda, Burundi, Sudan, Angola, the Congo, Sierra Leone, Somalia, Ethiopia, and Eritrea, with several other areas seemingly primed for similar disasters—a legacy of joint irresponsibility on the part of the former European colonial powers and the various African regimes that succeeded them.

Few states are ethnically and religiously homogeneous. What will happen if the nation-state system fails and many of the more than 5,000 identifiable ethnic groups in the world demand independence in a crescendo of worldwide identity politics? How will the chaos and violence be contained? If German militarism was the dominant fear after the First World War, and Soviet expansionism the concern following the Second World War, one of the post–Cold War nightmare scenarios is the collapse of the nation-state system itself, leading to chronic global instability, unprecedented communal violence, and war, with consequent increased risk of use of weapons of mass destruction. Whereas before we chiefly feared the spread of totalitarian control, we now fear the collapse of the central controlling force in contemporary world politics, the nation-state, and descent into a kind of hell in which such order and control as exists is exerted by thugs, gangs, and terrorist groups, armed with the latest and most lethal weaponry. This is what Hoffmann calls our "predicament," for which we most urgently need "a clear set of principles to set goals."

Such a set of principles must, we believe, constitute a *radical* agenda for the 21st century. In the two preceding sections, we have presented an outline of our moral and multilateral imperatives. They provide the intellectual foundation of the entire radical agenda to which we subscribe. Both are radical departures from the recent past. Both call to mind the crisis measures that Woodrow Wilson tried and failed to institute following the First World War, which became the trip-wire initiating history's most lethal century. In the remainder of this book, we will offer a more comprehensive outline of our agenda for the 21st century.

In Chapter Two we will discuss prevention of war among the Great

Powers. In particular, we will advocate that relations between Russia and the other Great Powers, and between China and the other Great Powers, must be as fully reconciled as those between France and Germany, and the United States and Japan, and with just as little likelihood of war between them.

Chapter Three will focus on all other forms of conflict between and within states. The following four steps will be paramount: the prevention of war and the termination of conflict in the event deterrence fails; establishing a multilateral mechanism for the application of force; guaranteeing the borders of all states against external aggression; and codifying and enforcing the rights of minorities and ethnic groups within states.

Chapter Four will explore actions to avoid nuclear war, reducing the risk that entire nations may be destroyed if collective security should fail.

This is an agenda to avoid catastrophic loss of life in the 21st century, an agenda easier to articulate than to achieve. It will not be achieved in a year, or even a decade. The actions required are too radically at variance with past practice to believe otherwise. It will be achieved, if at all, slowly and through small steps by leaders of dedication and persistence. Where will these leaders come from? The leadership role will no doubt shift among nations, depending on the issue at hand. But more often than not, no nation other than the United States will be capable of filling that role. But we cannot succeed in such an endeavor without the consultation and cooperation of other nations. And we will not receive the required cooperation if we continue to act unilaterally, as though we were omniscient. Clearly we are not.

Wilson's ghost looms large and foreboding before the world as we contemplate the 21st century. This is especially true for Americans. On July 10, 1919, in presenting the peace treaty to the U.S. Senate, President Wilson said: "The only question is whether we can refuse the moral leadership that is offered us, whether we shall accept or reject the confidence of the world."[86] The burden of responsibility for the 21st century is shared by all nations, but because the United States is by far the strongest nation, the largest single share of that responsibility belongs to it. Tragically, America refused its share of the burden following the First World War. The result was the violent death of approximately 50 million people in the Second World War. If we fail this time to act on the imperatives we share with Wilson, all of civilization may be at risk before the century is concluded.

My deliberate judgment is that our whole weight should be thrown for an armistice which will not permit a renewal of hostilities by Germany, but which will be as moderate and reasonable as possible within that condition, because lately I am certain that too much severity on the part of the allies will make a genuine peace settlement exceedingly difficult if not impossible. . . . Foresight is better than immediate advantage.

Woodrow Wilson, July 29, 1918[1]

It is going to take time for the new Russia to come to terms with itself. . . . But let us, in the meantime, not confuse ourselves, and let us not unnecessarily complicate our problem, by creating a Russia of our imagination to take the place of the one that did, alas, once exist, but fortunately is no more.

George F. Kennan, 1996[2]

Should the United States look upon China as a potential enemy and therefore seek to weaken or divide it, thereby creating the reality we seek to avoid? I believe the answer is no. To move in this direction would become a self-fulfilling prophecy. . . . The future well-being of the American and Chinese people depends on the ability of these two nations to cooperate.

Senator Sam Nunn, 1996[3]

2

Preventing Great Power Conflict

Bringing Russia and China in from the Cold

The terms of the Treaty of Versailles impoverished and humiliated Germany, which felt betrayed, because the Germans believed they had agreed to an armistice based on Woodrow Wilson's formula of "peace without victors." The betrayal felt by Germany fueled the rise of the Nazis, leading to the Second World War and, in fact, ensured that the 20th century would be soaked in blood. Wilson's ghost has already appeared in the 21st century, as Russia and China have become increasingly suspicious of the United States and the West for having betrayed them, reneging (as the Russians believe) on commitments not to expand the NATO alliance on Russia's western border; and (as the Chinese believe) on commitments to avoid supporting independence for Taiwan. Public opinion in the United States and the West dangerously fails to appreciate the possibility of a Great Power clash and/or to make plans to prevent it. We provide an approach to understanding why a conflict might arise via a lack of empathy for the situations faced by the Russians and Chinese; and by the failure to anticipate inadvertent conflict that is the unintended consequence of actions taken by a multilateral cast of characters over time, rather than a direct and present threat to U.S. interests.

"Wilson's Ghost," the Origins of the Second World War, and the Risk of a Third

As the 21st century begins, Wilson's Ghost may haunt us if we do not now begin to ask ourselves how a Great Power conflict might begin and what must be done to prevent it. Understanding Wilson's vision, however, can help us immeasurably in finally laying to rest Wilson's ghost. Woodrow Wilson and the other Allied leaders failed after the First World War to establish a sustainable peace with their defeated adversary, Germany. Almost alone among his contemporaries, Wilson understood the problem: If Germany was not, in the phrase of our own day, brought "in from the cold," if the Germans were instead to be humiliated, to feel betrayed, and to become ever more paranoid as they looked out on the world then, said Wilson, "I do not hesitate to say that the war we have just been through, though it was shot through with terror of every kind, is not to be compared with the war we would have to face next time."[4] Tragically, this is exactly what happened. The Allies' treatment of Germany after the First World War is a parable of how *not* to prevent Great Power conflict, the lessons of which apply to a principal task of the United States and the West in the 21st century: bringing Russia and China "in from the cold."

Here, in roughest outline, is how the seeds were planted that grew into the Second World War. On November 9, 1918, Kaiser Wilhelm II abdicated his throne as German emperor, in the wake of a popular uprising. There followed a meeting in a railway car in the forest of Compiègne, in France, where a representative of the new German government signed an armistice by the terms of which Germany agreed to lay down its arms. At the 11th hour of the 11th day of the 11th month in 1918, the armistice took effect, ending the First World War.[5]

The German government, in signing the armistice, had put its faith in Woodrow Wilson's "Fourteen Points" which, according to Wilson, would lead to "a peace without victors," chiefly by means of a nonpunitive peace treaty that would leave Germany with the capacity to rebuild itself into a democratic republic, and via the establishment of the League of Nations, which would enforce the European peace thereafter. At the time of the signing of the armistice, not a single foreign soldier occupied German territory. Indeed, many German soldiers and civilians believed, on the basis of Wilson's program to end the war and secure the peace, that Germany had not, in fact, *lost* the war. One German town famously erected a banner with which to welcome its returning troops that read: "Welcome, brave soldiers, your work has been done; God and Wilson will carry on."[6]

One can speculate as to whether God prevailed, but Wilson did not. To the representatives of France, Britain, and Italy—the three major allies of the United States—the Treaty of Versailles could have but one purpose: to punish Germany by extracting as much of its wealth and territory as possible, thereby leaving it too weak and destitute to threaten its neighbors thereafter. According to the terms of the treaty, the Germans lost a great deal: 25,000 square miles of territory containing approximately six million people; all their overseas colonies; and much of their natural resource base and industrial capacity.

But the aspect of the peace treaty that most angered the Germans was the humiliating clause 231, by which they were forced to accept all responsibility and guilt for the First World War. It read:

> The Allied and Associated Governments affirm, and Germany accepts, the responsibility of Germany and her allies for causing all the loss and damage to which the Allied and Associated Governments and their nationals have been subjected as a consequence of the war imposed upon them by aggression of Germany and her allies.[7]

The Weimar government, forced to agree to this, thereby forfeited a good deal of its credibility with the German people, who felt betrayed—by Wilson and by his European allies. Many Germans also felt betrayed by groups that would suffer grievously after the Nazis came to power in 1933: German pacifists, Jews, republicans, homosexuals, and socialists. They would be Hitler's scapegoats in the Nazis' successful transformation of the widespread feelings of betrayal and hatred deriving from the Treaty of Versailles into the basis for a fanatical war machine.

As the Yale historian Donald Kagan has written, the treaty "was neither conciliatory enough to remove the desire for change, even at the cost of war, nor harsh enough to make another war impossible."[8] In humiliating Germany, in pressing for every conceivable momentary advantage from her, and in giving rise to her feelings of betrayal and the need for vengeance, the Allies at Versailles helped sow the seeds of their own devastation at Germany's hands in the Second World War.

If the lessons of this Wilsonian parable are not heeded, a Third World War could result sometime in the 21st century. Such an event may seem highly improbable at the moment and may remain so for some time. But we nevertheless discern an eerie resonance between Germany's feelings of betrayal in 1919 with those of Russia and China following the Cold War. Even more troubling, we also see similarities between the victors' enthusiasm for humiliating Germany in 1919 and the lack of empathy so far shown in the West—particularly by the United States—for the situation of the major communist "losers" in the half-century–long Cold War. For these reasons, we believe, a Great Power conflict between Russia or China (or both) and the United States is not impossible and, in fact, the risk of such a conflict may rise over time, unless we act to lower that risk. In 1919, as the combatants in the First World War sat down to negotiate in Paris, the risk of another Great Power conflict was also low. By 1933, with the ascension of the Nazis to power, it may have been too late to prevent it. This, therefore, should be our objective: to prevent the 21st century from ever arriving at its own figurative "1933."

The Imperatives for Preventing Great Power Conflict

In Chapter One, we recommended that, in the 21st century, special emphasis should be placed on limiting the risk of war between and among Great Powers. The most critical task before us in this regard is the integration of Russia and China into relations with the other Great Powers as fully as France and Germany were reconciled after centuries of enmity, and as fully as the United States and Japan have been reconciled after one of the most brutal wars ever fought. It is easy to forget how astonishing was the reconciliation of Germany and Japan with the United States and other Western powers following the Second World War. Can it be done again? Can we not move to integrate both Russia and

China fully into the "global village" of the 21st century—into a prosperous, interdependent, cosmopolitan relationship with the other Great Powers, particularly the United States?

In seeking to address this question, it has become clearer than ever that, despite its peculiarities, the Cold War had many of the characteristics of a Great Power *war*. Before the astounding events of 1989, for example, little serious thought was given in the West, and particularly in the United States, to the reconciliation or integration of Russia and China into an international system of shared values, beliefs, and institutions. The communist "bloc" was the enemy, and it had its own system—its own mutual security and economic organizations. A principal purpose of such organizations, on both sides, was to *prevent* anything resembling integration between the two systems. Reconciliation on terms acceptable to both blocs was generally seen as an impossible pipe dream and suggestions to the contrary were customarily regarded on both sides as seditious, as caving into the enemy. The emphasis was on intra-bloc solidarity, not inter-bloc integration. Officials and ordinary citizens on both sides of the Cold War divide got up every morning and, in effect, went to war, a far colder war than the first two world wars but a war nonetheless, the outcome of which would be a winning side and a losing side.

The Cold War's principal surprise is that it never erupted into a full-blown military conflict between two or more of the Great Powers on either side. It ended instead with a sudden, unexpected communist "whimper" rather than with the "bang" of nuclear explosions that were the principal fear of the entire period. The Soviet Union collapsed, and communist ideology was globally and irreversibly discredited (although communist parties retained power in a few countries, including China). All this happened without Western military conquest and occupation, without any kind of official "surrender." That all this happened peacefully was both a shock and a blessing.

Yet this supreme blessing of the Cold War—its relative "coldness," including its peaceful conclusion—is, in a sense, the post–Cold War era's curse, because it mimics, in an eerie way, the conclusion and aftermath of the First World War. Just as the other Great Power signees of the Treaty of Versailles ensured that Germany entered the 1920s humiliated, destabilized, bankrupt, and bitter, Russia and China after the Cold War seem in many respects to feel alienated—politically, economically, militarily, socially, and psychologically—from the global community established by the other Great Powers. Russia and China, in their individual ways, still feel very much "out in the cold," just as Germany did 80 years before. While of course history never repeats itself exactly, the comparison with the aftermath of the First World War yields sobering scenarios regarding the potential consequences of leaving Russia and China alienated from the West.

It is useful to keep in mind why the end of the previous Great Power conflict, World War II, does *not,* in most respects, offer useful lessons for those seeking guidance on how to achieve the integration and reconciliation for Russia and China in the 21st century. The difference is obvious but critically important: The unconditional surrender, and subsequent extended occupation, of Germany and Japan made it possible for the United States and the West to *force* quick integration and eventual reconciliation with their former enemies. No such possibility exists with regard to Russia's and China's entrance into the mainstream of the 21st century.

In the absence of military occupation of Russia and China, and the consequent impossibility of their enforced tutelage in Western-style civil society, and political and economic affairs, by what indirect means might the United States and the West bring these powers "in from the cold"? How might this be accomplished, moreover, before Russia's and China's alienation from, and suspicion of, the United States and the West provoke a crisis, possibly leading to a military confrontation? If we cannot forcibly remold Russia and China according to Western political values, how can we reach them, make contact with them, develop a dialogue of mutual exploration, by the conclusion of which their integration and reconciliation might be achieved? These are the key questions regarding the prevention of Great Power conflict in the 21st century.

The First Imperative: Deploy Realistic Empathy

Our answer is to deploy "realistic empathy," a process that, we believe, must lie at the heart of any successful strategy of bringing Russia and China "in from the cold." With occupation neither a realistic (or desirable) option, a policy based on empathy is an idea whose time has come.

Think of it this way: a policy whose objective is not to preach but to listen; to learn something of the history and culture of Russia and China, rather than to proclaim the virtues of our history and systems; to treat them, in effect, as our equals, as peoples and cultures who seek peace and tranquility but also dignity and respect. Thus, a strategy of realistic empathy should emphasize, in the first instance, both the reeducation of Russians and Chinese *and* the reeducation of Americans and the leaders and citizens of the other Western Great Powers.

Empathy has nothing to do with sympathy, with which it is often confused. Ralph K. White, a former U.S. Information Agency official, later a political scientist and psychologist at George Washington University, was for a generation the foremost advocate of realistic empathy in foreign affairs, and he made exactly the distinction that must be made between empathy and sympathy. According to White:

> Empathy is the *great* corrective for all forms of war-promoting misperception. It means simply understanding the thoughts and feelings of others. It is distinguished from sympathy, which is defined as feeling with others—as being in agreement with them. Empathy with opponents is therefore psychologically possible even when a conflict is so intense that sympathy is out of the question. We are not talking about warmth or approval, and certainly not about agreeing with, or siding with, but only about realistic understanding.[9]

White goes on to explain what might be called the implementation of empathy in the cause of reducing the risk of conflict:

> How can empathy be achieved? It means jumping in imagination into another person's skin, imagining what it might be like to look out at his world through his eyes, and imagining how you might feel about what you saw. It means *being* the other person, at least for a while, and postponing skeptical analysis until later. . . . Most of all it means trying to

look at one's own group's behavior honestly, as it might appear when seen through the other's eyes, recognizing that his eyes are almost certainly jaundiced, but recognizing also that he has the advantage of not seeing our group's behavior through the rose-colored glasses that we ourselves normally wear. We may have grounds for distrust, fear, and anger that we have not permitted ourselves to see. That is the point where honesty comes in. An honest look at the other implies an honest look at oneself.[10]

The United States is at present the world's only superpower and is commonly regarded by friends and foes alike as arrogant and lacking in objectivity toward itself. Thus, it is possible that a principal benefit to Americans of the deployment of a strategy of realistic empathy would be an unprecedented "honest look at oneself." Should this occur, it could easily have a stunning effect upon the Russians and the Chinese, who have often expressed the view that it is useless talking to Americans because they refuse to believe that their political system has any faults or any limitations on its application anywhere in the world.

White also identified three critical mistakes in foreign policy making that prevent empathy from occurring: (1) not seeing an opponent's longing for peace; (2) not seeing an opponent's fear of being attacked; and (3) not seeing an opponent's understandable anger.[11]

❖

Robert McNamara: The mistakes identified by Ralph White—and others— were made in both Washington and Hanoi during the escalation of the Vietnam war between 1961 and 1968, but not during the short, intense period of the Cuban missile crisis. In what follows, I want to quote some key documentation: from a June 1997 conference on the Vietnam war, held in Hanoi, and from the transcript of the tape recordings made by President Kennedy on October 27, 1962, the most dangerous day of the Cuban missile crisis. Together, they illustrate two points: first, that without the sort of realistic empathy described by Ralph White, it is possible for two countries—the United States and North Vietnam—to fight a terribly destructive war with each other, even though they have almost no history of conflict, and no territorial disagreements of any kind; and second, when realistic empathy is deployed in the service of resolving a conflict, results approaching the miraculous are possible. President Johnson and his senior advisers had almost no realistic empathy during the escalation in Vietnam, especially between 1965 and 1968, when the war become an American war. President Kennedy and some of his associates, on the other hand, had it in abundance in October 1962.

Among the most difficult, but most fruitful, of the discussions in Hanoi were the initial exchanges on "mindsets." During this discussion, which lasted the better part of a day, representatives of each side explained to one another their own mindsets in the 1960s, and their perceptions of the mindsets held by their adversaries at that time. As you will observe in the following excerpt, it is not easy, even more than three decades after the events being reexamined, to clear the air and really "occupy" the mindsets of those whose views were so profoundly misunderstood at the time.

My interlocutors in the excerpt are the late Nguyen Co Thach, the former Vietnamese foreign minister, and leader of the Vietnamese delegation to the June 1997 conference; and Nguyen Khac Huynh, who was in the period under discussion one of North Vietnam's leading specialists on the United States.

Robert McNamara: Before discussing the U.S. mindset, I want to state, and I want to state it quite frankly, that if I had been a Vietnamese communist in January 1961, when the Kennedy administration came to office, I might well have believed, as I judge they did, that the United States' goal in Southeast Asia was to destroy the Hanoi government and its ally, the National Liberation Front—that the U.S. was an implacable enemy whose goal, in some fashion, was victory over their country.

However, if I had been a Vietnamese communist and had held those views, I would have been *totally mistaken*. We in the Kennedy administration had no such intention; we had no such aims with respect to Vietnam. On the contrary, we believed our interests were being attacked all over the world by a highly organized, unified communist movement, led by Moscow and Beijing, of which we believed, and I now think incorrectly, that the government of Ho Chi Minh was a pawn.

So, put very simply, our mindset was indeed one of what President Eisenhower identified as the fear of "falling dominoes."

Nguyen Co Thach: In my way of thinking, the principal problem in the evolution of these mindsets was that—especially in the 1950s and 1960s—the U.S. seemed to want to become the world's policeman. Mr. McNamara correctly quotes President Kennedy's Inaugural Address as evidence of a certain anti-communist mindset—a fear that communism would overrun the U.S., or something of the sort. Actually, it seemed to us that in Kennedy's inaugural, he was asserting that the U.S. wished to become something like the "master of the world." In this way, the U.S. would replace the British and the French, who had previously based their policies on such a wish. In our part of the world, this "fear of falling dominoes" was joined to the "threat of the yellow skin"—so those were two reasons, or excuses, really, why the U.S. felt justified in taking over as the new imperialists.

Therefore, I would say, with all due respect to Mr. McNamara, that the U.S. mindset, as he says, was incorrect, but also that the Vietnamese mindset—our assessment of the U.S.—was essentially correct.

Nguyen Khac Huynh: Mr. McNamara has said the U.S. did not have colonialist aims. The U.S. did not precisely follow the example of the English or French. When the English or French conquered an area, they established a colonial governor. The governor was all-powerful. If there was already a king or an emperor in place, then they usually retained him as a puppet, as long as he was compliant. The U.S. set up a puppet regime through the use of economic and military assistance that was under U.S. control. In this regime, the U.S. ambassador played the role of a French or British governor general. The U.S. ambassador took the orders he received from Washington and passed them on to the puppet government in Saigon. In case the government did not satisfy the U.S., the U.S. would not hesitate to replace it.

Here is the second point. . . . In the resistance war against the French, we lived in the jungles for nearly ten years and eventually defeated them without having much information about their policies and strategies. We nevertheless knew more about the French than the U.S., since we had to be with them for nearly 100 years. But our knowledge about the U.S., which became our enemy, was far from sufficient. That is true. It was natural that we did not know much about U.S. internal affairs, the role your domestic politics played in the war, especially in the early days of the war. And our knowledge about the U.S. relationship with the rest of the world, which Mr. McNamara has referred to as the "geopolitical factor," was quite limited. We therefore formulated our strategies and policies principally on the basis of our assessment of the actual situation on the battlefield.

In these circumstances, what more could we do to make the U.S. understand us? Truly, we did not know how to do it.

Robert McNamara: We certainly misunderstood Vietnam. But I believe in the discussions this morning and this afternoon, there has been strong evidence that you did then—and I suspect even today—that you misunderstood us and our evaluation of the situation in Vietnam. I think I can speak for Presidents Kennedy and Johnson, with whom I was very close. I can certainly speak for myself. We were *not* opposed to an independent, unified Vietnam. We were *not*!

So let me try again and I want to be blunt. What we feared was a Vietnam that was a pawn in the hands of the Soviets and/or the Chinese. . . . I believe we misunderstood each other. I think it is a tragedy. We were not opposed to your independence. Ho Chi Minh was correct when he quoted our Declaration of Independence in his early statements, in 1945, when he formed this country. We believed those sentiments then (in 1776), and we believe them today. I know we don't always act in accordance with those beliefs, but those *are* our fundamental beliefs. I don't think you appealed to them. I don't think you understood them. And I am damn certain we didn't understand that that was your belief. So I think it's a tragedy that we allowed that misunderstanding to exist and I hope we won't allow it to continue in the future.[12]

What a tragedy! We believed that the North Vietnamese were merely doing the bidding of the Soviets and Chinese, obsessed with spreading communism over all of southeast Asia. So we discounted their nationalism and completely missed the point of the war, as they saw it, which was to unify their country under Vietnamese leadership—not French, not Japanese, not Chinese, and certainly not American leadership. They, on the other hand, concluded that our aims were those of these other colonial powers, and went to war to throw us out when, in reality, we didn't want to be there in the first place, except to prevent them from spreading communism. There was approximately zero empathy on each side, no understanding in Washington and Hanoi of the values and assumptions that were driving the policies of their adversaries.

Contrast the absence of empathy between Washington and Hanoi regarding the escalation of the war in Vietnam with the following example of optimum empathy when the chips are down. Here was the situation. It was the climactic weekend of the missile crisis, the closest the United States and the Soviet Union would ever come to war—nuclear war—with one another. On Friday, October 26, 1962, President Kennedy received a private letter from Soviet leader Nikita Khrushchev, which was rambling and somewhat ambiguous—it appeared to have been dictated by a person under great stress—but which seemed to propose a resolution to the missile crisis that we could accept. The deal would be: Khrushchev would pledge publicly to remove Soviet missiles from Cuba; we would pledge publicly not to invade Castro's Cuba.

Then, overnight, before we could act on the offer, Khrushchev made a public announcement that was waiting for us when we gathered to resume our deliberations the following morning. This message described a public deal that many of those advising President Kennedy believed we could not accept: that in addition to the conditions of the previous letter, the Soviets would require us to remove what they called "analogous" NATO missiles on their southern rim in Turkey. Although the NATO missiles (U.S. Jupiters) were nearly worthless militarily, there were a host of reasons this condition was difficult for us to accept. The missiles were under the jurisdiction of NATO, not the United States, and both the Turks and the European members of NATO had made clear to us that such a deal would appear to be selling out a NATO ally in order to settle a local dispute in the Western hemisphere unrelated (as they saw it) to NATO at all.

At one point in the discussion, Llewellyn ("Tommy") Thompson, a former ambassador to Moscow who had vast experience with the Soviets and with Khrushchev personally, suggested that we simply ignore the second letter that contained the unacceptable deal, and reply to the first. President

Kennedy was skeptical of this strategy, and for good reason. The original offer had come via a private letter from Khrushchev, but the second one was public, leading the president to believe that the second letter must be operative in Moscow. There is where we come in on perhaps the single most important exchange of the entire crisis and, given the stakes at that supremely dangerous moment, one of the most important discussions of the entire Cold War.

President Kennedy: We're not going to get these weapons out of Cuba, probably, anyway . . . I mean by negotiation. . . . I don't think there's any doubt he's not going to retreat now that he made that public, Tommy. He's not going to take them out of Cuba.

Llewellyn Thompson: I don't agree, Mr. President. I think there's still a chance that we can get this line going.

President Kennedy: He'll back down?

Llewellyn Thompson: The important thing for Khrushchev, it seems to me, is to be able to say "I saved Cuba; I stopped an invasion," and he can get away with this, if he wants to, and he's had a go at this Turkey thing, and that we'll discuss later.

President Kennedy: All right.[13]

I still shiver every time I read those lines. On the one hand, here was the president, with time running out, looking for a way to resolve the crisis peacefully, but confused by the dual communications from Khrushchev. On the other was Tommy Thompson, a senior level foreign service officer but in terms of rank, one of the lowest ranking members of the group discussing how to respond to Khrushchev. But so great was the president's belief in Tommy's expertise—his empathy with Khrushchev and the leadership in Moscow—that he put the key question to Tommy, then and there, to vote it up or down. And Tommy, who was by nature a shy man of few words, stood his ground in the face of presidential skepticism. He told the president that if Khrushchev got the no-invasion pledge, he would declare victory to his people and get the missiles the hell out of Cuba, no matter which letter came first, and no matter which letter was public or private. And that is exactly what happened.

I thank God we had a president who was, in McGeorge Bundy's phrase, "fully on the job"—inquisitive, forceful, determined to find a way out short of war—and an adviser whose empathy with the Soviets allowed him to be, at that moment, virtually our in-house Russian.[14] Without that president, so full of determination to avoid a Great Power conflict, and that adviser, so full of empathy for our Soviet adversary, I shudder to think what the outcome of those dangerous days might have been.

❖

The great philosopher of empathy, Sir Isaiah Berlin, wrote that in addition to knowing the mind of an adversary, empathy requires one to grasp "the particular vision of the universe which lies at the heart of [an adversary's] thought." This capacity, he said, permits one to "to some degree re-enact the states of mind of men" who are fundamentally at odds with oneself.[15] This is what we call the "deployment" of empathy, the "occupation" of a mindset whose assumptions are fundamentally alien from one's own.

Michael Ignatieff has written that to refrain from the deployment of empathy in situations such as those described above is fundamentally immoral. To act uninformed by empathy, to refuse to occupy as fully as possible the mindset of an actual or potential adversary, is to submit to what he calls "autism," the behavior of those who are "so locked into their own myths . . . that they can't listen, can't hear, can't learn from anybody outside themselves." In these instances, according to Ignatieff, "What is denied is the possibility of empathy: that human understanding is capable of penetrating the bell jars of separate identities. But social peace anywhere depends for its survival on just this epistemological act of faith: when it comes to political understanding, difference is always minor, comprehension is always possible."[16]

But when empathy is embraced it is possible, as the example of Kennedy and Thompson demonstrates, to construct a peaceful solution even when all the momentum of history, politics, and military alerting schedules seem to be forcing the parties involved to calamitous hostilities. This option is fully available now to anyone in the United States, and the West generally, who seeks to find common cause with the Russians and Chinese.

The Second Imperative: Anticipate Inadvertent Conflict

This is our second imperative for preventing Great Power conflict: Anticipate that any military confrontation between the United States and either Russia or China may occur inadvertently. Inadvertent conflict is not "accidental" conflict. Rather, it is conflict that occurs due to the unintended consequences of actions taken by many actors, over an extended period, at the outset of which none of the actors will have anticipated a crisis leading to heightened risk of war between two or more of them.

It is becoming increasingly apparent that the gravest threats to Great Power security, and to the peace of the world, derive not from threats uttered or implied at the moment, but from *inadvertence*—from unintended consequences of hugely complicated interactions of policies, pronouncements, and actions taken over time by a multilateral cast of players. In fact, often some of the most important actions leading to conflict are taken years, decades, or centuries before the shooting begins. *History*—incommensurable interpretations of the "same" history—must also be taken into account as a potentially explosive factor in a process leading to increased risk of conflict.

No leader in U.S. history understood better than Woodrow Wilson the significance of preventing inadvertent conflict. Here is Wilson speaking to Congress on January 8, 1918, in the speech containing the original formulation of his Fourteen Points, leading to a "peace without victors":

What we demand . . . is that the world be made fit and safe to live in. . . . All the peoples of the world are in effect partners in this interest, and for our own part we see very clearly that unless justice be done to others it will not be done to us.[17]

Wilson was not driven to this view because he *knew* that a Second

World War would result if the United States and its allies in Europe did not think this way. He never claimed to know this much. He could not state the probability of a second cataclysm then, or later.

Rather, Wilson felt compelled to think in this radically multilateral fashion for two reasons, both of which apply equally to the 20th century and to the 21st. First, World War I was the first conflict to result in a global catastrophe. It must be kept in mind that no one saw this coming. A disaster on this scale was thought to be merely the stuff of science fiction. That is the first reason for Wilson's emphasis on inadvertence and multilateral thinking: Something had to be done, and quickly—something that might prevent it from ever happening again. The League of Nations, which was virtually Wilson's conception alone, was based on a revolutionary thought: that the affairs of nations might be decided within a multilateral organization of openness and transparency. Second, Wilson was convinced that the growing interdependence of the world and its technological development—what we today call "globalization"—had made obsolete the traditional view of security, which emphasized threat, deterrence, and secrecy in the service of maintaining optimum anxiety in an adversary as to one's political and military capacity to back up the threats.

It is a perversely fascinating fact of life as we enter the 21st century that, while our capacity to destroy our fellow human beings is in effect infinite, and the globalization and interconnection of the world is now almost beyond comprehension—in spite of these developments, concepts of national security and foreign policy still rely almost exclusively on assumptions of direct threat, counterthreat, and the like. To an extent, new ideas appeared in the late 1950s, as specialists began to study the implications of endeavoring to "defend" the country in a situation where there could be no meaningful defense against Soviet ballistic missiles tipped with nuclear warheads. In this singularly uncomfortable fact lay the origins of the so-called theory of nuclear deterrence, according to which each side in the Cold War sought to convince its adversary that an attack by the opponent very probably would result in unacceptable damage inflicted in a retaliatory strike.

The bottom line from these developments was even less comforting to Americans than the knowledge that the Russians (after 1949) and the

Chinese (after 1964) had nuclear weapons. It was this: that in order to avoid nuclear destruction, one must rely on the sanity and discretion of the enemy not to launch a devastating first strike against the United States. The Russians and Chinese, in other words, had to become our *collaborators,* and we had to become theirs, in pursuit of our mutual survival. We had to trust each other—no easy task for either side then or now.

One of the most influential American interpreters of this peculiar situation was the Harvard economist and strategist Thomas Schelling. His analysis of the Cold War suggested to him that the competition between Great Powers in the nuclear age was governed less by specific military capabilities than by what he called "competition in risk-taking."[18] Attempts at coercion, according to Schelling, now were principally "psychological"—consisting of efforts to manipulate the risk of producing a crisis that might *inadvertently,* by a process that could not be foreseen in detail, lead to nuclear war. Schelling speculated that perhaps the Great Power that was willing to tolerate greater risk of such a conflict would prevail in Great Power confrontations—that is, if a war was avoided, especially a war involving nuclear weapons.

Schelling also noticed that what he called "threats which leave something to chance" have a peculiar and unexpected result between Great Powers in the nuclear age: the threats are just as threatening to the threatener as they are to the side that is threatened. In such a situation, Schelling wrote, the threat becomes "more impersonal, more 'external' to the participants; the threat becomes part of the environment rather than a test of will between two adversaries."[19]

This was nowhere more apparent than in the Cuban missile crisis of October 1962, which became a kind of learning laboratory for all sides regarding the necessity for thinking deeply about how a war might start. Richard Neustadt and Graham Allison offer the following plausible reconstruction of President Kennedy's thinking during the crisis:

If the Russians held their course for a mere seventy-two hours, we would have to escalate a step, probably by bombing Cuban sites. In logic, they should then bomb Turkish sites. Then we . . . ; then they . . . *The third step* is what evidently haunted Kennedy. If Khrushchev's capability to calculate and control was something like his own, then neither's might suffice to guide them both through that third step without holocaust.[20]

Neustadt and Allison observe that "no event demonstrates more clearly than the missile crisis that with respect to nuclear war there is an awesome crack between *unlikelihood* and *impossibility*."[21] This is an absolutely critical point about focusing on inadvertent conflict: Probabilities concerning conflict, based on threat assessment, are no longer necessarily decisive; the missile crisis proved that the most dangerous kind of Great Power conflict might result from actions neither side intended to be threatening, but that were perceived as threatening.

❖

Robert McNamara: When it first became known that the Russians were building nuclear missile sites in Cuba, President Kennedy and many of his advisers believed that an attack on the missile sites was almost inevitable. The reason was this: The president had warned the Russians publicly the previous month that, if they were to put missiles in Cuba, "the gravest issues would arise"—which is a diplomatic way of saying that we would remove them by force, if necessary.[22] But of course, we never dreamed that they would actually do it, for the simple reason that we would find it totally unacceptable.

But after a few hours of discussion, it became obvious to some of us—certainly to me—that we had to consider what the Russians would do if we attacked and, depending on the level and location of their military response, how we might respond to their response. Dick Neustadt and Graham Allison are absolutely correct. I personally could not get beyond "the third step" without risking, in my own mind, a nuclear exchange that would have disastrous consequences for us, for the Russians and Cubans, and for the world. I wanted to do everything possible to avoid taking that risk.

The immediate provocation for the discussion in the following excerpt was the Soviets' shooting down of a U-2 reconnaissance plane over Cuba on Saturday, October 27, and the death of the pilot, Major Rudolf Anderson. My colleagues and I began to discuss how to respond. Some, like CIA

Director John McCone and Treasury Secretary Douglas Dillon, called for an immediate "reply" by taking out the missile site in Cuba responsible for the shoot-down. The pressure was building. Time was running out. Work on the missile sites by the Russians was proceeding 24 hours a day. At this point, the president left the room for a few minutes, and I used the opportunity to explain my own thinking in some detail to the others. As will be obvious, my proposal to "defuse" the NATO missiles in Turkey was an attempt to avoid "the third step," the nuclear step, the catastrophic step, taken first either by the Russians or by us, followed by retaliatory strikes. Never in my life, and I suspect never in the lives of my associates, did I experience a greater need for anticipating inadvertent war, for foreseeing the interactive decisions on each side that might lead somehow, at some point, to disaster, and thus the steps that must be taken to avoid it.

As we come in on the discussion, it is late in the afternoon of Saturday the 27th. All of us are exhausted. The news of the shoot-down has just come in. And there has been a lot of enthusiasm expressed for attacking the missile site that took out the U-2, possibly that same evening.

Robert McNamara: Let me state my propositions over again. First, we must be in a position to attack quickly. We've been fired on today. We are going to send surveillance aircraft in tomorrow. Those are going to be fired on without question. We're going to respond. You can't do this very long. We're going to lose airplanes, and we'll be shooting up Cuba quite a bit, but we're going to lose airplanes every day. So you can't just maintain this position very long. So we must be prepared to attack Cuba—quickly. That's the first proposition. Now the second proposition. When we attack Cuba we're going to have to attack with an all-out attack. . . . I personally believe that this is almost certain to lead to an invasion. I won't say certain to, but *almost* certain to lead to an invasion—

Douglas Dillon: Unless you get a cease-fire around the world—

Robert McNamara: That's the second proposition.

McGeorge Bundy: Or a general [nuclear] war.

Robert McNamara: The third proposition is that if we do this, and leave those missiles in Turkey, the Soviet Union *may*, and I think probably will, attack the Turkish missiles. Now the fourth proposition is, *if* the Soviet Union attacks the Turkish missiles, we *must* respond. We *cannot* allow a Soviet attack on the—on the Jupiter missiles in Turkey without a military response by NATO.

Llewellyn Thompson: Somewhere.

Robert McNamara: Somewhere, that's right. Now, that's the next proposition. . . . Now the minimum military response by NATO to a Soviet attack on the Turkish Jupiter missiles would be a response with conventional [nonnuclear] weapons by NATO forces in Turkey, that is to say Turkish and U.S. aircraft, against Soviet warships and/or naval bases in the Black Sea area. Now that to me is the absolute minimum, and I would say that it is *damned dangerous*—to have had a Soviet attack on Turkey and a NATO response on the Soviet Union. This is extremely dangerous. Now I'm not sure we can avoid anything like that, if we attack Cuba, but I think we should make every effort to avoid it, and one way to avoid it is to defuse the Turkish missiles *before* we attack Cuba. Now this . . . this is the sequence of thought.

George Ball: I would say that in the assumption that if you defuse the Turkish missiles that saves you from a reprisal, it may—may mean a reprisal *elsewhere*.

Robert McNamara: Oh, I think it doesn't save you from a reprisal.

George Ball: I think you're in a position where you've gotten rid of your missiles for *nothing*.

Robert McNamara: Well, wait a minute. I didn't say it saved you from a reprisal. I simply said it reduced the chances of military action against Turkey.

George Ball: Well, but what good does that do you in the event of action against Berlin, or somewhere else?

Robert McNamara: You have to go back in my proposition and say if there aren't Jupiter missiles in Turkey to attack, they're going to employ military force elsewhere. I'm not—I'm not at all certain of that.[23]

We now know from a variety of Russian sources, including Nikita Khrushchev's son and biographer, Sergei Khrushchev, that in the event of a U.S. air attack on one or more of the missile sites in Cuba, the likeliest Soviet response would indeed have been a strike at the Turkish missile sites. Nikita Khrushchev, like Kennedy, was trying to avoid a disastrous war, and the Soviet leader regarded a strike at Turkey as the minimum he could authorize that would satisfy his military commanders.[24] But would a strike on Turkey have been the end of the line of escalation, or the beginning? No one knows. But this is the kind of thinking—anticipating inadvertent, unintended paths to disaster—that, I believe, kept us from a spiral of escalation leading to nuclear war.

On October 27, 1962, my colleagues and I served our president well. The chips were down. We had Tommy Thompson, full of empathy for Khrushchev's situation and able to convey it credibly to the president. And many of us were intent on preventing that inadvertent fateful "third step" that would lead to the first direct military clash of the Cold War between the Russians and us.

Contrast our thinking during the missile crisis with that of another critical moment, in July 1965, when President Johnson and his closest advisers debated whether to send combat troops to Vietnam and, in effect, transform the conflict there into an American war. There is a world of difference. We did not, I believe, serve our president well on that occasion. I wrote in my memoir, *In Retrospect,* that "looking back, I clearly erred by not forcing—then or later, in either Saigon or Washington—a knock-down, drag-out debate over the loose assumptions, unasked questions, and thin analyses underlying our military strategy in Vietnam."[25]

Why the difference? To this day, I am not sure. But surely it had something to do with the dire urgency we all felt about removing the missiles from Cuba without a war—a war that would threaten the United States directly and disastrously— whereas in the July 1965 discussions of sending troops to Vietnam we did little or none of the kind of thinking that we had done in October 1962. We failed to ask the hard and necessary questions: If we do this, if we send the troops, what exactly will the North Vietnamese do? And of equal importance, whom do we have in the room at the moment with the required empathy for the situation of Ho Chi Minh, General Vo Nguyen Giap, and the other leaders in Hanoi? Do we, in fact, have anyone here who has ever met these men, talked with them, lived with them for a time, as Tommy Thompson had done with Khrushchev? We did not, and worse, we failed even to ask such questions.

So the key issue, for me, remains: How can we raise the odds that the sensitivity to inadvertent disaster that characterized the missile crisis debates be equally present in situations that I call "crises in slow motion"—like Vietnam, but also like our 21st-century relations with Russia and China?[26]

◈

What we are calling the "sensitivity to prevention of inadvertent conflict" is somewhat similar to what University of Maryland political scientist John Steinbruner has recently referred to as a shift from "deliberate threat" to "the threat emanating from *distributed processes*—the unforeseen interaction of deployed forces."[27] "It seems likely," he concludes, "that the process of globalization will make unintentional, distributed threats a much more prominent concern. . . . How then might the drama play out? Where might an impending transformation manifest itself most prominently? . . . The practice can be expected to develop most rapidly where the problem is greatest. In the first instance, that means Russia. . . . It also means China."[28]

Steinbruner believes that if we are successful in deepening the concern over inadvertent conflict with Russia and China, then the actions necessary to solve them will, if they occur, "be the occasion for fundamental revisions of security posture." But our failure to do so will, he fears, be "the source of massive grief if those revisions are not accomplished."[29] Thus we return again to the fundamental question for preventing Great Power conflict in the 21st century: Can we reorient ourselves to a concern for inadvertent conflict and can we do this in time to bring Russia and China in from the cold before a war-threatening crisis arises?

America's Post–Cold War Relationships with Russia and China

In the 21st century, the most destructive type of conflict would involve two or more Great Powers, armed with nuclear weapons, who find their interests so irreconcilable, their situation so perverse and non-negotiable, that the least bad option at some critical moment seems to be to go to war with one another. It strains many imaginations, at the moment, to articulate plausible scenarios by which the United States might become involved in a war with potential enemies that are, or likely will be, great military powers during the course of the 21st century. The leading candidates—virtually the only plausible candidates at present—are Russia and China, America's former Cold War rivals. Yet Russia is in terrible straits economically, psychologically, and militarily, whereas China remains militarily inferior to the United States at every level and also faces deep uncertainty about the future of its social, political, and economic systems. Each may be said to be, relative to the position of the United States and the West, deeply inferior, hardly in a position to risk war with the United States.

But what is not adequately appreciated, especially in the United States, is the potential significance of the reaction in Russia and China to what both perceive as post–Cold War U.S. unilateralism—what we referred to in Chapter One, following Samuel Huntington, as the phenomenon of America as a "rogue superpower." The key elements of their common reaction are: first, that due to the way the Cold War ended, the United States has become triumphalist and increasingly *arrogant* in the prosecution of its foreign policy, especially toward Russia and China, the "losers" in the Cold War struggle; and second, that this U.S. arrogance is not only irritating, it is also dangerous because it threatens a number of interests Russia and China consider vital. U.S. arrogance, in their view, is displayed most ominously in its *betrayal* of both Russia and China on pivotal and contentious issues, betrayals that demonstrate a U.S. disregard for its international commitments. To Russian and Chinese eyes, America appears to believe that as the world's only remaining superpower, it need not adhere to accepted norms of international behavior among Great Powers.

Many contentious issues divide the United States and the West from Russia and China. Both oppose the building of a U.S. national missile defense: Russia, because it will violate the terms of the 1972 Anti-Ballistic Missile Treaty between the United States and the Soviet Union; China because they believe it will compromise their relatively small nuclear deterrent force. Russia resents U.S. and Western accusations of human rights abuses in the ongoing war in Chechnya, which Russia regards as a purely internal matter. China takes the same dim view of Western criticism of its governance of Tibet. China also objects strenuously to the 1996 renewal of the U.S.-Japan Security Alliance, believing that it represents an attempt to encircle and contain China.

In 1997, Prime Minister Li Peng stated emphatically to Robert McNamara during a visit to his country that, whereas initially the treaty might have been directed against the Soviet Union, with the end of the Cold War it could have no purpose other than to contain and, ultimately, threaten China. He supported his argument by emphasizing that in contrast to Germany, Japan had never admitted or accepted responsibility for its role in the Second World War. To this day, the majority of Japanese citizens are ignorant of the degree to which their country's actions contributed to the initiation of the Second World War in the Pacific. For example, they are unaware that in August 1937, without provocation, Japanese aircraft bombed Shanghai. McNamara, serving on the *President Hoover,* a U.S. merchant vessel, witnessed the bombing. Li Peng claimed—perhaps with exaggeration—that Japan was responsible for 20 million Chinese dead. And he said he observed continuing signs of militarism in Japanese society. All of this was spoken with enormous intensity and vehemence.

There is some basis for China's fear of Japanese militarism. Although the Japanese constitution, shaped by the United States, prohibits Japan from developing "military" forces, a small but vocal and influential minority continues to press for their creation. In September 2000, it was reported that the mayor of Tokyo had called out 7,000 members of the Self-Defense Forces for highly visible drills that included helicopters, light tanks, troop transport vehicles, and landing craft.[30] The drills sparked a major debate in Japan. Antimilitarists suspected that an unstated goal of the exercise was to raise the profile of the armed forces and improve the prospects of revising the constitution to allow Japan to form an army for the first time since the Second World War. This incident followed by a few months a statement by Japan's deputy minister of defense (who was later removed from office) that the nation should move to acquire nuclear weapons, an action that would be viewed as hostile, not only by China but in all of Asia as well.

Economic issues are also contentious: Russia is resentful due to what it regards as a "too little too late" assistance program from U.S.-dominated institutions such as the World Bank and International Monetary Fund; China is resentful of economic sanctions of various sorts due to what the United States regards as unacceptable human rights abuses in China and unacceptable Chinese arms export policies.

The lists of Russian and Chinese grievances are long and their resentment is, in some cases, strong—leaving open the question of whether it is justified. Our purpose here is not to try to "resolve" all these issues, but rather to penetrate as deeply as we can in a brief space into the Russian and Chinese mindsets that harbor this substantial resentment toward the United States. We are convinced that the resentment is real and growing. It is in many ways remarkable that in the space of a single decade since the conclusion of the Cold War, U.S. relations with Russia and China have plummeted from an initial heady optimism to their present testy, occasionally very tense state. It would be an exaggeration to say that we are in the midst of a new Cold War with either country. But we believe that Russian President Boris Yeltsin did not exaggerate when he warned in December 1994 of an imminent descent into a "cold peace," caused, he said, by attempts of the United States and the West to "bury democracy in Russia."[31] As we see it, the "cold peace" predicted by Yeltsin in late 1994 has now arrived.

We will focus on brief case studies of two issues: the reaction of Russia to the U.S. decision to enlarge the North Atlantic Treaty Organization (NATO); and the reaction of China to what it perceives as a shift in U.S. policy toward Taiwan, from the "one China" policy inaugurated by the Nixon administration, to one favoring independence for the island. We focus on these for four related reasons:

- *U.S. "Arrogance."* Each issue seems to Moscow and Beijing to epitomize the arrogant refusal of the United States to grant Great Power status to any country other than the United States itself.

- *U.S. "Betrayal."* Both the Russians and Chinese interpret U.S. actions as fundamental betrayals of previous U.S. pledges and commitments.

- *U.S. "Threat."* These ostensible betrayals threaten the legitimacy and security of the Moscow and Beijing governments.

- *U.S. "Flashpoint."* Each issue could become a "flashpoint" in which the current testy relationships explode into a dangerous crisis. Indeed, each has recently come close to doing so.

To reiterate: We do not necessarily agree with these Russian and Chinese assessments. In fact, we do not believe that their accuracy—as to whether they represent a true understanding of U.S. motives—should be the principal issue, either for scholars of foreign policy or U.S. and Western foreign policy makers themselves. Far more important, in our view, is this: We believe Russia and China see the United States and, to a lesser extent, the other Western powers, as pushing them into a corner over these issues, raising the risk not only of regional confrontations but also of a military clash that would not be in the interest of any of the countries involved. Such a clash would almost certainly be a disaster for all sides.

John Steinbruner, in his new book *Principles of Global Security,* has argued that what is needed to reduce the risk of Great Power conflict of this sort will require a major adjustment in the way U.S. officials understand international security in the post–Cold War world. What is needed, he believes, is a "conceptual shift from deterrence to reassurance" as a function of which the "core security relationship" of the United States with Russia and with China will be "redesigned." According to Steinbruner, "the relentless fact is that Russia cannot live with . . . [its] situation and neither, therefore, can anyone else." He adds that "China presents a variation of the same problem . . . of comparable significance."[32]

This is the absolutely central proposition, the beginning of wisdom for preventing Great Power conflict in the 21st century: If Russia feels severely threatened by NATO expansion on its western border, and if China feels similarly threatened by what it believes to be growing U.S. support for Taiwan's independence and for Japan's rearming, *then the U.S. and its allies, including Japan, should feel similarly threatened.* We must recognize that if Great Powers go to war in the 21st century, whole nations are likely to disappear. This is why we emphasize the primacy of comprehending the Russian and Chinese views, rather than arguing with them or lecturing them. An ounce of empathy and anticipation of inadvertent paths to conflict will be worth a pound of disputation, and a ton of traditional "deterrence."

The "Betrayal" of Russia: NATO Expansion

On March 12, 1999, U.S. Secretary of State Madeleine Albright hosted the foreign ministers of Poland, Hungary, and the Czech Republic at the Harry S. Truman Library in Independence, Missouri. The occasion was the formal accession of these three former members of the Warsaw Pact into the NATO alliance, the culmination of decisions made by the Clinton administration beginning in late 1994. According to Deputy Secretary of State Strobe Talbott, the Clinton administration's coordinator of Russia policy, the post–Cold War preservation and expansion of NATO was required to provide "the means of deterring or, if necessary, defeating threats to our common security," and to provide "newly liberated and democratic states . . . [with] the security that the Alliance affords."[33]

The Russian view is totally different. They see NATO expansion as part of an American post–Cold War doctrine of neo-containment, whose purpose is the encirclement and neutralization of Russia in its traditional European sphere of influence. Any Russian diplomat can recite the litany of ostensible U.S. betrayals leading up to NATO expansion. In 1989–1990, for example, the Soviet government believed that the United States had pledged never to expand NATO eastward, if Moscow would agree to the unification of Germany. In their book, *At the Highest Levels: The Inside Story of the End of the Cold War*, Michael

Beschloss and Strobe Talbott report the following conversation on February 9, 1990, between Soviet President Mikhail Gorbachev and U.S. Secretary of State James Baker:

> The Secretary of State knew that Gorbachev and his colleagues were worried mainly about a recurrence of Germany's historical ambition to seize territory to its east. He asked Gorbachev, "Would you prefer to see a united Germany outside of NATO and with no U.S. forces, perhaps with its own nuclear weapons? Or would you prefer a unified Germany to be tied to NATO, *with assurances that NATO's jurisdiction would not shift one inch eastward from its present position?*"
>
> Gorbachev replied, "Certainly, any extension of the territory of NATO would be unacceptable." He spoke of the deep Soviet fear of the Germans, the impact of the Nazis, the deaths of tens of millions of Soviets. From this Baker concluded that Gorbachev might be willing to accept a united Germany as a NATO member if the territory of the former East Germany could be excluded from NATO deployments and maneuvers.[34]

"Not one inch eastward," Baker said. Did Gorbachev misunderstand him? Perhaps. But the Russian interpretation was and remains that the United States had pledged not to expand NATO even to deployments in the territory of the former East Germany.[35] Thus the decision in favor of NATO "enlargement" was considered a U.S. betrayal, one that directly threatened Russian interests.

The former director of Russia's Institute of the USA and Canada, Sergey Rogov, has written of NATO's decision to expand: "It is very difficult to not interpret this step as an expression of deep Western skepticism about future developments in Russia and as a kind of delayed containment, containment in a different form."[36] Many Americans share Rogov's assessment. For example, *Washington Post* columnist Charles Krauthammer wrote in the spring of 1998: "Is NATO expansion directed against Russia? Of course it is."[37] During the 1998 Congressional debate over NATO expansion, Senator Dale Bumpers of Arkansas, typically a supporter of the Clinton administration's foreign policy initiatives, made a speech criticizing expansion. "The Russians would have to be incredibly naive beyond all imagination," he asserted, "not to believe that

. . . NATO enlargement is designed to hem Russia in."[38] The *New York Times* joined the critical chorus toward the end of the debate, stating in an editorial: "It is delusional to believe that NATO expansion is not at its core an act that Russia will regard as hostile."[39]

The next critical act of betrayal began in May 1997, with the signing in Paris of the "Founding Act" of cooperation between Russia and the West, in which Russia sought to obtain a written commitment that NATO would:

- limit the expansion of its military capabilities even as its membership grew;

- disavow any intention to use force against any state except in self-defense or unless authorized by the UN Security Council; and

- grant Russia a role in NATO's political decision making.

Russia achieved the first two objectives but failed in the third.[40] The result, in the Russian view, was another betrayal in March 1999, when NATO began its bombing campaign against the Serb government in Belgrade, in an effort to force the Serbs to stop their ethnic cleansing of Albanians in Kosovo. In the West, the intervention was portrayed as an attempt to avert a humanitarian disaster caused by the racist and fascist policies of Serb leader Slobodan Milosevic. To the Russians, however, the NATO intervention was, first, an outrage, in part because it was directed against their fellow Slavs, the Serbs; but more important, it flagrantly violated the Founding Act's commitment that both NATO and Russia would refrain "from the threat or use of force against each other as well as against any other state, its sovereignty, territorial integrity or political independence in any manner inconsistent with the United Nations Charter."[41] As the Russia specialist Celeste Wallander of Harvard University has written: "Kosovo is about more than Serbia, and about even more than NATO. For Russia, Kosovo is about the management of post–Cold War security problems, including the kinds of ethnic and territorial conflicts that threaten its own borders and territory."[42]

But Kosovo, for the Russians, was also more than a little frightening. They watched helplessly as NATO conducted a high-tech air war against the Serbs, seemingly invulnerable to any sort of defense the Serbs could muster using their antiquated Russian equipment. One principal implication of NATO's success was drawn by Russian Defense Minister Igor Sergeev following Russian maneuvers in June 1999 that simulated a NATO attack on Russia in the Kaliningrad Oblast region, using only conventional forces. "Russia was able to defend itself," he said of the training maneuvers, "only by using nuclear weapons."[43] This led Russian President Vladimir Putin to endorse in 2000 what he calls Russia's "new concept of security"—renouncing its stated policy of "no-first-use" of nuclear weapons and relying increasingly on early use of such weapons if Russia should be attacked, presumably by NATO forces.[44] More recently, Putin authorized a 15-year plan to modernize Russian conventional forces, while reducing the strategic nuclear arsenal to approximately 1,500 warheads.[45] Celeste Wallander draws the bottom line. "For Russia," she says, "the lesson of Kosovo is that power matters," including both nuclear power and conventional military power.

This is what it has come to: NATO, via its betrayal (as Russia sees it) of its commitments, has forced Russia to accept perhaps the most dangerous feature of traditional NATO strategy during the Cold War: possible nuclear First Use. Even more distressing, the war in Kosovo has evidently convinced many Russians that they may be next—that NATO may continue to flex its muscles when and where it sees fit, perhaps even in Chechnya, where Russia is engaged in a long-term war with Chechen rebels who seek secession from Russia. As one Russian military official put it: "NATO is metastasizing all over Europe."[46]

President Putin was interviewed recently by three Russian journalists regarding his view of the significance of NATO expansion to former Warsaw Pact countries:

Question: What's wrong with our relationship with NATO?

Putin: We don't feel like we're full-fledged participants in the process. If we were granted full-fledged participation in decision making, then things wouldn't be so terrible.

Question: Why . . . if a weakened Russia could not do anything?

Putin: That's not true. Even in its current state, there's a lot that Russia can do. We should have analyzed the situation earlier—before the bombing of Yugoslavia—to see how we could have influenced our partners' decision. We could have worked more actively with the countries that did not agree with the turn of events.

Question: They said that Kosovo would remain within Yugoslavia, and yet they brought in the troops.

Putin: That's why we are not agreeing to any options like Kosovo. Nothing analogous to the Kosovo events is possible. And it will never be possible. Everything that the NATO allies actually achieved in Kosovo directly contradicted the goals that NATO had established for itself.

Question: You say, "We are not agreeing." Have they really made such offers?

Putin: Let's say we are being offered mediators to help resolve the Chechen conflict. We don't need any mediators. That is the first step toward internationalizing the conflict—first come the mediators, then someone else, then observers, then military observers, and then a limited contingent of troops. And away we go . . .

Question: So should we reconsider joining NATO?

Putin: We can consider it, but not at this moment. It's a question of *what kind* of NATO we're talking about. If we're talking about the NATO that acted in Kosovo in direct violation of UN decisions, that's not even of theoretical interest for us to discuss. If we're talking about a serious transformation of this bloc into a political organization prepared to have constructive interactions with Russia, then there is a topic for discussion.

In sum, I don't see any reason why cooperation between Russia and NATO shouldn't develop further; but I repeat that it will happen only if Russia is treated as an equal partner.[47]

It seems to us that two somewhat contradictory strains of thought are obvious in Putin's views. First, he remains convinced, as he has said many times, that the place of Russia is "as part of the West"; but second, he is also a fervent Russian nationalist, almost the epitome of the sort identified by Isaiah Berlin—a Russian with an "inflamed condition" brought about by "national humiliation."[48] Such people, Berlin pointed out, are sometimes capable of extreme actions they believe will earn them the respect they believe they deserve.

Sergey Rogov said recently that this history of betrayal has led the Russian foreign policy establishment to begin to contemplate, for the first time since the end of the Cold War, "a new geopolitical split of the world . . . between the West on one side and Russia, China and India on the other"—a new Cold War.[49] This bears some resemblance to what Samuel Huntington has referred to as "the West against the rest."[50] There is a fundamental difference, however, between the origins of such a new Cold War, should it happen, and the sort of "clash" Huntington envisions. Huntington predicted a "clash of civilizations," for example, Western Judeo-Christian culture versus Islamic fundamentalism, foisted on the West by aggressive non-Western peoples. But in the confrontation Rogov refers to, the arrow of causation would point in the opposite direction. By forcing other Great Powers such as Russia and China into a corner on key issues and by attempting to deny them membership in the club of Great Powers, the United States may cause these states to formally ally with one another in order to resist what they regard as U.S. hegemonic impulses. Moreover, the split would not be primarily along "cultural" lines. It would simply constitute a means, in Berlin's terms, for "humiliated" sovereign states in "an inflamed condition" to refight the Cold War for nonideological reasons. And the United States would have itself primarily to blame.

Jack F. Matlock, Jr., former American ambassador to the Soviet Union, recently wrote that many U.S. difficulties with Russia derive from American historical blindness, our inability to understand and appreciate the significance of the fact that "the Cold War we won was against the Soviet Union, not Russia."[51] For just this reason George Kennan has called NATO expansion "the most fateful error of American policy in the entire post–Cold War era."[52] What particularly worries Kennan, and worries us, is the emphasis placed by the United States on NATO, on the military dimension of its relations with its European allies and with Russia. According to Kennan, all the emphasis on NATO and NATO expansion, in the absence of an ideological Cold War, seems to indicate that the United States and the West are oblivious to the probable outcome "if new orgies of military destruction should be added to those in which Europe has already indulged within the memory of many of us alive today."[53] Treating the new Russia more or less as the Soviet Union was treated — giving the Russians the impression that they are being encircled and "contained" once again by the military might of a technologically superior West, Kennan says, "can only have suicidal significance."[54]

The "Betrayal" of China: The Status of Taiwan

Ever since the 1972 opening to China by the Nixon administration, the formal U.S. position on Taiwan has been one of "strategic ambiguity." According to this policy, the United States recognizes "one China" whose capital is in Beijing, a China to which Taiwan belongs. At the same time, the United States provides military hardware and political backing for the (now) democratically elected and (at times) independence-minded government in Taipei, in an effort to deter Beijing from attempting to conquer the island by force. Washington has hoped thereby to delay indefinitely a final resolution of its contradictory policy, which it regards as reflecting the reality of Taiwan—this disputed remnant of the still incompletely resolved Chinese civil war between Mao Zedong's Communists and Chiang Kai-shek's Nationalists, a war that began before the Second World War.

Yet in Beijing, the feeling of U.S. betrayal on the central issue of Taiwan is powerful and growing. It derives from the U.S. failure (at least in China's eyes) to adhere to the "one China" policy it agreed to in 1972. Indeed, Beijing believes that the United States, via its arms sales and military advice to Taiwan, has sought instead to make the island an impregnable fortress and in this way to force Beijing into accepting an eventual "two-China" reality.

As further proof of the validity of this view of U.S. motives, Chinese officials cite the continued U.S. military presence in East Asia. Especially worrisome to the Chinese was the reaffirmation of the U.S.-Japan Security Alliance in 1996, which the Chinese regard as directed principally against themselves, and especially at their efforts at reunification with Taiwan. In this way, Beijing's feeling of U.S. betrayal on the Taiwan question has fueled broader suspicions that the United States has "hegemonic" objectives in East Asia. While the situation is intermittently tense, the governments in Taipei, Beijing, and Washington have, at least so far, backed off at key moments.

Many believe, however, that the day of reckoning over Taiwan is coming. Increasingly, the Beijing government threatens to intervene militarily if the Taipei government and its more than 20 million constituents choose independence. Once every four years, during Taiwan's presidential elections, some political candidates court voters with pledges to move toward the full independence that Beijing says it will never permit. The United States is, as always, caught in the middle. It seeks better relations with an increasingly prosperous and powerful China, but it is also committed to protecting Taiwan militarily, should Beijing try to conquer it by force. One analyst has maintained that "the question of Taiwan's affiliation" is "the single most serious jurisdictional issue to survive the Cold War."[55] It is a very dangerous situation.

In recent years, the perpetually smoldering danger has twice exploded into crises. Beijing believes that the U.S. betrayal began in earnest in 1995 when, under pressure from Congress, the Clinton administration authorized the visit of Taiwan's President Lee Teng-hui to the United States, ostensibly on an "unofficial" visit to attend a class reunion at Cornell University. But Lee had just previously raised the ante in the war of words between Taipei and Beijing by seeming to Beijing to have openly advocated separatism, and by initiating a campaign to get Taiwan readmitted to the UN, where it had been replaced by Beijing in 1971. In retaliation, the Chinese government flexed its muscles in the lead-up to Taiwan's March 1996 election by firing three intermediate-range "M-11" missiles at what they called "target zones" in the Taiwan straits. They landed close enough to Taiwan's two largest ports, Keelung and Kaohsuing, to disrupt shipping. The Chinese then expanded military exercises in the area, simulating the kind of maneuvers required to invade the island.[56] The

United States responded by deploying two aircraft carrier battle groups nearby and by warning Beijing not to deepen the crisis.

In a recent memoir, former U.S. Secretary of Defense William Perry has written that "in retrospect it seems clear that Chinese government officials had misunderstood the seriousness with which the United States viewed unprovoked military actions against Taiwan. The CBG [carrier battle group] deployment straightened out that misunderstanding."[57] In fact, however, the Chinese by no means regarded their actions as unprovoked. They viewed them as required by the shrillness and boldness of the preelection rhetoric of several presidential candidates in Taiwan urging a declaration of full independence from Beijing. Predictably, the Chinese then regarded deployment of a U.S. carrier battle group as a provocation. Prime Minister Li Peng responded by reminding the Americans that "with a concentrated fire of guided missiles and artillery, the People's Liberation Army can bury an intruder in a sea of fire."[58] The confrontation ended in a standoff. The United States had signaled its willingness to use force to protect Taiwan from a forcible takeover. China had indicated that any move toward Taiwanese independence would be regarded in Beijing as an act of war by both Taiwan and the United States.

After the crisis, the Beijing government pointedly refused to renounce the use of force if, at some point in the future, progress had not been made toward reunification of Taiwan with the mainland.[59] Beijing backed up its rhetoric by focusing its military development and acquisition efforts on building the capability to coerce Taiwan militarily. As Perry points out, after the 1995–1996 crisis, "the PLA [People's Liberation Army] appears to share the Chinese government's overall preoccupation with the Taiwan question . . . [which] is now driving PLA reform and modernization programs."[60] As for Taiwan, it ranked second only to Saudi Arabia throughout the 1990s as the largest recipient of foreign arms—nearly $12 billion worth, the majority coming from the United States, including a vast array of missiles, tanks, warplanes, and advanced computer systems to link all of the weapons systems together. In Beijing, it appears that the Taiwanese military and their U.S. advisers are preparing for the kind of high-tech air war that characterized the 1991 Persian Gulf War and the 1999 war in the Balkans.[61]

The escalating war preparations on both sides provided the backdrop for the latest flare-up over Taiwan. Taiwanese President Lee Teng-hui threatened in July 1999 that Taiwan might move toward unilaterally abandoning the "one China" doctrine. This was interpreted in Beijing as virtually an open declaration of Taiwanese separatism.[62] Rhetoric escalated once again, with the approach of the Taiwanese presidential election in March 2000. On February 21, Beijing issued a policy paper, "The One-China Principle and the Taiwan Issue." Its most noteworthy point was this: that indefinite delay in serious negotiations leading to the full reunification of Taiwan with the mainland would result in a military attack on the island.[63] As the election drew closer, Beijing escalated its rhetoric even further, especially against eventual winner Chen Shui-bien, the candidate of the Democratic Progressive Party, which in the past had supported full independence.

On the eve of the election, Chinese Prime Minister Zhu Rongji warned that Taiwanese advocates of independence from Beijing would "not end up well."[64] This time, Zhu took the unusual step of going into detail regarding China's lack of fear regarding war with Taiwan and the United States. Of those who think China would be afraid to initiate a conflict with the United States, he said: "They do not know the history of China and that the Chinese people will use all of their blood to defend the unity of the Chinese nation." He added that "we must trust that our Taiwan compatriots will make a sensible choice." But if they did not, he said, they might not "get another opportunity."[65] While this crisis did not escalate to the firing of missiles or the deployment of carrier battle groups, it was taken even more seriously in Europe than was the 1996 crisis. Officials in Britain and France worried especially that they would face an agonizing decision were war to break out, as to whether or not to send their forces to assist the Americans in Taiwan.[66]

What is all this about? Why does Beijing believe that, according to Li Daoyu, its former ambassador to the United States, "Taiwan is the most important and most sensitive issue in China–United States relations"?[67] How is it that, as John Steinbruner has written, the Taiwan issue is "a major strategic accident waiting to happen"?[68] Why has this relic of a Cold War long since over become a potential flashpoint for a Great Power conflict in the 21st century?

The Beijing government's view of the Taiwan problem mirrors Russia's perception of NATO expansion. Beijing believes that U.S. policy since 1995 represents a betrayal—a unilateral reversal of U.S. pledges and written commitments over nearly three decades. It believes it has a strong case. Here are the relevant passages from the "Shanghai Communiqué" of February 27, 1972, that concluded the epochal visit of President Nixon to China and established the ground rules for U.S.-China relations ever since:

The Chinese declared:

The Chinese side reaffirmed its position: The Taiwan question is the crucial question obstructing the normalization of relations between China and the United States; the Government of the People's Republic of China is the sole legal government of China; Taiwan is a province of China which has long been returned to the motherland. . . . The Chinese Government firmly opposes any activities which aim at the creation of "one China, one Taiwan," "one China, two governments," "two Chinas," and "independent Taiwan," or advocate that "the status of Taiwan remains to be determined."

The United States declared:

The U.S. acknowledges that all Chinese on either side of the Taiwan Strait maintain there is but one China and that Taiwan is part of China. The U.S. Government does not challenge that position. It reaffirms its interest in a peaceful settlement of the Taiwan question by the Chinese themselves. With this prospect in mind, it affirms the ultimate objective of the withdrawal of all U.S. forces and military institutions from Taiwan.[69]

The meaning seemed transparently clear to the Chinese: politically, the United States had committed itself, during the so-called transitional era leading to reunification, to a steady withdrawal of its presence. Beijing believed it would be followed quickly by Beijing's recovery of its sovereignty over Taiwan. This was reinforced in two subsequent documents: the Joint Communiqué on the Establishment of Diplomatic

Relations Between China and the United States of 1979, and the Joint Communiqué of August 1982 concerning U.S. arms sales to Taiwan. In all these agreements, the United States agreed that "there is but one China and Taiwan is part of China." The identical phrase appears in all three documents. These are the agreements that Beijing felt were being violated by U.S. support of separatist sentiments voiced by Taiwanese leaders in March 1996 and March 2000.

Yet the U.S. commitment to Beijing in these three communiqués is contradicted by the language of the Taiwan Relations Act of 1979, which governs the U.S. relationship with the Taiwanese government itself. According to this act of Congress:

> It is the policy of the United States . . . to consider any effort to determine the future of Taiwan by other than peaceful means, including boycotts or embargoes, a threat to the peace and security of the Western Pacific area and of grave concern to the United States [and] . . . to maintain the capacity of the United States to resist any resort to force or other forms of coercion that would jeopardize the security, or the social and economic system, of the people on Taiwan.[70]

In other words, Taiwan believes that the United States has made a commitment to Taiwan that, in the event of hostilities between Taiwan and China, the United States is legally bound to enter the conflict on the side of Taiwan. Taiwan looks upon this as an ironclad security commitment, of the sort that characterized the security relationship among the NATO countries during the Cold War, in the event of an attack on any of them by Soviet forces.

The conflict arises because the Shanghai Communiqué is based on the assumption that all or most of the people on both sides of the Taiwan Strait believe that Taiwan is part of China. This is certainly not true as we enter the 21st century. Henry Kissinger, the principal U.S. author of the Shanghai Communiqué, wrote in his memoirs that "the Taiwan paragraph of the communiqué put the Taiwan question in abeyance, with each side maintaining its basic principles."[71] But Kissinger's claim to have put the issue in "abeyance" is valid only if the assumption in the communiqué continues to be accepted by both parties. Otherwise, as the

American journalists Richard Bernstein and Ross Munro have written, "the United States is committed in theory to the untruth that all of the people involved in this unique historical situation see themselves as belonging to the same country, even as it is in practice committed to preserving the real truth, which is that they do not."[72]

This is what arouses such anger among the Chinese leaders over the Taiwan issue: They believe the United States has committed itself repeatedly for more than a quarter of a century to *their* view of the matter—to the view that Taiwan has always been a province of China and should, as soon as possible, be returned officially to the one "China" whose capital is Beijing. It was on that basis that Mao Zedong and Zhou Enlai decided to open up relations with the United States in 1972; it was on that basis that Deng Xiaoping decided to normalize relations with the United States in 1979. It is on that basis that a Washington-Beijing relationship exists at all. This is what the Chinese can read in the documents. Yet ever since 1972, peaking during the Clinton administration, what do they see? A huge military buildup on Taiwan, involving overwhelmingly American equipment and American advisers, building a virtual "Great Wall" between the island and the mainland. In Beijing, it seems that the Americans are attempting to show them that Taiwan will never be part of China, an outcome the Americans appear to believe they can guarantee by a show of overwhelming, high-tech military force.

The former *New York Times* Beijing bureau chief Patrick Tyler recently recounted a conversation he had in the spring of 1995 with Wang Jisi, a senior member of the Chinese Academy of Sciences. Wang Jisi had just returned from a retreat for Chinese specialists on the United States. He said:

> I want to tell you the consensus of the retreat. The first point was that America is in decline and, therefore, it will try to thwart China's emergence as a global power. In the opinion of the participants, the United States is the only country that poses a threat to China's national security. You know, for historical reasons, Japan has always been the most unpopular country for the Chinese, but I can tell you that among China's senior leaders, the United States is [now] the most unpopular country.[73]

The United States, in short, had become China's number one enemy by the spring of 1995. This was before the March 1996 Taiwan Strait confrontation; before the accidental May 1999 bombing of the Chinese embassy in Belgrade; and before the March 2000 Taiwan election crisis.[74] Each of these episodes further inflamed U.S.-Chinese relations. But even before they occurred, according to Wang Jisi, those in Beijing who know America best regarded the United States as their principal enemy.

What is the solution to this downward spiral of relations that is driven by the Taiwan issue? What should be done about what seems to be a "crisis in slow motion," with a steadily increasing risk of a conflict involving the United States and China?[75] Michel Oksenberg of Stanford University, a leading U.S. specialist on China, believes that above all else, Americans must begin to show more "empathy and understanding . . . in thinking about the problems the leaders of China confront."[76] In particular, he points out, we must try to understand their sense of betrayal, and how it feeds suspicions going back to the 19th century, when China, which had long seen itself as the "Middle Kingdom," the center of civilization, entered the modern world only to be occupied, humiliated, and exploited. They recall vividly, as does Robert McNamara, that in the 1930s Shanghai contained two huge foreign zones, one governed by the British and one by the French in which appeared signs reading, "No dogs, cats or Chinese allowed." Oksenberg concludes that, "to a considerable extent, Chinese foreign policy in the twentieth century involves a quest to redress national grievances and to restore the lost greatness."[77]

In addition, there seems to be considerable concern within the post–Cold War leadership in Beijing regarding the firmness of their grip on power and the possibility that China might follow in the path of the Soviet Union, breaking up into pieces, no one of which approaches the power and influence of the former union.[78] This is a potentially deadly combination: the aspiration to recover the past glory and position of China, coexisting with the fear that even its current position could be undermined by U.S. and Japanese "encirclement." Taiwan symbolizes everything the Chinese leadership seeks (reunification and recovery of at least its past geographical borders) and fears (the loss of Taiwan, loss of face and prestige, and loss of the credibility even of its claim to regional hegemony, let alone Great Power status). Whether or not one agrees with the policies of the Communist government in Beijing, empathy for the pressure its leaders feel seems to us a bare minimum for lowering the odds of conflict over Taiwan. At a minimum, the United States should urge Taiwan to avoid actions that appear to be contradictory to a one-China policy.

The ambiguous status quo may not be completely satisfying to either side, but it is surely better than a war—which is likely if Taiwan proceeds down the road to independence and/or Beijing continues periodically to threaten the island militarily. The former U.S. assistant secretary of defense Joseph S. Nye, Jr. (currently the dean of the Harvard's Kennedy School of Government), has proposed a useful formula: Beijing should pledge not to use force against Taiwan, which, in turn, should pledge not to declare independence.[79] While this is not an ultimate solution, it would buy much precious time that is needed to arrive at one.

Finally, we believe the United States should strive to play the role of mediator in pursuit of such an ultimate solution. In the past, Beijing has rejected U.S. mediation because it has claimed, not without reason, that the United States is far from neutral in the dispute. Yet we believe it is well worth exploring with both Beijing and Taiwan whether U.S. mediation might be useful if the first interim objective were an agreement along the lines suggested by Nye.[80]

Dangerous Misconceptions of Great Power Conflict

How do U.S. and other Western observers interpret the prospects for Great Power conflict between the United States on the one hand, and Russia and China on the other? Have they noticed the disagreements we have noted? Do they believe these reflect only the "growing pains" of post–Cold War international relations? Or do they express concern that these differences indicate big trouble for Great Power relations on the horizon of the 21st century? Most do not. We judge typical U.S. approaches to the problem to be both insensitive and unimaginative. Empathy for the Russians and Chinese is virtually nonexistent. There appears to be little recognition of potential inadvertent paths to conflict with these Great Powers and the steps necessary to prevent it.

We believe that the approaches and assessments in the United States and the West generally regarding Great Power conflict have become part of the problem, rather than part of any realistic solution.

The most common "reaction" in the United States is no reaction at all. The Cold War is over. The United States stands alone astride the world. What else need be said? The American people have lost interest in world affairs generally, which is bizarre in light of the warp speed with which globalization is taking place. Funding has been cut drastically for foreign missions run by the U.S. State Department. U.S. foundations have cut back their philanthropy in international security generally; almost none are now funding research that is focused on the prevention of Great Power conflict. This is totally different from the situation prevailing as recently as ten years ago, and reflects the current received wisdom that the great Cold War danger of East-West conflict has passed and no new danger of Great Power conflict has replaced it. Likewise with media coverage: Coverage of international geopolitical affairs, insofar as it exists at all in the United States, is devoted largely to humanitarian disasters containing dramatic images that stand a chance of getting the attention of those watching television, the principal source of news for the vast majority of Americans. Most Americans are thus simply oblivious to the danger of any 21st-century Great Power conflict. This view might be summarized as follows: There is only one Great Power—the United States. How can a Great Power conflict develop in a world in which we, a benign superpower, are the only Great Power?

In fact, it also seems to be difficult for many foreign policy professionals to take seriously the possibility of conflict with Russia and/or China, in the absence of imminent Cold War threats, such as a nuclear attack from Russia or "falling dominoes" toppled by China. Journals that a few years ago were full of cautionary scenarios of possible conflict with the Russians or Chinese are now almost devoid of them. Just to take an example: The Fall 1999 issue of *Foreign Affairs* magazine, the most influential in the field, carried several examples of this failure of imagination in the West regarding the need to reduce the risk of Great Power conflict in the 21st century. The subtext of each article is: How can Russia and China still be considered threats to the United States? They are simply the Cold War losers.

In an article called "Russia's Collapse," Anders Aslund, a sometime consultant to the Yeltsin government, relates a joke making the rounds in Moscow: "There are two ways out of the Russian economic crisis: the natural and the miraculous. The natural way is that the archangel Michael and all the angels come down to earth and work twelve hours a day to save the Russian economy. The miraculous way is that the Russians do it themselves."[81] In another joke, the Russian power utility announces that the light at the end of the tunnel has been turned off temporarily for lack of fuel.[82] Aslund, who has a reputation as a staunch optimist on Russian affairs, further notes that the government has reverted to billboard exhortation, reminiscent of the Soviet era, for example: "Nobody will help Russia apart from ourselves."[83] While true enough, the slogan has the hollow, desperate ring of the ubiquitous Cuban billboards exhorting Cubans to "Be like Che." Russia is, as financier George Soros recently said, experiencing a complete financial "meltdown" and its "prospects are dim" for recovery, because international institutions do not want to risk trying to bail Russia out.[84] Russia is a basket case. So why worry?

In a companion piece, Gerald Segal, the former director of studies at the International Institute for Strategic Studies in London asks, in the title, "Does China Matter?" According to Segal, the answer is "no," or at least "not much." The Middle Kingdom is but a Middle Power. "Odd as it may seem," he says, "the country that is home to a fifth of humankind is overrated as a market, a Power and a source of ideas. At best, China is a second-rank Middle Power that has mastered the art of diplomatic theater."[85] Conclusion: There is little or no reason to worry about Beijing.

But there is no apparent awareness in either of these pieces that if the United States fails to treat them now and in the future as *actual* Great Powers, Russia and/or China might eventually confront the United States militarily such that a disastrous war could result. We believe that those inclined to see Russia primarily as a "basket case" and China as a barely second-rate power suffer from a failure of imagination—an inability or unwillingness to imagine what it must be like to have "lost" the Cold War, to face the post–Cold War world not as the sole triumphant superpower.

What must it be like for proud peoples and leaders in Russia and

China to confront lectures and insults from the self-appointed, ostensibly benign U.S. hegemon, a Cold War adversary they have for a generation considered their geopolitical equal, but which now seems inclined to treat them more like ignorant children than as serious rivals? Should we be surprised at the accumulation of resentments by the Cold War's communist losers who were, and still are to a considerable extent, on the wrong side of history? Is it possible that we too, under such circumstances, would strenuously resist what seems like hypocritical betrayal and preaching? Were the roles reversed, might we regard a Russian or Chinese geopolitical behemoth as arrogantly meddlesome and imperialist to the core? And might we take concrete steps to rectify the situation, even though the hegemon is likely to regard them as provocative—so provocative that a serious crisis could result, one that might conceivably escalate to a military confrontation?

We believe the answer to all such questions is "yes." But many Americans, exulting in their Cold War victory over Russia and China, have turned away from foreign affairs generally. Feeling secure in their obliviousness, they never even ask themselves such questions.

Whereas the Cold War victors are oblivious of any risk of Great Power war between the United States and Russia or China, another group of scholars and practitioners—calling themselves "*realists*"—incline to the belief that the present immediate post–Cold War period is but the relative calm before the Great Power storm. One gets the impression from some of them, in fact, that a Great Power threat to the United States, far from being unthinkable, is virtually inevitable. It is, they believe, in the nature of the system of sovereign states to generate cycles of relative peace, and cycles of conflict, as the power, wealth, and influence of the major states ebbs and flows. That is how they read the history of the Great Powers since at least 1648, when the nation-state system in Europe was written into the Treaty of Westphalia, concluding the Thirty Years' War. In fact, the realists' focus is almost exclusively upon the Great Powers—the history of Great Power diplomacy and warfare, and the international relations theory they derive from it.

There are several reasons why the realists are so pessimistic about Great Power conflict in the 21st century. Perhaps the most fundamental is their belief that the nation-state has been, and will continue to be, the basic unit in international relations, and that relations between states exist in a condition of anarchy, in which they must protect themselves and look out for their own interests. The distinguished British historian Sir Michael Howard is among those who hold this view. According to Howard:

> It is hard to deny that war is inherent in the very nature of the state. States historically identify themselves by their relationship to one another, asserting their existence and defining their boundaries by the use of force or the immanent threat of force; and so long as the international community consists of sovereign states, war between them remains a *possibility,* of which all governments have to take reasonable account. . . .
>
> Who fights with Dragons, said Nietzsche, shall himself become a Dragon. . . . [But] the other horn of the dilemma is: he who does not fight with Dragons may be devoured by them.[86]

This is the world of the realists, a world in which the Great Powers dominate and in which war is integral to that domination. Need it be so? Or might war—especially Great Power war—be relegated, perhaps like slavery, to a cruel and primitive past? For those hoping for this, according to Howard, "the history of mankind chronicles few more cruel disillusions than that which these hopes suffered during the nineteenth and twentieth centuries."[87]

Nor, according to the realists, is this state of affairs likely to change anytime soon, because the state system is not going to change. This deterministic belief in the primacy of *the international system* of nation-states, each selfishly pursuing its own interests under a condition of anarchy, can lead to some remarkable opinions. For example, John Mearsheimer of the University of Chicago, an influential realist scholar of military affairs, wrote the following in 1992, following the collapse of the Soviet Union:

> [W]ith the Cold War now relegated to the dust bin of history . . . optimists believe these changes can serve as the basis for a more peaceful world in the 21st century.

In fact, however, *there have been no fundamental changes in the nature of international politics since World War II.* The state system is still alive and well, and although regrettable, military competition between sovereign states will remain the distinguishing feature of international politics for the foreseeable future.[88]

The end of the Cold War, the collapse of the Soviet Union, the disappearance of its Eastern European and Central Asian empires—all of these events have produced "no fundamental changes" in international relations. How is this possible? Because according to the realists, the end of the Cold War has left the state system intact, a system whose nature is *competitive,* rather than cooperative.

Another reason for the pessimism of the realists, in addition to the characteristics of the state system, is their belief that the rise and fall of Great Powers tends to occur in *cycles,* which are invariably accompanied by increased competition among the states, often resulting in war. According to Kenneth Waltz, a leading contemporary realist, the structure of the international system provides important information regarding whether or not the risk of Great Power war is increasing or decreasing. In general, according to Waltz, multipolar systems tend to be more stable, with alliances being formed with which the states seek to balance power between them. Unipolar systems, such as some believe exist in the wake of the Cold War, tend to erode, as states try to preserve their independence and security by seeking alliances that help to offset the power of the hegemon. When this happens, one or more rising states eventually challenge the leading state, a situation that often leads to Great Power war.[89] Thus begins another cycle in the history of the dog-eat-dog world of international politics, as interpreted by the realists.

Most realists subscribe to such a cyclical view of Great Power warfare. Perhaps its best-known exponent is the Yale historian Paul Kennedy. Musing over the end of the Cold War in 1993, he wrote, "The lack of a global sovereign, and the competitive instincts of nation-states as their relative influence waxes and wanes, give reinforcement to the arguments of today's Realist school that it would be unwise to assume a lasting Great-Power peace in the decades ahead."[90]

As he looks ahead, Kennedy writes that "we may have reason to be concerned about the future of world peace, stability and legitimacy. Truly, as the Chinese curse puts it, we are fated to live in interesting times."[91] This cyclical variant of the realist group is carried to its logical conclusion by international relations theorist Immanuel Wallerstein, who, using mathematical models of historical change, concluded that each of these cycles is 50–60 years in length, implying (to him) that peace and stability should return to the 21st century by about 2070, should there be anyone left to enjoy it, following the intervening Great Power war.[92]

All these speculative realist notions regarding Great Power war would be just so many abstract tempests in the teapots of academics, were it not that they imply important and dangerous policy choices for the United States in the years ahead. John Mearsheimer has for the past decade been among the most forthright and controversial of the realists in articulating what the United States must do to survive in a 21st century in which other Great Powers will challenge its supremacy, even its survival. He asks: "What should be the guiding principles of American national security in the decades ahead?" His answer is twofold:

- Prevent Great Power war by quickly and forcefully balancing against potential aggressors. (That is, retain military dominance, in the interest of security and stability.)

- Avoid military intervention in nonstrategic areas as a matter of policy, without exception. (This applies to the entire Third World.)[93]

Mearsheimer has also argued that the United States could stabilize post–Cold War Europe by encouraging "the limited and carefully managed proliferation of nuclear weapons."[94] This recommendation has prompted the Yale historian John Gaddis to remark that this is "what happens when theory is pursued beyond common sense."[95]

How does the realists' analysis apply to Russia and China in the 21st century? The Princeton political scientist Robert Gilpin, one of the most venerable of the realists, warns that Russia and China will likely re-emerge as Great Powers in the 21st century. "Russia," according to Gilpin, "has been a Great Power for two centuries and has vital interests in Eastern Europe, the Middle East, and East Asia. It is highly unlikely that either a democratic or authoritarian Russia will neglect these long-established interests."[96] Gilpin's view of China is that "the most critical issue . . . facing Asia and the world" is "how the Chinese will choose to use their rapidly growing economic and military power."[97] This is a typical realist analysis, and it is consistent with the theory of sovereign states operating in an anarchical environment.

One of the most fundamental aspects of the realists' analysis and policy prescriptions is their view, usually implicit, that the end of the Cold War changes *nothing* significant about potential threats of other Great Powers to the United States. In particular, they are inclined to see post-Soviet Russia as the most dangerous threat to peace and to U.S. interests. Former Secretary of State Henry Kissinger, a longtime realist, recently wrote that the central problem of American security will likely be Russia, "historically imperialist, whose identity has been tied up with expansion." According to Kissinger, "historically, the Russians' tragedy is that they have not been able to find security in their own development."[98] The key task for U.S. policy, he says, is not to bring democracy to Russia. Rather, "it means convincing Russian leaders that if Singapore, Japan, Austria, and almost every country in the world could grow and develop without expansion, it is absolutely a possibility for a country with ten time zones."[99]

How is this to be accomplished? Former national security adviser Zbigniew Brzezinski, also a realist, believes strongly in what he calls the preservation of "a benign American hegemony" throughout "Eurasia . . . the world's axial super-continent."[100] The task, for Brzezinski, is more or less what it was during the Cold War, as he practiced it when he was a member of the Carter administration: constraining the Russians on the West via strong NATO ties and on the East via a mutually useful condominium with the Chinese. In the post–Cold War era, however, Brzezinski believes that the United States has opportunities it did not have during the Cold War: expanding NATO as quickly and comprehensively as possible; and nurturing relations with Beijing, in part by making an ironclad recommitment to the one-China policy, and in other ways by facilitating China's very gradual emergence as a dominant regional power. As Brzezinski sees it, while China is potentially a rival of the

United States in Asia, it will be incapable of challenging the United States for many decades and can thus be given plenty of space to maneuver in its region (a point also made by Kissinger). While China may be a U.S. rival down the road, the more immediate problem to these realists is constraining Russia.

Does a resulting potential eruption in U.S.-Russian relations worry Brzezinski? No. Such a strategy will, he believes, "encourage Russia to make its long-delayed post-imperial decision in favor of Europe."[101] In any case, "Russia's longer-term role in Eurasia will depend largely on its self-definition," rather than anything done to it by other countries or alliances.[102] Most of all, according to Brzezinski, Russia needs to understand that its former empire in Central Europe is permanently off-limits, and the best way to send that message is to absorb all of that former empire into NATO as quickly as possible.

He recommends, for example, that even the Baltic states, with their sizable ethnic Russian populations, be admitted to NATO not later than 2003.[103] It is difficult for us to imagine a more provocative move, short of a NATO military intervention in Russia itself, for example in Chechnya. Some believe that NATO absorption of the Baltic republics would lead immediately to a dangerous crisis reminiscent of the Cold War crises between East and West. But firm in his belief that the U.S. mission is to remain a "benign hegemon," and concerned that the United States seize the advantage while the Russians are preoccupied with their disastrous internal situation, Brzezinski appears unworried about the eventual outcome. In any case, he writes, "Russia's first priority should be to modernize itself rather than to engage in futile efforts to regain its status as a global power."[104]

In this way, Russia and China in the 21st century are understood by realists to be sovereign, potentially belligerent states, bent on challenging what they take to be U.S. hegemony—Russia sooner, China later. This sort of behavior is driven by aggressive motives that, if left unchecked, will eventually threaten U.S. vital interests. This is why the Americans must always try to signal preemptively to Russia now, and China later, if necessary, that the United States is too strong militarily to be seriously challenged, let alone defeated in war. This, they say, will keep the peace and prevent the kind of ambiguity and uncertainty in the international system of states that could lead to a Great Power war in the 21st century.

We reject this entire analysis. It seems to us that the realists are in fact *unreal* in their analysis of the world of the 21st century. In particular, they are blind to the lessons of the Wilsonian parable with which we introduced this chapter, especially the danger of trying to intimidate, humiliate, or coerce a nation whose self-image is that of a Great Power. We may intimidate them into compliance in the short run. But the memories of the humiliated tend to be long ones, and the emotions generated by the sort of U.S. hegemonic supremacy recommended by the realists tend to be especially intense.

That is why this view, in which Russia and China are believed to aspire to challenge and defeat the United States in the 21st century is so perverse. It creates enemies where there need not be enemies. It leads to missed opportunities for sustainable peace that may never come again. It leads to self-fulfilling prophecies of Great Power conflict that the realists mistake for naturally occurring phenomena. Needless to say, it is utterly devoid of empathy for modes of human history and existence different from the Western liberal norm of its proponents. And while it shows cleverness in articulating scenarios of Great Power conflict, all such dangers derive from irreconcilably hostile *threats*, rather than from inadvertent paths in which a multilateral cast of characters, including the United States and the West, contribute unwittingly to the evolving danger.

.   .   .

We believe all of these U.S. approaches to Russia and China in the 21st century are dangerous. The danger lies in the combustible combination of two simultaneous perceptions in Moscow and Beijing. The first is that the United States will betray its international commitments when it feels so moved. The second is the deep feeling of inferiority felt in Moscow and Beijing with regard to U.S. power—both (what Joseph Nye has called) the "hard" power of U.S. military superiority at all levels, and the "soft" power of the U.S. economic juggernaut and of U.S. cultural influence around the world.[105] Russia and China have thus become angered at the United States and at the same time fearful of U.S. capabilities.

What has occurred among the ruling elites in Russia and China, it seems to us, is a surge of post–Cold War, chauvinistic *nationalism* of a particular kind that is directed primarily at the United States. In a famous essay, Isaiah Berlin put it concisely: "Nationalism," he wrote, "is a pathological form of self-protective resistance. . . . It animates revolts . . . for it expresses the inflamed desire of the insufficiently regarded to count for something among the cultures of the world."[106] At bottom, what the Russian and Chinese leaders at the dawn of the 21st century seem to have felt most acutely in their relations with the United States is that Americans do not regard them as fully legitimate, as occupying the same rung on the ladder of the international order that Americans occupy. Thus they resist and can be counted on to continue to resist, precisely because their sense of having been betrayed seems to them to reveal in the Americans the insufficiency of U.S. regard for them as fellow Great Powers, as cultures, and as peoples.

They feel that, by our manner and bearing, we insult them at every turn. And lacking cognizance of the necessity of empathy between Great Powers, we seldom notice that we are insulting them. And even if we notice, too often we lack the imagination to see the ways these sorts of interactions might lead inadvertently to confrontation, to crisis, even to military conflict.

Thus it is that Russia and China have entered the 21st century full of mistrust of the United States, suspicious that the United States seeks worldwide hegemony to which even the other Great Powers (as the Russians and Chinese regard themselves) are expected to knuckle under. Were this trend to continue, we believe U.S. foreign policy specialists in the future will have little or no trouble articulating plausible scenarios at the end of which the United States and either Russia or China (or both) push one another to the brink of a Great Power war. Even now, it is relatively easy to imagine dangerous arms races, as the Russians and Chinese frantically try to catch up. And it is already too easy to imagine confrontations with the United States caused, in part, by a felt need by the Russians or Chinese to challenge the Americans, to create crises if necessary, as a way to make the Americans understand that while the United States may be the world's only superpower, other Great Powers exist that cannot be betrayed, whose interests cannot be compromised, without penalty.

"We Must Reverse the Course of History"

One question dwarfs all others regarding the prevention of Great Power conflict in the 21st century: Can we in the United States and the West bring Russia and China in from the cold? Woodrow Wilson's heroic effort to bring Germany in from the cold after the First World War failed. Will Wilson's ghost haunt the 21st century in this respect, as it has haunted the 20th, with catastrophic war and suffering? This is an issue that should be paramount in the minds of all who seek actively to prevent the 21st century from becoming a bloody repetition of the 20th.

We have argued that we must always think and act cognizant of, and in unison with, a global or regional coalition. We must seek to "deploy realistic empathy," and we must muster the imagination to "anticipate inadvertent conflict." If we are able to "occupy" the mindsets of Russia and China, and to focus on the ways and means by which conflict might result later as unintended consequences of actions taken now, then we can significantly lower the likelihood of a Great Power conflict in the 21st century.

We should have no illusions about the difficulty before us. The degree of that difficulty is illustrated in the following story of the evolution of one individual's thinking. At a 1991 meeting called by the Carnegie Corporation of New York to discuss post–Cold War security needs, a participant suggested to the assembled group a program somewhat similar to the one we propose here. The chair of the meeting, Senator Sam Nunn of Georgia, stifled any further proposals along these lines by replying: "Well, you have human nature and all of history going against you there. What have you got going for you?"[107] That was in 1991. In the summer of 1999, Senator Nunn (since retired from elective office) again chaired a meeting of specialists in international security, this time under the auspices of the Aspen Strategy Group. On this occasion, having witnessed the devolution of the 1990s into escalating tension between Russia and China, on the one hand, and the United States and the West on the other, he said simply, "we must reverse the course of history."[108]

How difficult will *that* be? In our terms, will the required multilateral imagination materialize? Where will those of us in the United States and the West find the empathy to occupy the mindsets of the Russians and Chinese, whose people were victims in the 20th century of repeated terror, violence, and catastrophe? Most Americans and many others in the West have no acquaintance with these horrors. To what extent will these (to us) utterly foreign experiences make Russians and Chinese impervious to our efforts to meet them on the common ground of liberal Western values? Will we, should we, meet them on any other ground?[109] And who will bet that Americans, the supreme unilateralists, will develop a taste for multilateralism, for the humility to consider that their actions, if unilateral, may raise the odds of an inadvertent Great Power conflict later on in the 21st century? The odds seem stacked against success. Yet we must succeed.

President John F. Kennedy, having been through his own kind of terror in the Cuban missile crisis, saw the world in an irrevocably transformed way—a post–Cold War way—thereafter. Once a cold warrior who was willing, as he said in his inaugural address, to "pay any price" in the fight against communism, he made a very different speech on June 12, 1963:

> And if we cannot now end our differences, at least we can make the world safe for diversity. For in the final analysis, our most basic common link is that we all inhabit this small planet. We all breathe the same air. We all cherish our children's future. And we are all mortal.[110]

Can we achieve this degree of empathy with the Russians and Chinese without another brush with nuclear oblivion or another disastrous Great Power war? Will we work with them to reduce the risk of inadvertent conflict? As Michael Ignatieff has written: "When it comes to political understanding, difference is always minor, comprehension is always possible."[111] Possible, yes. But will we make the effort? And will we do so in time?

National aspirations must be respected; peoples may now be governed only by their own consent. "Self-determination" is not a mere phrase. It is an imperative principle of action. Peace must be planted upon the tested foundations of political liberty.

Woodrow Wilson, May 19, 1919[1]

[The] post-Cold War international system [is] characterized by the presence of many dangerous, troubled, failed, and murderous states. . . . Military intervention is ethically justified when domestic turmoil threatens regional or international security and when massive violations of human rights occur.

Stanley Hoffmann, 1998[2]

[L]iberal imperialism may be the best we are going to do in these callous and sentimental times. . . . The alternative is not liberation or the triumph of some global consensus of conscience, but to paraphrase Che Guevara, one, two, three, many Kosovos.

David Rieff, 1999[3]

3

Reducing Communal Killing

Intervention in "Dangerous, Troubled, Failed, Murderous States"

At the Paris Peace Conference in 1919, Woodrow Wilson naïvely put forth a proposal that appeared to promise national "self-determination" to all those who wished to claim it. That has proven to be a prescription for disaster. In fact, the modern origins of recent communal conflicts in the Balkans, including Bosnia and Kosovo, lay in the misguided, uninformed idealism of Wilson. As we enter the 21st century, increased Western awareness of the horror of communal violence has led to interventions in the former Yugoslavia, East Timor, and various parts of Africa. Public support for these sorts of interventions has been momentarily strong but fleeting. In this chapter, the problem of intervention to prevent or stop communal killing is framed within the dilemma posed by the necessity to confront the many moral blind alleys involved in "doing evil in order to do good."

Self-Determination:
Wilson's Dream, Our Nightmare

We enter the 21st century shocked by what seems to be an epidemic of communal violence and killing. We in the West, particularly in the United States, simply cannot comprehend the world as it appears in the wake of the end of the Cold War. Nor do we know how to prevent or stop the violence and killing. Michael Ignatieff expressed the feelings of many when he wrote:

> [T]he twenty-first century . . . began in 1989. When the Berlin Wall came down, when Vaclav Havel stood on the balcony in Prague's Wenceslas Square and crowds cheered the collapse of communist regimes across Europe, I thought, like many people, that we were about to witness a new era of liberal democracy. . . . We soon found out how wrong we were. For what has succeeded the last age of empire is a new age of violence. The key narrative of the new world order is the disintegration of nation-states into ethnic civil war; the key architects of that order are warlords. . . . The repressed has returned, and its name is nationalism.[4]

This virulent nationalism had been repressed, for the most part, for a very long time—this notion that the world is divided into "nations," linked by blood ties, to which one belongs and owes everything, including the right and duty to protect the "nation" through violence perpetrated on those who would infringe upon its right to organize itself into a sovereign nation-state.

This repressed nationalism is yet another guise of Wilson's ghost. Many, perhaps most, of the instances of communal killing witnessed since the end of the Cold War derive historically from mistakes first made at the peace conference in Paris in 1919. It was there that the idealistic Woodrow Wilson proclaimed the dawn of the era of universal self-determination. It was there that old empires were pronounced dead and new borders were established in Europe, Asia, and Africa, borders that too often created or exacerbated conflicts between rival ethnic or religious groups, conflicts that were repressed, to a large degree, through the remainder of the colonial period and until the end of the Cold War. In Paris Wilson argued that self-determination would bring an end to violent conflict. It did not. Instead, his emphasis on self-determination helped sow the seeds of the conflicts whose recent eruptions have perplexed and troubled so many in the West. Many of us, like Michael Ignatieff, believed that such tribal warfare had died out long ago. But it had not. It had merely gone underground and has now returned to the surface.

Woodrow Wilson was the first American president to travel to Europe during his term in office. The occasion for this precedent-setting trip was the need, as Wilson saw it, to use his personal powers of persuasion to ensure that the peace agreement reached at the Paris conference was consistent with his notion of a "peace without victors." He went to Paris against the advice of many of his aides, who tried to persuade him that he would inevitably be overwhelmed by the complexity of the arrangements that must be made, by the need to resist every hour of every day the urge on the part of Britain, France, and Italy to take revenge on the Germans, and by the effort that would be required to bridge the chasm that divided his vision of the postwar world from that of the allies of the United States.

In addition, Wilson had been intermittently ill for some time. Many close to him feared for his health if he were to try to single-handedly resist the efforts of the other Great Powers to dismember the German, Austrian, and Ottoman empires to their own mutual benefit and satisfaction. These fears proved prescient, as Wilson suffered two strokes in the autumn of 1919, brought on by extreme exhaustion, paralyzing his left side and rendering him virtually incompetent.

Herbert Hoover, who arrived in Paris in late November 1918 to take charge of American relief efforts and aid distribution, argued to Wilson that he should absolutely abstain from participation in the detailed discussions of what was called "the settlement of Europe"—a euphemism in whose two incompatible meanings was captured the central drama of the Paris conference. Would Europe be settled by carving up the empires of the losers and incorporating them into the empires of the winners? Or would Wilson's vision prevail, with independent nation-states established along ethnic lines and according to historical precedents?[5] Hoover feared that Wilson would feel compelled to resist every attempt by the victorious allies at "horse-trading" territories, peoples, and resources, that Wilson in the end would not prevail, and that his immersion in the myriad details of the settlement would prevent him from exercising the kind of leadership the conference would need to become something other than a party for the winners held at the expense of the losers.

Alas, Wilson, supremely confident that he saw the right and that right would prevail, did not share any of Hoover's concerns. Upon arriving in Paris on December 14, 1918, he went straight to work endeavoring to convince the Allies of the justice of his vision of the postwar world. That vision was already well-known in Europe. Wilson had first enunciated it in February 1918 in two speeches to Congress. In the first speech he stated his position baldly on self-determination, without refinement or development. "National aspirations," he proclaimed, "must be respected; peoples may now be governed only by their own consent."[6] He pronounced colonialism dead. In its place, throughout Europe, Asia, and Africa, subject peoples in colonies were henceforth to determine their own fate and govern themselves according to democratic principles. Peoples who had been subjugated for decades or centuries would now govern themselves.

Then on February 11, Wilson gave a second speech in response to Congressional criticism that he was naïve to think that, in effect, European, African, and Asian variants of the United States of America—liberal democracies—could be constructed as easily as he seemed to indicate. This speech contained a caveat. "All well-defined national aspirations," he said, "shall be accorded the utmost satisfaction that can be accorded them without introducing new or perpetuating old elements of discord and antagonism. . . ."[7] So while there would undoubtedly be competing claims regarding borders and other matters, these differences of opinion would, Wilson believed, be resolved peacefully at the conference table. Each claimant would have to give a little to get a little.

Wilson saw himself as the best arbiter of these differences because, as he often said, he was a disinterested and idealistic American who sought no territory for his country, and would thus be an honest broker. Wilson, a distinguished historian and political scientist before becoming presi-

dent, protested to skeptics that he had long known all about the antago-
nisms, the suspicions, and so on that he would face. Thus did Wilson
arrive in Paris, intending to facilitate the world's transition from colonialists and colonized to freely self-determined peoples and states, one
and all. Perhaps, some skeptics remarked, he innocently expected the
debates over self-determination and sovereignty to resemble the discussions at the Faculty Club at Princeton University, where he had once
been president—that is, detached, polite, and reasonable.

Whatever Wilson might have expected, what he actually found
shocked him, according to Herbert Hoover. This was the reality that Wilson had to face in Paris:

> When the president arrived, the delegations of twenty-seven nations of
> the Allied and Associated Powers had been approved to sit at the peace
> table. The delegations of seven nations who had declared themselves
> self-governing peoples, not yet "recognized," and seven little nations
> neutral in the war came there to peer into the windows, anxious for
> their future. . . . The issue at Versailles was the rough job of making
> peace among 400,000,000 people in Europe living cheek by jowl amid
> economic desperation, ancient and rival traditions of power and vio-
> lent forces of hate and revenge. . . . In the blood of many delegations at
> Versailles were the genes of a thousand years of hate and distrust, bred
> of religious and racial persecution and domination by other races. The
> impelling passion for vengeance of past wrongs rose with every hour of
> the day.[8]

All of this antagonism Wilson no doubt knew about from his studies—
from books. Yet he totally lacked the kind of experience, and the tem-
perament, that would have prepared him for what he encountered. As
Hoover put it delicately, regarding these eruptions in Paris of passion for
vengeance: "As a historian, Mr. Wilson was no doubt familiar with their
age-old background, but he did not seem to realize their dynamism."[9]

Thus it was that the passions of decades and centuries became
unlocked by the collapse of empires in the wake of the First World War.
Emboldened by Wilson's declarations of universal self-determination,
and seeking to take advantage of the anarchy of the moment, new states

were proclaimed daily, sometimes hourly, by the various delegations. Armenia alone was "represented" by no fewer than 47 separate delegations, each suspicious of the others, each burning with hatred for the Turks who had ruled them, and each fearful of the Russians, who were already moving in to fill the void left by the collapse of the Ottoman Empire.

States were also proclaimed elsewhere in Europe during the course of Versailles conference. In the former Austro-Hungarian empire, as the historian John Morton Blum has observed, "the quarrels of self-generated self-determination, complicated by revolution, were forging in malice the states which were to speckle the map of central and eastern Europe whether the men at Paris willed it or not."[10] Already on July 20, 1917, a year and a half before the Armistice, the South Slav Federation (what would become Yugoslavia) had been proclaimed by a group of idealistic Serbs, Croats, and Slovenes in exile on the Greek island of Corfu. In this "unauthorized" act of self-determination, which Wilson and the other Allies eventually had no choice but to ratify, was contained the seed of the Yugoslav tragedies—first in Bosnia, then in Kosovo—of the 1990s. This particular exercise of self-determination "from below," independent of the Great Power discussions, proved unsustainable following the end of the Cold War.

But tragedies of self-determination also occurred "from above"— deriving from decisions made by Wilson and his colleagues in Paris. From what had been German East Africa, for example, a League of Nations Protectorate called Ruanda-Urundi was established, to be administered by Belgium as part of the Belgian Congo. Wilson's dream was that in such territories, liberal democracy could be nurtured, as conditions permitted, from which independent, self-determined nation-states would emerge and gain admittance to the League of Nations.

The Belgians, however, did not share Wilson's dream. They administered the territory chiefly via two monarchs from the Tutsi ethnic group, who carried out the orders given them by their colonial masters, even though Tutsis made up only a little more than 10 percent of the population, the rest being mainly of a rival ethnic group, the Hutus. This system, abetted in 1926 by the introduction of mandatory ethnic identity cards, virtually ensured that enmity between the Hutu majority and the Tutsi minority would grow. In 1962, the independent countries of Rwanda and Burundi were created, and almost at once Hutu extremists began to take revenge on the Tutsis for what they regarded as decades of abuse. Violence ebbed and flowed for three decades, culminating in the genocide of Hutus against Tutsis, which began on April 6, 1994, and lasted for approximately 100 days, during which nearly a million people were killed.[11]

Harold Nicolson, who had been a British delegate to the Paris conference, characterized Wilson's failure this way: "America, eternally protected by the Atlantic, desired to satisfy her self-righteousness while disengaging her responsibility."[12] Why self-righteous? Because, although Wilson lacked direct acquaintance with the way life was lived and the way states were governed beyond the borders of the United States, he nevertheless believed that people would in the end be reasonable, and that compromise would prevail in disputes involving self-determination. Why irresponsible? Because once proclaimed by Wilson, the right to self-determination was demanded by hundreds of groups throughout the former Austro-Hungarian and Ottoman empires—groups that sought power and advantage over others in their immediate vicinity. This phenomenon, and the accompanying communal violence and killing, would of course profoundly complicate life in Europe, while the Americans simply went home to relative peace and tranquility.

In fact, it is clear in retrospect that Wilson was profoundly mistaken in believing that the right to national self-determination can in general be exercised widely, freely, and peacefully. Wilson himself, in a rare public moment of self-doubt, seemed to realize that his assumption to the contrary had been tragically wrong. During the ratification debate in 1919, he told the Senate Foreign Relations Committee:

> When I gave utterance to those words ["that all nations had a right to self-determination"], I said them without the knowledge that nationalities existed, which are coming to us day after day. . . . You do not know and cannot appreciate the anxieties that I have experienced as the result of many millions of people having their hopes raised by what I have said.[13]

In proclaiming the universality of the right of self-determination of nations, he had not meant, he said, "to inquire into ancient wrongs."[14]

But this was of course Harold Nicolson's point. The representatives of the victorious European Great Powers understood the incompatibility of universal self-determination with peace and tranquility, even if Wilson did not. They knew all too well that it was seldom possible to raise the subject of self-determination without also raising the issue of "ancient wrongs." Unfortunately, Britain, France, Italy, and the other victors sought only to perpetuate the colonial system, preserving their positions of preference against both local and foreign parties. Wilson, on the other hand, came to Paris with nobler aspirations, yet he failed utterly to understand that not all European (or African or Asian) problems of nations and nationalities had an American solution—a peculiar instance of immodesty that many believe has become, in the post–Cold War era, the quintessential American national "disease," and which Samuel Huntington has called the phenomenon of "the rogue superpower."[15]

The journalist Michael Hirsh has written that, in the post–Cold War world, "most of the rest of the world is insisting on fulfilling Wilson's dream, and that has become our nightmare."[16] In this chapter, we will consider what should be done—what sort of *interventions* should be undertaken—to stop and prevent communal violence and killing. The problems are complex. Easy answers are nonexistent. The beginning of wisdom, we believe, is to renounce Wilson's dream of universal, conflict-free self-determination as a fantasy. Once this is understood and accepted we can begin to awaken from the nightmare of communal killing that had already become the diabolical signature of Wilson's ghost in the 1990s, and which continues unabated into the first decade of the 21st century.

Approaches to Reducing Communal Killing

For hundreds of years, international relations have been characterized by a strong presumption in favor of state sovereignty. A state's borders are held to be inviolable, and exceptions are considered acts of war.

This norm of nonintervention was applied by the European Great Powers to one another but not, until very recently, to states outside of Europe. The nonintervention norm was strengthened during the post–World War II liberation of the European colonial empires. In fact, the postcolonial states of Asia, Africa, and Latin America became, and remain, among the staunchest advocates of an absolute prohibition on the right of one state to intervene in the affairs of another, no matter what the alleged cause. The reason is obvious: Many of these postcolonial states tend to be small and weak and therefore fearful of being exploited by larger states that may have "neo-imperialist" ambitions.

The strong presumption for state sovereignty has been challenged repeatedly since the end of the Cold War. With the end of East-West tensions and the mutually obsessive concern each "bloc" had with the designs of the other, the larger and wealthier states in the West, particularly the United States, now have the luxury of taking a broader view of whatever threats to the peace may exist, no matter where they are located, and no matter what form they may take. That is the first change: No longer required to equate foreign threats with "Moscow," "Beijing," and their "satellites," many in the West are noticing things that escaped them before. Second, the end of the Cold War has unlocked a Pandora's box of contending claims of self-determination, sometimes accompanied by violence and killing on a scale that those in the West find shocking. The violence and killing, however, tend to occur *within* the boundaries of established states. Many violent locales come to mind: the former Yugoslavia (first Bosnia, then Kosovo), countries on the southern tier of the former Soviet Union (Tajikistan, Moldova, South and North Ossetia, Abkhazia), Rwanda, Somalia, Haiti, Colombia, East Timor, Aceh, and various other provinces of Indonesia.

So we *see* more violence and bloodshed than before. And it appears to many as if there *is* more than before. Our television news is flooded with horrible human disasters, often the result of great cruelty originating in the kind of nationalist furies of which few in the West have any direct experience. We want to do something to stop it; we want *somebody* to do something to stop it. In this way, as legal scholar Anne-Marie Slaughter Burley and economist Carl Kaysen have written, "the simmering tension . . . between the norm of nonintervention and the norm of self-determination in cases of internal repression is now brought to a boil by the desire to promote an entire range of human rights in addition to political autonomy."[17]

It is widely believed that "we"—the United States, the UN, NATO, the West—can make a difference by intervening to stop the killing. But how? By whom? Under what conditions? With what objectives and with what projected likelihood of success should such interventions be undertaken? Let us return to the moral and multilateral imperatives for the 21st century that lay at the heart of our "radical agenda." The moral imperative is to reduce human carnage in the 21st century. First, the moral corollary for stopping communal killing:

The Moral Corollary: Confront "Moral Blind Alleys"

This is our moral corollary for stopping communal killing: Face squarely the fact that many instances of communal killing will present those who would intervene with excruciating moral dilemmas involving conflicts between our wish to do something now to stop the killing, on the one hand, and, on the other, our ability to do so at acceptable cost and the risk of exacerbating the situation and thus inadvertently becoming accomplices to a tragedy in progress. Moral philosophers believe that "ought implies can"—that we are morally bound to do only that which it is possible to do. But in extreme cases of communal killing we may be driven by our feelings of horror and common humanity to believe we can stop it, when in fact we cannot. In these cases, we encounter a "moral blind alley," from which there may be no completely acceptable escape.

In retrospect, the Cold War seems to have been all blacks and whites, morally speaking, with the forces of light on one side, and those of darkness on the other. We in the West imagined all too often that orders given in Moscow or Beijing were carried out by dutiful, brainwashed automatons in Hanoi, Pyongyang, Havana, Luanda, or wherever else we believed the evil empire of communism had spread its tentacles. Likewise, all too often, officials in Moscow or Beijing imagined vast Western conspiracies to entrap them or destroy them, when in fact the noncommunist leaders in the West felt they were on the defensive most of the time. And so it went: good guys and bad guys; and easy justifications for almost any policy, weapons system, or intervention. There was much tension, of course, due chiefly to the intermingling of nuclear danger with the Cold War confrontation. Geopolitical life wasn't easy. But from the standpoint of our entry into the 21st century, we seemed to have inhabited an extraordinarily simple world.

The theologian and moral philosopher Reinhold Niebuhr labored in vain throughout the early Cold War period to encourage his fellow Americans to take what he believed was a more realistic view of the world. Niebuhr's message, while complex and nuanced, can in a sense be reduced to a single question, a question he believed Westerners, and Americans in particular, should address to themselves, though they seldom did so: "*How much evil must we do in order to do good.*"[18] During the Cold War, the typical American answer was "zero." The communists were evil; we resisted them; thus we were good. We did what we had to do.

But the post–Cold War epidemic of communal violence and killing, driven by incompatible claims of self-determination and nationalist extremism, no longer allows for such a simple response to Niebuhr's central question. As he might have put it, since 1989, we have known sin. We intervened in Somalia in 1992–1994, made a bad situation worse, witnessed the killing of nearly two dozen Americans, and retreated in shame. We closed our eyes in 1994 to perhaps the worst case of genocide since Hitler's "final solution"—in Rwanda—and did nothing to stop it. We have repeatedly intervened in the former Yugoslavia—the UN in Bosnia, and NATO in Kosovo—yet failed to completely eliminate ethnic cleansing and communal killing.

Niebuhr's question seems prescient at the outset of the 21st century. Now, confronted with evil all around us in the form of communal killing, we find that in order to stop the killing—to do good—we must, in fact, be prepared to commit evil ourselves. This became clearer than ever in the spring of 1999, as NATO forces bombed a modern European city, Belgrade, for weeks, killing innocent civilians and making life miserable for those who survived. And in Kosovo, the NATO bombing campaign greatly accelerated the Serbian forced removal of ethnic Albanians already underway. Because of these results, guilt was and remains palpable in the West, despite claims of "success." Writing in 1952 of America's new responsibilities in the Cold War, Niebuhr observed that "the perennial moral predicaments of human history have caught up with a culture which knew nothing of sin or guilt."[19] Few heard the message then. Now it is inescapable.

Niebuhr's outlook and central question form key elements of the view of one of America's most insightful contemporary philosophers of war and peace, Thomas Nagel of New York University. What is permissible in warfare? How much killing, and what kind of killing, is permissible before justifiable acts of war become immoral atrocities, massacres, and other acts categorizable as criminal? These problems—the problems of the proper relation between ends and means in violent conflict—have occupied Nagel for more than thirty years, since he began writing about the American war in Vietnam in the early 1970s. For heads of state, civilian officials, field commanders, foot soldiers or common citizens of nations in conflict, Nagel asks: Which ends justify which means? Nagel, a secular philosopher of the Anglo-American school, asks the same question as the Lutheran theologian Niebuhr: How much evil for how much good?

Nagel's principal contribution has been to locate the core tension which generates the moral dilemmas involving ends and means in warfare, a tension that derives from the interaction of our human capacity to attend to both the projected *outcome* of our actions and also to what we, in fact, are *doing* in our efforts to produce that intended outcome. The former capacity he calls "utilitarian"; the latter, "absolutist":

> Utilitarianism gives primacy to a concern with what will *happen*. Absolutism gives primacy to a concern with what one is *doing*. The conflict between them arises because the alternatives we face are rarely just choices between *total outcomes*: they are also choices between alternative pathways or measures to be taken. When one of the choices is to do terrible things to another person, the problem is altered fundamentally; it is no longer a question of which outcome would be worse . . . [I]t is perfectly possible to feel the force of both types of reason very strongly; in that case, the moral dilemma will be acute, and it may appear that every possible course of action or inaction is unacceptable for one reason or another.[20]

This is what Nagel calls a "moral blind alley," in which one cannot find a way to refrain from doing (or not doing) that which one believes in morally wrong.[21]

It is this feeling that has become so familiar and so unwelcome a psychological accompaniment to our entry into the 21st century. Confronted, even bombarded, daily with vivid reports of communal killing on a scale many find incomprehensible, we instantly feel that it must be stopped, that perpetrators must be apprehended and punished, that things should be put right. But how, now that we have also seen UN peacekeepers held hostage and murdered in Rwanda and Sierra Leone; when U.S. Marines have been killed and humiliated in Somalia; and when, after months of bombing Yugoslavia, with all the mayhem and suffering that it produced, we still saw in newspapers and on television, for more than a year after the bombing, the smiling face of Serb President Slobodan Milosevic—a man indicted in May 1999 as an accused war criminal? These are the moral blind alleys of the post–Cold War world, the moral cul-de-sacs in the midst of which we continue to squirm, groping for a morally acceptable way out.

These moral blind alleys seem virtually inescapable now, at the outset of the 21st century, no matter what one's view of a particular intervention may be. For example, General Wesley Clark, commander of NATO forces during the 1999 intervention in Kosovo, strenuously objected to constraints placed on him by his political masters. Clark wanted to "go downtown" with the air war on the first night of NATO's attack, knocking out the power in Belgrade and endeavoring to liquidate Milosevic and his inner circle. But NATO said no, the attacks must initially be light. It was called a "phased air operation."[22] Clark also wanted authorization to send in NATO ground troops, which was also refused.

Clark necessarily took what Nagel calls the *utilitarian* view, concerned to achieve the most decisive military outcome as soon as possible. What was the actual outcome? Kosovo was systematically "cleansed" of Albanians. Milosevic remained in power for more than a year after the bombing was terminated. And the Serb forces were decidedly not defeated in the field. In fact, as they withdrew northward in June 1999, Serb soldiers in sunglasses made obscene gestures for the benefit of Western television crews covering their withdrawal. The evil Serb warriors against which NATO had flown over 34,000 sorties in 78 days left Kosovo hardly "defeated" in any meaningful sense.[23] Clark felt a strong moral obligation to defeat and remove the Serbian government of Slobodan Milosevic and was, in effect, removed from his command for arguing publicly that he was prevented from doing so by the constraints placed on him by the NATO political leaders.

On the other hand, the nongovernmental organization Human Rights Watch, which had been insistent that a military intervention be carried out to halt ethnic cleansing in Kosovo, has severely criticized NATO for *its* human rights violations—of both Serbs and Albanian Kosovars. In their *WorldReport 2000,* they cite three categories of such violations: (1) failing to provide assistance on the ground to the Kosovars; (2) killing more than 600 innocent civilians, in spite of rigorous attempts to avoid collateral damage from the high-altitude bombing; and (3) NATO's attacks on a wide variety of targets in Belgrade and elsewhere in Serbia that caused suffering to millions of noncombatants—in effect, the entire civilian population of Serbia.[24] In Nagel's terms, Human Rights Watch is an *absolutist* organization, concerned especially to monitor *what is being done* to people during conflicts. The organization thus found the Kosovo campaign as morally unsatisfactory as did Wesley Clark and his military colleagues at NATO headquarters in Brussels, though for quite different reasons.

Both Clark and Human Rights Watch agreed on the moral need to stop the Serbian ethnic cleansing of Kosovo. Yet Clark et al. regretted the failure to achieve their moral objective—elimination of the Serb threat to Kosovo—while those at Human Rights Watch regretted the failure of NATO to strictly observe the moral responsibility to avoid doing harm to those not directly involved in the fighting. In each case, the regret was strong. NATO was therefore condemned for what it did not do, and for what it did do. The Protestant theologian Paul Ramsey puts the general case this way:

For us to choose political or military intervention is to use power tragically incommensurate with what politically should be done, while not to intervene means tragically to fail to undertake the responsibilities that are there, and are not likely to be accomplished by other political actors.[25]

This is precisely the kind of outcome Nagel described in 1971 as a moral blind alley in which, regardless of whether the decision is to intervene or not to intervene, it is impossible "to feel that a moral dilemma has been resolved."[26] If the Kosovo conflict was, as has been claimed, an "anti-heroic war," it seems that one of its chief characteristics is moral discomfort with the results, no matter what one's view of the outcome.[27]

One of the most interesting and important recent attempts to confront these moral blind alleys head-on is *The Harvest of Justice Is Sown in Peace*, a 1993 statement by the National Conference of U.S. Catholic Bishops.[28] The American bishops invoke St. Augustine, who said, "Love may require force to protect the innocent," making a point similar to that made by Niebuhr.[29] The bishops, working within the centuries-old tradition of Just War Doctrine, offer not a way out of the moral blind alleys of the 21st century—for it does not exist—but rather a way to engage more fully the conundrums facing citizens and their leaders contemplating humanitarian intervention.

It is worth recalling the basic issues addressed by Just War Doctrine, the tradition within which the bishops' analysis is made. They are two: *jus ad bellum* (the decision whether to intervene militarily), and *jus in bello* (what is justified in the actual application of military force). The relevant questions to be asked under *jus ad bellum* are: (1) Will the intervention being contemplated be carried out by the right authority? (2) Does the intervention have the right intention, that is, rescuing those in need and establishing longer-term safeguards for their peace and security? (3) Is the use of military force being undertaken, as it should be, only as a last resort? (4) Does the intervention have a reasonable hope of success? and (5) Will the proportionality of the good achieved likely justify the evil required to achieve it? For *jus in bello,* the relevant questions are: (1) Have innocent noncombatants been sufficiently protected from harm during and following the intervention? and (2) Is the degree of military force used proportionate to the ends the intervention is supposed to achieve?[30] The bishops' goal was to establish the terms, or categories, within which morally responsible debate concerning humanitarian intervention might take place. They recognized the risk they were taking in situating the debate about intervention within the categories of Just War Doctrine: that leaders and citizens may apply the categories selectively to justify positions at which they have already arrived for other reasons. They warn against doing so by arguing that, in effect, the various categories of *jus ad bellum* and *jus in bello,* properly understood, provide a framework for asking questions, not a mechanical algorithm for reaching certainty, let alone justification, regarding the moral probity of military interventions. Indeed, even a cursory glance at the questions required by Just War Doctrine reveals that assessing the moral standing of any military intervention is no simple matter. One needs to ask, for example, about the Kosovo intervention: Were innocent combatants sufficiently protected? And were the military means used proportionate to the end which was achieved? Clearly NATO took extra-ordinary measures in these regards. But did they succeed? Was the outcome therefore *morally justified?*

When we read the bishops' statement, it becomes evident that not even they could escape the effects of moral blind alleys, for they too are human beings who can become outraged and driven to seek redress in ways that seem to require bypassing the very categories of Just War Doctrine they hope to promote. For example, the bishops quote approvingly this statement by Pope John Paul II:

> . . . [When] populations are succumbing to the attacks of an unjust aggressor, states no longer have a "right to indifference." It seems clear that their duty is to disarm the aggressor if all other means have proved ineffective. The principles of sovereignty of states and noninterference in their internal affairs . . . cannot constitute a screen behind which torture and murder may be carried out.[31]

On the one hand, this statement is eerily prescient, coming just months before the Hutu genocide against the Tutsi in Rwanda in the spring of 1994. The Pope's warnings, in effect, were not heeded in Rwanda, where many states, including the United States, seem indeed to have used the principle of noninterference as a "screen" for inaction.

Yet it is pertinent to ask what might have happened if the Pope's injunctions had been heeded, keeping in mind the size and speed of the systematic program of atrocities in Rwanda—nearly a million people were killed in less than three months. Would a Kosovo-style bombing campaign have been sufficient to prevent or end it? We believe the answer is very likely no. Would air power backing up an airborne invasion of Rwanda have stopped the genocide? We believe it is doubtful. In any case, no such force was available, or could be made available in time.[32] How large an invasion force would have been necessary to prevent or significantly reduce the carnage via an airborne invasion (leaving aside, for the moment, the critical practical issue of where they would have come from)? It is difficult to say.

And what would have been the probable outcome of a war fought by a large contingent of foreign combat troops in central Africa? Using air power and all other means that might have been, in principle, at the disposal of such an intervention force, how many Rwandans, Hutus and Tutsis alike, would have been killed? How many refugees would have been produced? How many hostages taken? How long do we suppose such a war would have been sustainable to the governments that had sent troops, in light of the evident necessity of taking significant casualties in the effort to subdue and disarm the Hutu extremists? Days? Weeks? Months? And if it had failed, how would this have affected the international community's inclination to intervene in the midst of similar tragedies in the future? The Pope states that it is our *duty* to intervene in such cases. Yet in the case of Rwanda, it is not at all clear that an attempt to carry out this "duty" would have led to a morally satisfactorily conclusion. Yet the inverse is also true: not intervening was clearly not morally satisfactory.

So we are back again in one of Thomas Nagel's moral blind alleys. "The moral dilemma in certain situations of crisis," he writes, "will be acute" because it will "appear that every possible course of action or inaction is unacceptable for one reason or another."[33] Notice that Nagel does not say that in such situations one chooses "the lesser of two evils." He says that we will find all available courses of action and inaction *unacceptable,* because any conceivable act of intervention to prevent or ameliorate a tragedy will, or very likely will, require that we do exactly what we must avoid, which we must never do, which is immoral. The Rwandan genocide of April 1994 is an illustration of this. Of course it would be desirable to stop communal killing such as he describes, and such as occurred in Rwanda. Yet in the attempt to do so, would Rwanda itself be destroyed? Would a failure in Rwanda lead to worse humanitarian catastrophes elsewhere?

Nagel's conclusion is discomfiting: "[G]iven the limitations on human action, it is naïve to suppose that there is a solution to every moral problem with which the world can face us. We have always known that the world is a bad place. It appears that it may be an evil place as well."[34] As Niebuhr understood, the confrontation with evil necessarily produces guilt because "power cannot be wielded without guilt . . . even when it tries to subject itself to universal standards and places itself under the control of a nascent world-wide community."[35]

Recognizing these facts of life is doubly difficult for Americans, who are inclined to celebrate their leadership of the forces of good that triumphed over those of evil in the Cold War. In addition, the United States, unlike Europe, Africa, and Asia, has been free of large-scale armed conflict since the American Civil War nearly a century and a half ago. No American now living recalls the circumstances of the communal conflict and killing in which nearly 600,000 Americans perished, nor therefore the force of General William T. Sherman's reply to the mayor of Atlanta, who had begged him to spare the civilian population of the city. Sherman's terse reply, just before giving the order to burn it to the ground, was that "war is cruelty and you cannot refine it."[36]

Thomas Nagel's characterization of evil is, as the political philosopher Michael Walzer has acknowledged, deeply troubling, especially for political and military leaders on whose shoulders inevitably falls most of the responsibility for deciding whether to intervene or not.[37] It is they, Walzer notes, who will rightly bear the lion's share of the guilt for the choices they make. Following Nagel and Niebuhr, Walzer agrees that no matter what the choices, guilt will be involved—and for good reason. Walzer says:

> Were there no guilt involved, the decisions they make would be less agonizing than they are. And they can only prove their honor by accepting responsibility for those decisions and by living out the agony. A moral theory that made their life easier, or that concealed the dilemma from the rest of us . . . would miss or . . . repress the reality of war.[38]

Fair or not, this burden of responsibility will be a fact of life for those who would seek to fulfill the moral imperative to reduce communal killing in the 21st century.

Even after the fact, it may be difficult to judge whether an intervention was justified. The Oxford scholar and journalist Timothy Garton Ash recently confessed that answers to the central questions of the Kosovo conflict remain elusive. Why did Slobodan Milosevic reject NATO's terms and carry out the ethnic cleansing of Albanians in Kosovo? "The truth is," according to Garton Ash, "that we simply do not know why Milosevic and his tiny clique of cronies and advisers behaved as they did."[39] Likewise, why did Milosevic finally cave in? "Once again," Garton Ash concludes, "we really don't know what made the difference to that poisoned but calculating mind."[40]

Garton Ash is as astute an observer of Central European politics as exists in the West. Yet we suggest that the very terms in which he addresses these key issues betrays a lack of appreciation for the way the prospect and actuality of massive bombing affects people who must live under the bombs. We have not the slightest inclination to defend an opportunistic demagogue like Milosevic. But to characterize him as a devil with a "poisoned mind" does not help us understand the defiance of NATO by the majority of Serb citizens, many of whom despised Milosevic before the bombing began. Their responses to the intervention reflected wounded national pride; reflected the fact that the war was about their country, about its nature and definition, about whether it would continue to exist; and reflected how people pull together when their backs are to the wall, no matter their personal opinions of their political leadership.

Those who intervene, as NATO did in Kosovo, will frequently face these attitudes—which are so at variance with their own experience. Failing to take these disconnects into account may lead to an immoral result, in which the ends do not justify the means. This is hardly an argument for avoiding intervention when the situation calls for it. It is rather meant to caution those who would embark on an intervention to correct egregious evil that the morality of the outcome will be determined by far more than the intention to do good. One must also ask how much evil will be required to accomplish the good. That NATO may have given insufficient attention to these "evil" aspects of intervention is implied by Garton Ash's reference to critics of the NATO intervention. Although his metaphor is medical rather than moral, the point is identical. It is possible, he concludes, that "NATO's action was the disease for which it claimed to be the cure."[41]

The Multilateral Constraint

We wrote in Chapter One that with the exception of responding to a direct attack on the American homeland, the United States should never apply its military power unilaterally. That is our multilateral imperative for the 21st century. We now discuss its application to reducing communal killing.

This is our multilateral constraint on reducing communal killing: The United States must practice "zero tolerance" multilateralism—unilateral interventions are proscribed, without exception. As the only country with genuine global military reach, the United States will, in many instances of military intervention to stop communal killing, be required to take the lead in implementation. It should do so preferably under the aegis of the UN Security Council, or of appropriate regional organizations such as NATO, the Organization of American States (OAS), or the Organization of African Unity (OAU). But in no case should the United States decide unilaterally to intervene. U.S. leaders are not omniscient, even though they sometimes act as if they are. Wisdom and local knowledge are essential for successful interventions, and others with similar concerns may well have more of it than the Americans. Because armed intervention is a very risky business, we should practice the democratic principles we preach by subjecting our beliefs and inclinations to critical reviews by like-minded allies with similar values and interests.

In our 1999 book, *Argument Without End: In Search of Answers to the Vietnam Tragedy,* we listed what we believed were the essential lessons of the Vietnam war for the 21st century. We consciously tried to draw lessons that might apply across the board, to any sort of armed intervention by one or more countries across the borders of another. One of those lessons provides the basis of our multilateral constraint on reducing communal killing. In our analysis of the U.S. decision-making process regarding the intervention in Vietnam, it became obvious just how monumentally wrong were so many of the U.S. assumptions, perceptions, judgments, and calculations that led to the Americanization of the war—under five presidents of both major political parties (Truman, Eisenhower, Kennedy, Johnson, and Nixon). It was also obvious that many, perhaps most, of these mistakes could have been corrected had the United States seriously consulted other nations who were similarly concerned but better informed, had listened open-mindedly to their criticisms, and had incorporated their views into the U.S. decision-making process. The tragedy of Vietnam was, in many ways, a tragedy of American unilateralism. For that reason, we concluded that U.S. power should be applied "only in a context of multilateral decisionmaking."[42]

The post–Cold War era began with a powerful display of multilateralism: the U.S.-led, but Security Council authorized, multinational force's expulsion of the Iraqis from Kuwait in the Persian Gulf War in early 1991. The perceived success of Operation Desert Storm led many to speculate about the possibility of building a new international order, one in which just this sort of U.S. leadership without unilateralism would become the rule for military interventions. Here is Yale historian John Lewis Gaddis, waxing optimistic in an essay published in *Foreign Affairs* magazine at the conclusion of Desert Storm:

> Woodrow Wilson's vision of collective international action to resist aggression failed to materialize in 1919–20 because of European appeasement and American isolationism, and again after 1945 because of the great power rivalries that produced the Cold War. Neither of these difficulties exists today. The world has a third chance to give Wilson's plan the fair test it has never received . . . by acting through a reinvigorated United Nations—*not* through the unilateral action of the United States.[43]

President George Bush spoke in the aftermath of the Gulf War of the advent of a "new world order." Anthony Lake, national security adviser to Bush's successor, Bill Clinton, described the Clinton administration's post–Cold War foreign policy as one of "Wilsonian enlargement," aimed at expanding democracy and free trade, and protecting and promoting human rights.[44]

It was an optimistic moment for American foreign policy makers, who wondered whether Wilson's vision, long delayed, might become a reality. Would the UN Security Council, free at last after the Cold War from its ideological straitjacket, begin to embody Wilson's dream of a U.S.-led, but genuinely multilateral, global police force? Much that Wilson sought but failed to achieve seemed possible in the months immediately following the Gulf War. The political philosopher Michael J. Smith of the University of Virginia has picturesquely but aptly named this period, lasting approximately from 1991 to 1993 as one of "Dudley Do-right euphoria" for U.S.-led multilateralism, evoking the Royal Canadian Mounted Policeman of cartoon fame, who is constantly galloping off on his horse to set things right.[45]

What a difference a decade makes! We enter the 21st century not anticipating the realization of Wilson's dream, but pursued by Wilson's ghost—by the failure, once again, to achieve effective multilateralism, with regard to competing claims of self-determination and communal conflicts that the international community has failed repeatedly to resolve. What seems to have happened is that the United States and other Western nations committed an error that cognitive psychologists call *overgeneralization*. They observed the results of the Gulf War, assumed (perhaps not always consciously) that the Gulf War was the model for 21st-century conflict, and generalized from these considerations that the future looked rosy indeed for the effective application of multilateral force. But many characteristics of the Gulf War have not been replicated in the subsequent communal conflicts. In fact, the Gulf War was an example of what appears to be an increasingly rare form of conflict: an old-fashioned cross-border war of aggression by one sovereign state against another and one, moreover, that seems to threaten a vital interest of the rich and powerful Western democracies—in this case, access to Persian Gulf oil.

One of the West's most incisive observers of this sea change in attitudes toward the possibilities of multilateralism is David Rieff. He notes in a September 2000 essay that "after Somalia and Bosnia, Rwanda and Kosovo, the heady optimism of the immediate aftermath of the Cold War seems almost as culpably naïve as Woodrow Wilson's assertion in 1918 that World War I had been 'the war to end all wars.'"[46] In Wilson's time and in ours, stopping communal killing within state borders has proven to be a virtually insoluble problem for outsiders.

There are many reasons why this is so. Those undertaking an intervention must first overcome the strong traditional presumption in favor of state sovereignty. In addition, interventions with the objective of stopping communal violence must usually be justified by an appeal to *values* rather than state interests. Coalitions of nations must be assembled that adhere to such values. The biggest difficulty, however, one that has caused many a potentially willing intervener to halt at the brink, is the typical ferocity of communal killing such as has been unleashed by the end of the Cold War. To enter the killing fields of Somalia, Rwanda, Bosnia, or Sierra Leone is to bear witness to a level of man's inhumanity to man that few in the West can comprehend, let alone resolve. Throughout the post–Cold War period of communal conflicts, Western governments and publics have had a kind of approach-avoidance reaction to the killing. The horror that has attracted them to the *idea* of humanitarian intervention has also caused them to recoil when, as Jim Hoagland of the *Washington Post* puts it, it is time to "put up or shut up."[47] Alas, as Hoagland notes, many in the West refuse to "shut up" about their profound moral obligations to stop such killing, even as they also refuse to "put up" the funds, forces, and advanced weaponry for the kind of operations required to succeed.

David Rieff uses an arresting metaphor for the evolution of the West's response to communal killing. According to Rieff, it "eerily mirrors Elisabeth Kubler-Ross' famous scheme of the five stages of dealing with death: denial, anger, bargaining, depression and acceptance . . . leading to the conclusion that, except in a few rare cases, there was little that could be done."[48] This is closely related to what Michael Ignatieff calls "the seductiveness of moral disgust," brought on by "compassion fatigue," which "represent[s] an active repugnance at the inability of societies that receive help to do anything to cure themselves" of their murderous impulses.[49] Such an attitude is, as Ignatieff points out, often equivalent to the position that we should "let the brutes exterminate themselves," since that is apparently what they want to do anyway.[50]

To the extent that this has become a dominant attitude in the United States and the West with regard to communal killing, we deplore it (as do Rieff and Ignatieff). It is totally unacceptable to embark on a *policy*, whether formalized or not, of standing by passively while fellow human beings slaughter each other in appalling numbers over differences of ethnicity, religion, and the right of self-determination. Stanley Hoffmann of Harvard has issued an apt warning about the danger of this kind of apathy in the wake of the disasters in Rwanda and the former Yugoslavia. "Apathy about 'far away countries of which we know nothing,'" Hoffmann has written, quoting British Prime Minister Neville Chamberlain's pitiful response to Nazi Germany's invasion of Czechoslovakia, "can all too easily lead—through contagion, through the message that moral passivity sends to troublemakers, would-be tyrants, and ethnic cleansers everywhere . . . to a creeping escalation of disorder and beastliness that will, sooner or later, reach the shores of the complacent, the rich, and the indifferent."[51] To remain passive, to maintain an attitude of "acceptance" of such atrocities, Hoffmann rightly warns, "would be politically nefarious and ethically scandalous."[52]

To convince Western publics of the wisdom, let alone the necessity, of multilateralist activism will of course require leadership. In fact, leadership of the highest order will be required to instruct, to inspire, to cajole, and to decide wisely regarding military interventions. In the United States, strong and wise leadership will especially be required to convince the body politic of the virtues of multilateralism when, left to its own devices, it tends to oscillate wildly between, on the one hand, enthusiasm for morally messianic unilateralism and, on the other hand, morally disgusted isolationism. In other words, we advocate what may be called "*leadership multilateralism,*" a multilateralism that is goal-directed and activist, and which leads to action. This stands in opposition to "*I'll-go-if-you-go multilateralism,*" the kind of multilateralism that is in reality simply timidity and inaction.[53]

A thoroughgoing multilateral approach to intervention, one with "zero tolerance" for unilateralism, has at least four advantages over traditional U.S. unilateralism: (1) legal; (2) institutional; (3) perceptual; and (4) cognitive. By "advantages," we refer to consequences of multilateralism that seem to us to reduce the risk of a disastrous intervention caused wholly or in part by misinformation, misperception, misjudgment, and/or miscalculation.

First, there are *legal* advantages. According to legal scholars, multilateral or collective military intervention has, under certain conditions, the sanction of international law. While it is true that a strong presumption in favor of state sovereignty is written into the UN Charter, it also contains an important caveat. Article 2(7) of the Charter reads as follows:

> Nothing contained in the present Charter shall authorize the United Nations to intervene in matters which are essentially within the domestic jurisdiction of any state or shall require Members to submit such matters to settlement under the present Charter; *but this principle shall not prejudice the application of enforcement measures under Chapter VII.*[54]

The caveat regarding Chapter VII involves "threats to the peace, breaches of the peace, and acts of aggression."[55] According to Lori Fisler Damrosch of Columbia University Law School, "there is ample warrant for invoking the Security Council's powers to respond to 'threats to peace' . . . even if the conflict had no transboundary elements. The salient difference is between unilateral and collective action."[56] Anne-Marie Slaughter Burley of Harvard Law School agrees, noting that we enter the 21st century in the midst of "a shift in the paradigm of conflict" from interstate wars to communal violence. "As the paradigm shifts," she contends, "the old norm [of nonintervention] is stretched to accommodate the shift."[57]

Based on these considerations, we draw the following conclusions: Unilateral intervention is simply prohibited by international law; multilateral intervention can be legally sanctioned, if the level of communal violence is sufficiently great to produce either "threats to peace" in the surrounding area or a humanitarian catastrophe or both. In either case an appropriate institutional sanction is required by the UN Security Council or an appropriate regional organization. Moreover, it is always an advantage to act in accordance with international law, which contains a body of precepts that represent an important thread of the fabric of civilization that binds human societies together.

Second, important *institutional* advantages accrue to those adhering strictly to a multilateral approach. Any multilateral intervention must be implemented by a bona fide multilateral organization with proper authority to carry out the intervention as the representative of the wishes of the world's nations, or at least the nations of the region in which the communal killing is occurring. The leading candidate for sanctioning any such military intervention is of course the UN Security Council.

During the Cold War the Security Council was severely constrained by the ideological confrontation between its leading permanent members. Except in rare cases, the United States, Britain, and France could be expected to join on one side of an issue, and the Soviet Union and China on the other (following the Beijing government's replacement of Taiwan in the UN in 1971). It was the hope of many that the Security Council would, following the end of the Cold War, be able to act more freely and effectively as the arbiter and executor of proposed interventions to stop communal killing.

Yet in the view of most observers, including the two most recent post–Cold War UN Secretaries General, Boutros Boutros-Ghali and Kofi Annan, the Security Council has not proven equal to this task. This is especially true of its difficulties in dealing with what Boutros-Ghali has called "the culture of death"—killing fields in which warring groups of citizens of a common state are primarily animated by the urgent need to exterminate one another utterly.[58] He lamented in July, 1995: "We are not allowed to intervene on one side. The mandate does not allow it."[59] Annan has labeled this the "the dilemma of so-called 'humanitarian intervention,'" in which the UN Security Council, like a collective Hamlet, is immobilized by its need to respect national sovereignty and not to take sides despite its collective horror at the killing and the resulting urge to stop it.[60] Thus far in the post–Cold War period, this dilemma has proven insoluble, and it is exacerbated by the veto power wielded by each of the five permanent members of the Security Council—the United States, Russia, China, Britain, and France—and its unrepresentativeness as regards the world of the nascent 21st century.

Examples of the Security Council's ineffectiveness abound. The United States, reeling from the perceived fiasco of its 1993 intervention in Somalia, did not want to involve itself in Rwanda in the early spring of 1994, and its reticence helped to frustrate efforts to intervene there in a timely fashion. And in 1999 with regard to Kosovo: The United States and its NATO partners, convinced that Russia and China would veto any proposed military intervention targeted at Yugoslavia, bypassed the UN altogether, arguing that the NATO imprimatur was sufficient. But as Kofi Annan observes, "the choice must not be between Council unity and inaction in the face of genocide—as in the case of Rwanda—and council division but regional action, in the case of Kosovo."[61]

If the UN Security Council is to be the international body responsible for such interventions, it badly needs reform. The United States should take the lead in reshaping and reinvigorating the Security Council. It should promote Security Council enlargement to make it more representative of the world of the emerging 21st century, rather than the world that emerged from the Second World War, when the UN was founded. And it should press, as well, to eliminate the veto of individual members. Such reforms as these are taken up in a later section of this chapter, "A Program for Rescue and the Restoration of Peace in Failed States."

We also believe that the sooner the United States begins to act in this thoroughly multilateral fashion, the sooner new norms of intervention will be established—norms appropriate to the new era of failed states that are chiefly characterized by unacceptable levels of communal violence and killing. Stanley Hoffmann has compared the situation at the outset of the 21st century to a medical epidemic. "We cling to the notion of peace as the norm," he has written, "which results in states not moving until that norm has been broken." Instead, according to Hoffmann, "we should accept sickness as the norm, with actions being necessary in order to contain these sicknesses."[62] This is the ultimate objective: an institution ready, willing, and able to *prevent* communal killing, as well as contain it and terminate it. But the UN Security Council is far from able to achieve this with its current constituency, voting rules, and resources.

There is a third category of advantages to zero-tolerance multilateralism that we call *perceptual*. The United States needs urgently to begin to combat the perception throughout the world that it has become a "rogue superpower."[63] Nations of the developing world are virtually united in their suspicion of what they perceive to be American hegemonic tendencies, culturally, politically, and militarily. Some may say that this is just sour grapes on the part of the small, weak, and poor—that it is in the nature of international politics for the powerful to impose their will upon the weak. This is the view of the realists' school, who are fond of quoting Thucydides's account of the confrontation between the Athenians and the Melians in ancient Greece. The Athenians gave the much weaker Melians an ultimatum, following a revolt against Athenian authority: They could fight and be destroyed or they could surrender. The Melians responded that they were fighting for their freedom, to which the Athenians replied, "The strong do what they have the power to do and the weak accept what they have to accept."[64] In other words, power matters, perceptions do not.

International relations are no longer as simple as they were for the ancient Greeks, as power is now measured by many means other than raw military capacity. Japan, for example, is a Great Power on the world scene, even though it has only a rudimentary military capability. More to the point, the power wielded by the United States is often the "soft power" of its cultural, economic, and political institutions and traditions, which continue to have tremendous influence throughout the world.[65] America's unilateralist tendencies are of special interest to small countries suspecting that they too might one day be regarded as a target of a unilateral U.S. intervention. Yet the small, weak, and poor nations are far from alone in their suspicion of the United States. America's allies also often feel this way, none more volubly than France. French Foreign Minister Hubert Védrine, for example, has referred to the United States as the "hyperpower," a country determined to eradicate all vestiges of cultural and linguistic pluralism.[66]

The United States should be concerned about such attitudes because the period of U.S. dominance of the post–Cold War world is bound to be but a fleeting moment. We will need friends—reliable allies who trust us and smaller friends who are willing to give us the benefit of the doubt. And now is the time to start building trust, by practicing a little humility, by occasionally admitting that we are wrong, by listening to the concerns of others. We may be, as Joseph Nye has written, "bound to lead," but we should not confuse this with what may appear to others as a policy of being "bound to bully." The United States should in fact be "bound to lead *multilaterally*."

But there is a potentially much more serious perceptual issue at stake:

the view of the United States held by Russia and China. Consider, for example, the December 1999 joint communiqué issued following a summit meeting between Russian President Boris Yeltsin and Chinese President Jiang Zemin. The communiqué focused on the need to resist U.S. unilateralism:

> The two sides point out that negative momentum in international relations continues to grow and the following is becoming more obvious: the forcing of the international community to accept a unipolar world pattern and a single model of culture, value concepts and ideology . . . and the jeopardizing of the sovereignty of independent states using concepts like "human rights are superior to sovereignty" and "humanitarian intervention."[67]

U.S. unilateralism was what that summit was about—the Russian and Chinese perception that the United States believes it has the right to intervene as it sees fit in the internal affairs of other sovereign states with or without proper institutional sanction. Coming as it did just months after the NATO intervention in the Balkans, it was, British scholar Gwyn Prins has written, "the raw nerve which evidently ran, exposed and twitching, through the meeting."[68]

It may be true, as many point out, that such statements as the December 1999 communiqué are simply self-serving, used merely as diplomatic "cover" by two governments trying preemptively to defend themselves against criticism of aspects of their domestic behavior: for example, Russia's brutal mishandling of the war in the rebellious republic of Chechnya or China's cruel mistreatment of the indigenous population of Tibet. While not denying that such statements may indeed be self-serving, we believe that they nonetheless reflect the deep beliefs of the Russian and Chinese leadership and that we therefore need to take them into account. As has often been said, in international affairs, perceptions matter because, so often, perceptions are mistaken for reality. Thus, if the Russians or the Chinese say they feel their sovereignty is threatened, and that the international order is put at risk by U.S. promotion of human rights and humanitarian intervention, we had better listen and work harder at engaging them in a dialogue about this sensitive but unavoidable subject.

Fourth and most important, multilateralism has important *cognitive* advantages. By inviting others in to join the deliberations as to whether or not to intervene, nations are better able to transcend their inevitably provincial outlook—their cultural and historical limitations—and thus to develop the capacity to see the situation more or less as others with similar interests see it, and thus to reach a more objective and better-informed conclusion. The process may not be quite as neat and effort-less as one that omits "foreign" points of view. But by widening the field of inquiry, by seeking the views of others with similar concerns but different perspectives, policy makers contemplating military intervention can better avoid errors caused by what political psychologists call *cognitive biases*.[69] These include both biases that are "unmotivated"— caused by the complexity of the situation and inherent limitations on human capacities—and biases that are "motivated"— caused by the efforts of policy makers to seek premature closure on an issue, or to take a position that may be politically convenient but operationally unwise.

The presence or absence of these biases has considerable significance for the quality of decisions regarding military intervention to stop com-munal killing. The environment is typically extraordinarily complex. There are few "fronts," for example, in the fighting on the ground. The warring ethnic or religious groups swarm over the countryside as they attempt not so much to defeat as to annihilate one another, or at the very least to remove the enemy from disputed territory. In many respects, the pattern of fighting more closely resembles that of gang violence.

In addition, the information available to outsiders—to those who would intervene to stop the killing—about what is happening on the ground is usually sketchy, contradictory, and highly unreliable. Ever since the Persian Gulf War, all sides in conflicts, including the United States, have found it very useful at times to rely on CNN and other tele-vision network news for real-time information about these rapidly evolving situations, whose rate of change tends to swamp even the most sophisticated intelligence-gathering capability. In such situations of high stress, poor information, and public outcries of one sort or another, policy makers may be inclined toward knee-jerk reactions that simply reflect their need to mollify their own domestic political constituen-cies—either those favoring or opposing intervention. In this way, so-called unmotivated biases caused by the mismatch between the clarity needed by decision makers to make relatively rational choices and the chaos they have to deal with combine with "motivated" biases toward premature closure to yield poor-quality decisions. Instances of communal killing tend to involve the kind of emotionally charged, high-pressure perversity that produces poor, provincial, hasty judgments that are often regretted by those who make them.

To illustrate what some call the extreme "otherness" of the phenomenon of communal killing to most Westerners (including Western leaders), consider the process described by psychologist and poet Sam Keen in "Faces of the Enemy":

> *Start with an empty canvas*
> *Sketch in broad outline the forms of*
> *men, women, and children.*
> *Obscure the sweet individuality of each face.*
> *Erase all hints of the myriad loves, hopes,*
> *fears that play through the kaleidoscope of*
> *every finite heart.*
> *Twist the smile until it forms the downward*
> *arc of cruelty.*
> *Exaggerate each feature until man is*
> *metamorphosized into beast, vermin, insect.*
> *Fill in the background with malignant*
> *figures from ancient nightmares—devils,*
> *demons, myrmidons of evil.*
> *When your icon of the enemy is complete*
> *you will be able to kill without guilt,*
> *slaughter without shame.*[70]

What do U.S. decision makers—and the American people—know about the process described by Sam Keen? What do the NATO civilian and military leaders assembled at headquarters in Brussels know about it? The probable answer is little or nothing. Yet this process—what the American psychoanalyst and social critic Erik Erikson referred to as "pseudo-speciation," or reducing one's enemy, in the mind's eye, to something less than a member of the human species—is at the heart of outbreaks of communal killing.[71] This is the very phenomenon that must be reversed, yet it is paradoxically a phenomenon of which those invested with the inclination and power to intervene are unlikely to have any experience. On what basis, then, are they to decide whether to intervene, whether an intervention will stop this process, or whether it will exacerbate it? It seems to us obvious that parties who have this kind of experience need to be brought into deliberations about intervention.

There is no algorithm for optimal decision making in such circumstances. The only effective way to counteract the biases that tend to flourish in these situations is to embed decision making in a multilateral context, taking advantage of more information, discrepant but sympathetic points of view, and thus probably more wisdom, than one can expect from the deliberations within a single government. As Anne-Marie Slaughter Burley has written: "Collective intervention assumes deliberation, which itself assumes prudence, thereby minimizing the number of actions taken and advancing the goal of conflict containment."[72]

These cognitive advantages of rigorous multilateralism are the most important because military intervention to stop communal killing involves going to war on behalf of the international community. By "intervention," we are not referring to "peacekeeping"—placing soldiers in blue berets at borders to keep the peace between two hostile countries. In fact, those intervening militarily to stop communal killing will almost always face a nearly opposite situation. As Michael Ignatieff has written, communal wars today "are about the destruction of states and the creation of new forms of ethnic majority tyranny, backed by ethnic cleansing." This is why, he argues, "to be neutral in Sierra Leone [in May 2000] is to be an accomplice in crime. To keep the peace there is to ratify the conquests of evil."[73] Or as the political scientist Chaim Kaufmann puts it: "Direct intervention is viable, but only when the interveners choose a side and concentrate their efforts on gaining the best, safest territorial settlement for the client group."[74] Use whatever term one desires, according to Kaufmann, but those who would stop communal killing must "plan . . . for a limited war of conquest."[75]

Going to war to stop communal killing inevitably involves confronting the fog of war and inadvertent errors, some with serious ramifications. An example of this was NATO's bombing of the Chinese embassy in Belgrade in May 1999, believing it was a supply depot. This led to riots near the U.S. embassy in Beijing and, ultimately, a downward spiral in U.S.-Chinese relations—all because of the misidentification of a target in downtown Belgrade. We reiterate: Going to war in an effort to stop communal killing in the 21st century is a very serious matter, requiring the best information and greatest wisdom available—requirements best met by embedding decision making in a multilateral context.

The cognitive advantages of multilateralism, finally, provide the key link with the moral corollary—to confront moral blind alleys. Instead of endeavoring to ask and answer variants of the fundamental moral question on its own, a nation contemplating intervention asks for help in answering the question, "How much evil must we do in order to do good?" Other nations also ask themselves this question. True multilateralism requires that they also ask one other, that they listen to one other, and that deliberations give provisional credence to all perspectives. Mistakes will still be made, for such is war. But as Homer's Odysseus was lashed to the mast of his ship to avoid acting on his urge to respond to the song of the Sirens, decision makers in the 21st century should proceed multilaterally to avoid becoming imprisoned within their own biases.

❖

Robert McNamara: My personal conversion to a zero-tolerance multilateralism—with no exceptions allowed—began more than three decades ago. It was then that I began to reflect on the opportunities we in the Kennedy and Johnson administrations missed to end the conflict in Vietnam in the 1960s. One of these was an offer by French President Charles de Gaulle to broker a neutral government in Saigon. The deal de Gaulle had in mind would, I believe, have been in everyone's interest, including ours, for it would have allowed us to exit that conflict before it became an American war with the tragic results that are well-known. But we refused even to consider de Gaulle's participation. We distrusted his motives. Some disliked him personally. But mostly, we thought—wrongly, as I now believe—we knew better than he did.

I cannot say exactly when I began to reflect on the missed opportunity connected with our refusal of de Gaulle's assistance, but I can specify with some precision the date on which my "conversion" was complete. That occurred on or perhaps slightly before August 22, 1967. I discovered this as I was researching my memoir of the Vietnam war, *In Retrospect*.[76]

By August 1967, I was directing a secret peace initiative code-named PENNSYLVANIA, which, had it succeeded, could well have established a neutral, coalition government in Saigon for some period of time, prior to the reunification of Vietnam under the leadership of the Hanoi government. Back in 1962, a "neutral solution" had been President Kennedy's preferred "exit strategy" from Vietnam. It could have succeeded, but it ultimately failed due to a number of unfortunate misunderstandings between Washington and Hanoi.[77] Averell Harriman had been President Kennedy's emissary to the North Vietnamese at the July 1962 Geneva conference to establish a neutral government in Laos. Averell was also involved in the effort to move to negotiations in 1967.

While doing the research on my memoir, I came across a memorandum "for the file" written by Averell following a conversation with me on August 22, 1967. Averell began by saying that the North Vietnamese would never surrender, thus we had better redefine our war objectives. I agreed, saying that we must "make up our minds that the only way to settle this is by having a coalition government. We cannot avoid that." Averell agreed.[78]

It never happened. In the summer of 1967, many in the U.S. government believed that "neutral" meant simply "communist-in-disguise." In addition to their misconceived notions, North Vietnamese military actions at the time did nothing to convert President Johnson to the cause of neutralism in Vietnam. They continued to increase their level of infiltration down the Ho Chi Minh Trail all through 1966 and 1967. After the Tet Offensive of January–March 1968, involving simultaneous attacks on more than 40 cities and towns in South Vietnam, the possibility of a neutral solution was no longer discussed.

What exactly is the connection between a neutral solution in Vietnam and my conviction that military interventions should be multilaterally supported? It is this: Ideas for a neutral solution, and pledges of assistance in its implementation, had been proposed to us on at least three occasions by Charles de Gaulle: (1) in August 1963; (2) immediately following the assassination of South Vietnamese President Ngo Dinh Diem in November 1963; and (3) again in July 1964. De Gaulle had the requisite experience, of course. France had been the colonial power in Vietnam, and in all of Indochina, for more than a hundred years. De Gaulle also had the necessary contacts in both Saigon and Hanoi, as well as good relations with others in the area who were anxious to see an end to the conflict in Vietnam, especially Prince Norodom Sihanouk, the Cambodian head of state. Moreover, de Gaulle had an important political objective in putting himself forward as the facilitator of neutrality in Indochina: He wanted to help reestablish France on the world scene as a major player. I now believe that had we responded positively to any one of de Gaulle's offers to facilitate neutrality, the odds were good that we would have reached an acceptable solution.[79]

But we didn't properly explore with de Gaulle what he had in mind. We were virtually alone among our major allies in believing we had to "hold the line" against communism in Vietnam. Secretary of State Dean Rusk repeated over and over again that the Southeast Asia Treaty Organization (SEATO) treaty required us to come to the aid of an ally (South Vietnam) because it had been attacked by a foreign aggressor (North Vietnam). He added that, if we did not, our major allies (including of course France and Britain) would lose faith in the security guarantees we had given them. Yet France and Britain were also signatories to the SEATO Treaty, and had the same obligations we did. But both refused to support us in Vietnam. So we acted alone, believing we knew best.

De Gaulle's understanding of the situation in Vietnam, and his proposal, seem quite plausible in light of what we now know about North Vietnamese intentions in 1963–64. His basic idea was to begin the negotiating process by reconvening the conference held in Geneva in the summer of 1954, which set the terms for the French withdrawal from Indochina, drew a temporary border between North and South Vietnam at the 17th parallel, and sanctioned all-Vietnam elections for July 1956, following which Vietnam would be unified. Here is exactly what he proposed at a news conference in Paris on July 23, 1964:

A military solution [in Vietnam] cannot be expected. . . . Failing a military decision, peace must be made. Now, this implies returning to what was agreed upon ten years ago [in Geneva] and, this time, complying with it; in other words, this implies that in North and South Vietnam, in Cambodia, and in Laos, no foreign power may any longer intervene in any way in the affairs of these unfortunate countries. A meeting of the same order and including, in principle, the same participants as the former Geneva Conference would certainly be qualified to make a decision and to organize a means for impartial control. That is what France is proposing to the states concerned. This meeting, to which each participant must come without conditions or recriminations, would successively deal with the international aspects of the Laotian, Cambodian, and Vietnamese situation and as an essential first step, with their neutrality. No other road can be visualized which can lead to peace in Southeast Asia. . . . France, for her part, is ready.[80]

There is good reason to believe that de Gaulle's scheme would have worked, if only we had explored the idea with him and had worked with him. We now know that there were important voices at that moment in both the Hanoi and Saigon governments who would have welcomed the proposal of a reconvened Geneva conference, and who would have found a provisional neutral solution in Saigon acceptable, even preferable. But the United States would have had to take the lead in responding to de Gaulle, and we did not. Deeply fearful of "falling dominoes" in Southeast Asia, we continued—essentially alone—on a course of action that seems to have been doomed from the start.

Imagine, if you will, the discussions that would have been necessary to prepare for the kind of conference proposed by de Gaulle, and consider especially what we in the U.S. administration might have learned from it. What would de Gaulle and his French colleagues have told us, if only we had agreed to listen? First, I believe they would have tried to convince us that the Vietnamese thought of the conflict as less pro-communist (in the sense that it would lead to "falling dominoes" in Southeast Asia) than it was anti-imperialist (in the sense that our Vietnamese adversaries, north and south, considered us to be the successors of the French colonialists). They were wrong in important respects to have believed this. But it is clear from our collaborative research with Vietnamese scholars and former officials that they did believe it, and this information alone, presented to us by a relatively disinterested European ally—not as a hypothetical possibility but as a fact based on their knowledge and experience—would have made life difficult for those around President Johnson who dogmatically opposed opening negotiations.

Second, I am certain de Gaulle and his subordinates would have spent a great deal of time attempting to get us to understand the level of the commitment the North Vietnamese and National Liberation Front had to their cause. We knew some things, of course, but we did not absorb their importance. We knew that Vietnam had been occupied by China for a millennium, by the French for more than a century, briefly by the Japanese at the end of the Second World War, again by the French until they departed in 1954. We knew all this. But it did not somehow translate for us into a gut-level appreciation of the unshakable commitment that the Vietnamese communists, north and south, had to the cause of outlasting the Americans and reunifying their country. The French, who also had underestimated the Vietnamese in exactly the same way, had valuable lessons to teach us, if only we had been willing to listen.

Dealing with de Gaulle, especially in the role he sought as an arbiter for all of Indochina, would not have been easy. Dean Rusk, who as secretary of state spoke on many more occasions with de Gaulle than I did, wrote in his memoirs that "talking with de Gaulle was like crawling up a mountainside on your knees, opening a little portal at the top, and waiting for the oracle to speak. . . . Then he would say, 'Je vous écoute,' meaning 'Well Mr. Secretary, I am listening.'"[81] When he made his periodic offers to provide assistance in moving to negotiations, we made much of how difficult he was. But so what? The man had what we needed—the experience of having been dealt a decisive defeat in trying to achieve a military victory over Ho Chi Minh and his colleagues. He had learned lessons. He offered to share them with us. He offered to facilitate. We refused. History proves we were wrong to do so.

What is more, neither the defeat in Vietnam, nor anything else, seems to have diluted the strong strain of unilateralism running through the recent history of U.S. foreign policy. I have discovered this over the past several years, during private and public discussions in which I have advocated zero-tolerance multilateralism. Skeptics have included former secretaries of state and defense, as well as others who argue that as the only superpower, the United States must be guided by its own lights in many of its really important decisions. But I repeat: We are not omniscient. We need all the help we can get in decision making and in the sharing of financial costs and "blood" costs, and we had better ask for it—we had better require it—if we wish to avoid in the 21st century the kind of tragedies that Vietnam became.

❖

The Restoration of Peace and Long-term Reconciliation

Suppose the United States consults widely before attempting an intervention. Suppose, further, that it can even secure the votes required by the UN Security Council to authorize the intervention. And suppose, finally, that the chief result of the multilateral deliberations has been a commitment to what Stanley Hoffmann refers to as not only "rescue" but a full "restoration of the peace"? What should the intervention force expect to happen after they cross the borders of another of what Hoffmann calls these "dangerous, troubled, failed, and murderous states"?[82]

To put it bluntly, the interveners should understand that they must be prepared to spend a very long time and a lot of resources, and they should expect an enormous amount of frustration. This is why: The level of communal violence warranting a multilateral intervention will tend to be horrendous. And an extreme level of violence and atrocities means that a "restoration of the peace" will not be achieved easily. It will generally take a long time—perhaps a generation, perhaps more—before many of the combatants find reconciliation more satisfying, more *necessary*, than continued communal killing. Michael Ignatieff is eloquent on this point:

Reconciliation means breaking the spiral of intergenerational vengeance. It means substituting the vicious downward spiral of violence with the virtuous upward spiral of mutually reinforcing respect. Reconciliation can stop the cycle of vengeance only if it can equal vengeance as a form of respect for the dead. . . . This last dimension of reconciliation—the mourning of the dead—is where the desire for peace must vanquish the longing for revenge.[83]

But what will it take for Serbs to mourn the dead of the Bosnian Muslims? For the Tutsi to mourn the dead of the Hutu? It will be a long haul, but if we are serious about stopping communal killing *as a policy,* we must be prepared to see it through.

David Rohde of the *New York Times* has remarked that "the concept of individualized guilt remains alien in Kosovo. Most Serbs and Albanians whom I interviewed roundly denounced all members of the opposing ethnic group, making little distinction between how individuals acted during the conflict."[84] U.S. Army Sergeant William Burns, who has one black parent and one white one, told Rohde that the hatred he has seen in Kosovo reminds him of "racism in its most basic form" in the United States. Moreover, Burns added, "They don't understand democracy. They just look at you like you're crazy. They're like, 'When are you going to come rebuild our country?' I'm like, 'When are you going to roll up your sleeves?'"[85] What America is doing is not working in Kosovo. One gets the strong impression that all sides are merely biding their time until the Westerners leave, so they can once again seek the vengeance they all believe they are owed.

If the West, and the United States in particular, is to stay the course in places like Kosovo, we will have to implement a 21st-century equivalent of Woodrow Wilson's notion, put forward at the Paris peace conference, of taking control of those areas where conflicting claims of self-determination have led to unacceptable levels of communal violence. It may mean—as it has in Kosovo—that Western liberals, backed by NATO forces, involved in the effort to restore the peace will have to adopt some attitudes and practices with which they are both unfamiliar and distinctly uncomfortable. They may, we believe, be forced to adopt the stance of *an occupying power that has accepted the unconditional surrender of the state being occupied.* They may, in other words, be forced to adopt something like the attitude of General Douglas MacArthur, during the postwar occupation of Japan. Here is MacArthur's view of those whose country he and his forces occupied after August 1945:

If the Anglo-Saxon was say 45 years of age . . . the Japanese in spite of their antiquity measured by time, were in a very tuitionary condition. Measured by the standards of modern civilization, they would be like a boy of twelve as compared with our development of 45 years.[86]

In current vernacular, this is a supreme example of intercultural "political incorrectness."

Such an attitude may be difficult for Western liberals to adopt and sustain in practice, but if we fail to do so, observes David Rieff, "the alternative is not liberation or the triumph of some global consensus of conscience, but to paraphrase Che Guevara, one, two, three, many Kosovos."[87] As we prepare for the long haul to stop communal killing in the 21st century, it may be helpful to keep in mind that the reconciliation brought about by the man who held this attitude—MacArthur—was quite remarkable. A civil society was created and sustained where nothing remotely like it existed before. Democratic institutions were created from the ruins of a fascist military dictatorship. Most important, Japan and the United States, whose conflict in the Pacific in World War II was arguably the most brutal of the war, were reconciled, and remain reconciled to this day.

A Program for Rescue and the Restoration of Peace in Failed States

In contemplating an intervention in failed states, the United States and other nations need to consider these issues: institutional requirements, assumptions regarding the central issues of sovereignty and self-determination, decision rules for intervention, and the outcomes or ultimate objectives to be kept in mind. The following is our breakdown of what is required to implement the view that an intervention should not just rescue innocents today, stop the killing tomorrow, and enforce the peace for a week or a month, but should instead restore (or perhaps build for the first time) the conditions under which peace can be sustained. Only with a systematic and long-term approach can existing vicious cycles of communal violence and killing be broken, and new ones prevented.

While many will agree with our assessment of the situation, some will find unappealing, even repellent, the term some have used to describe the approach: *liberal imperialism.* The term was coined in 1999 by journalist David Rieff.[88] A "liberal imperialist" is one who believes that the long-term restoration of order in a murderous failed state requires those who intervene to impose liberal values of tolerance, pluralism, and democracy, and to control such states in the role of benevolent dictators until the communal factions are capable and willing to act in accordance with such values on their own. We agree with those who are repelled by the term "liberal imperialism," but we support the view of those who believe that in certain situations outside forces, multilaterally directed, must impose order to stop communal violence and killing over the long haul of the entire 21st century. As we write, in fact, what might be called a "liberal imperialist" multilateral regime is beginning to form in Kosovo, in an attempt not only to stop the brutality between Serbs and Kosovars, but also to build the kind of institutions and civil society with which such brutality, and the attitudes that sustain it, are utterly incompatible.

Enforcement: Reform of the UN Security Council

Without significant reform of the UN Security Council, little can be done to stop communal killing around the world. Many schemes have been proposed, but none have been taken seriously. The Security Council is often ineffective, as no one can say whether, or when, or by what means, it will authorize an intervention. And it is even more difficult to say whether any intervention undertaken will be effective, even with very short-term rescue operations. The propositions immediately following, therefore, may seem wishful but are essential prerequisites for dealing with communal violence and killing.

- The United States must lead.

- The Security Council must be expanded, become more representative, and the veto of the (current) five permanent members must be phased out and replaced with decision making by a "qualified" majority—for example, 75 percent.

- A (roughly) 10,000-strong international volunteer police force, under the command of the secretary general, must be authorized, financed, organized, trained, and made ready to move quickly when intervention is required to stop communal killing.

- Massive human rights violations and widespread ethnic or religious conflict must be accepted as a "threat to the peace" justifying intervention under Chapter VII of the UN Charter.

- If, prior to reorganization, the entire Security Council is unable to agree to an intervention, a "shadow" Security Council or a "coalition of the willing" should be assembled to approve the intervention and authorize it.

Philosophy: Positions on Sovereignty and Self-Determination

It is crucial that we not make in the 21st century the mistake Wilson and his colleagues made early in the 20th. Wilson issued a carte blanche to groups that wanted statehood, creating anarchy and animosity, leading to violence and killing on a wide scale. We must take the opposite approach, and give strong preference to the sanctity of existing borders. This will mean, in most cases, rejection of urges to create new states that are more ethnically "pure" than those presently in dispute. We should accept that:

- State sovereignty is not a given; it implies obligations to citizens, especially in the "zone" of human rights.

- State sovereignty is subject, therefore, not only to treaties, but to the norms established by international and regional organizations.

- A strong presumption should be made in favor of existing state borders; claims to other borders, or discrepant claims to jurisdiction within a set of existing borders, should be regarded as exceptional and treated skeptically.

- Secession should be a last resort, after all bilateral negotiations have failed, and after mediation by all international or regional organizations has been exhausted.

- Secession and the redrawing of borders should be considered only in those cases in which the actions do not threaten the vital interests of neighbors.

Operations: Carrying Out the Intervention

The following list of requirements for successful intervention is as revolutionary as anything we are suggesting. They require, under certain circumstances, that the secretary general of the UN become, under the direction of the Security Council, the commander-in-chief of a fighting force that can invade, conquer, occupy, and pacify an area. None of these attributes are, by usual interpretations, elements of the UN Charter. Our view is that the charter is, in significant respects, out of date and needs revising to take account of the needs of the 21st century. This will be contentious, to say the least, because it will require a dilution of national sovereignty not only of the states into which interventions occur, but also, at times, of the states participating in the intervention, under the banner and with the auspices of the UN. In most cases, any intervention force, let alone an occupying army, will have to be much larger than any "police force" the secretary general may have at his disposal on a permanent basis. Such larger forces would be commanded, as at present, by national governments selected by the Security Council.

Without the will and capability to intervene in the manner indicated below, the fashionable sentiment and rhetoric in the West regarding human rights will remain cheap, paper-thin, and thus hypocritical.

- The UN Security Council, and regional organizations involved in decisions regarding whether to intervene, must have early warning of violence and killing, and thus must also have access to state-of-the-art intelligence supplied, in most cases, by member states.

- UN or other international intervening forces must be prepared to act in a partisan fashion, rescuing those in groups that have been targeted for atrocities. This is not a peacekeeping operation. It is, in fact, an invasion and, as such, the forces must be prepared to take casualties on the ground, to shoot to kill when necessary, and to take and hold territory.

- Interventions must be carried out in close consultation with elements of the international justice system, especially the International Criminal Court (proposed in 1999, though still far from being established), and any other tribunals the UN has set up for specific instances of communal killing. In this way, the pursuit, capture, and trial of suspected war criminals may be facilitated. The exercise of such a judicial capability will in itself act as a deterrent.

- The intervention force may in some cases be followed by an occupation force, the aim of which is not unlike that of U.S. forces occupying post–World War II Japan: guarantee law and order, sow the seeds of civil society, and "force-feed" liberal values, attitudes, and institutions to the inhabitants.

Outcomes: What Kind of States Should Be Created?

The desired outcome of action that begins with an intervention will, in most cases, be a multiethnic state. This is because ethnically "pure" areas that are large enough and diverse enough in other ways to be economically sustainable will be rare. This, in turn, implies a serious commitment by the international community to follow up a military intervention with an occupation that not only is as benign as the conditions will allow but begins as soon as possible to point the warring factions toward what may at that point seem to be a distant outcome: a successfully functioning society in which members of groups recently intent on exterminating one another develop the will and ability to work together to achieve a common outcome. This of course will be in some ways even more difficult than implementing a successful military intervention that stops the communal killing. But a military intervention is not an outcome. It is only a prerequisite to the desired outcome, which is the creation of a peaceful and harmonious society. This will be difficult. Yet we know of no other way to break the cycles of feuding and violence that have become such common features of the early 21st-century world.

.   .   .

This program, according to Stanley Hoffmann (who also advocates most of its propositions), "gets us close to the shores of utopia."[89] But the key issue is not the size of the gap between the real and the ideal, but rather the size of this particular problem with which the 21st century must deal: communal killing. Can the citizens and governments of the West, led by the United States, develop and sustain in the 21st century an imperial zeal for preventing and resolving conflicts, and restoring order, that is akin to the zeal they displayed in previous centuries for economic exploitation? If not, the likely consequence will be communal violence and killing on a scale that is morally unacceptable by any standard, and detrimental to the self-interest of America and the West. So while we may not like to think of ourselves as imperialists or dictators, even liberal ones, we think that in doing so, we are better able to focus on the need to begin the difficult, dangerous work that lies ahead.

Unilateral Last Resort: The Human Rights Critique of Zero-Tolerance Multilateralism

America's instinctual unilateralism is not the only obstacle to acting multilaterally when deciding whether to intervene militarily to stop communal killing. A large and passionate group of Westerners who will find our zero-tolerance multilateralism objectionable are those we call the human rights absolutists. The most passionate of these are, in their way, as dogmatic as old-fashioned absolutists who hold that under *no* circumstance is it permissible to intervene in violation of a state's sovereignty. Human rights absolutists, conversely, argue that under *all* circumstances involving intrastate atrocities it is *necessary* to intervene, unilaterally if necessary.

The unilateral intervention they often seek is from the United States, the only country with the military "power projection" capability to intervene virtually anywhere in the world. Whereas the absolutists for sovereignty deny the possibility of morally correct intervention, human rights absolutists deny the possibility of morally correct nonintervention in cases involving communal killing. This is what we call the doctrine of *unilateral last resort,* according to which the United States is said to have the duty to intervene, if it proves impossible to assemble a multilateral force to intervene.

A leading advocate of human rights absolutism is the Frenchman Bernard Kouchner, one of the founders of the organization Médecins sans Frontières—Doctors Without Borders. For more than 30 years, Kouchner has promoted the idea of *le droit d'intervention humanitaire*— the right to intervene across state borders whenever states oppress their own citizens.[90] Kouchner, to his credit, has recently attempted to put some of his ideas personally into practice as the Special Representative of the UN Secretary General in Kosovo. It did not go well. "I've been a human rights activist for 30 years," he recently said, "and here I am unable to stop people being massacred."[91] Indeed, as David Rohde has reported, despite the efforts of Kouchner and many others, and despite the presence of much foreign good will and resources, Kosovo remains "corrupt, lawless, intolerant of both ethnic and political minorities, and a source of instability." The situation, he says, is "a recipe for a quagmire."[92]

For many involved in the human rights movement, this so-called right to intervene is really a *duty* to intervene, regardless of the precepts of international law, or even the preferences of any government or collection of governments that may be involved. The government responsible for the atrocities (or for not preventing them) is said to have no options. It can either issue an invitation to prospective interveners, or be invaded. According to political philosopher Michael J. Smith, an advocate of unilateral intervention, while such an action may be "presumptively illegitimate," that presumption nevertheless "can be overridden."[93]

This is because "a blanket requirement for multilateral approval or participation in a case of humanitarian intervention may have the unfortunate effect of insuring that nothing is done."[94] Michael Walzer expresses the same view this way: "Humanitarian intervention is justified when it is a response . . . to acts 'that shock the moral conscience of mankind.'" In such situations, he writes, there is no excuse for adopting "that posture of passivity that might be called waiting for the UN (waiting for the universal state, waiting for the messiah. . .)."[95]

Human rights absolutists have been aided in recent years by the so-called CNN effect—telecasts, often live, of the kinds of atrocities (in the Balkans, in the Great Lakes region of Africa, in various parts of Indonesia, in Colombia) that human rights organizations were created to oppose and prevent. Indeed, as William Zartman of Johns Hopkins University has written: "In the current era, foreign affairs has become a macabre sort of entertainment."[96] This is not necessarily a bad thing altogether, as the nightly viewing of filmed results of atrocities can produce empathy, however shallow and fleeting, for the victims, along with the feeling that something should be done to stop the killing.[97] Yet too often, this shallow commitment by Western citizens leads to an equally shallow commitment by leaders to rectify the problems. Sensing that the public wants something done but may not want to sacrifice much, if anything, on behalf of the victims, leaders often settle for token measures like ineffective economic sanctions, strong rhetoric, humanitarian relief, or the promise of contributing peacekeepers to a UN force, should peace ever be established.

Yet there is no doubt that a revolution has occurred in the last half century regarding the role that human rights should play in international politics. Before World War II, few believed that nations should act according to the Biblical injunction to be "our brother's keeper." But beginning with the signing of the Universal Declaration of Human Rights in 1948, and followed in the next half century by many more such proclamations and the founding of hundreds of organizations worldwide devoted to monitoring and promoting human rights, we in the West now take it as self-evident that actions of leaders of sovereign states like Indonesia, Yugoslavia, Colombia, and others may warrant military intervention to set things right.[98] In the United States, the traditional

American confidence in our ability to fix any problem has thus become married to the belief, derived from the human rights revolution, that many international problems involving communal killing within state borders can and must be fixed via a military intervention.

The 1994 genocide in Rwanda seems to have had a sobering impact throughout the human rights community, because *no one* intervened until it was too late. Beginning on April 8, when the presidents of Rwanda and Burundi were assassinated as the aircraft in which both were passengers was shot down, government officials in the United States and Europe and at the UN knew what was going on in Rwanda. And yet those with some means to stop the killing did nothing to stop it, nor did they respond positively to the urgent requests from Kofi Annan, who was then head of UN peacekeeping operations, to mobilize for an intervention. According to Stephen Lewis, the former Canadian ambassador to the UN and a member of an Organization of African Unity (OAU) panel that investigated the Rwandan genocide, "the United States . . . knew exactly what was going on," leaving what he calls "an almost incomprehensible scar of shame on American foreign policy." Indeed, he adds bitterly, "I don't know how Madeleine Albright [then the U.S. ambassador to the UN] lives with it."[99] There was no intervention. And, in less than 100 days, nearly a million human beings were killed, most at close range with knives or machetes.

Stanley Hoffmann, who is sympathetic to the views on intervention of many in the human rights community, is skeptical that the UN can be reconfigured to act in time to prevent the kind of communal killing that occurred in Rwanda, or in the former Yugoslavia, or anywhere else, for that matter. Alas, Hoffmann observes:

> This is an ungoverned world. The UN has no autonomous power; it is what its members want it to be, and usually its members don't want it to be anything much. . . . When it is said that it is better if things are done multilaterally, too often this means accepting the lowest common denominator. . . .[100]

Nor is Hoffmann optimistic that the United States can fill the void politically, though it has the only government that possesses the physical capability to intervene worldwide. He chides U.S. leaders, in fact, for what he calls the requirement of "combatant immunity" in any intervention to stop communal killing.[101]

Nevertheless, Hoffmann is absolutely clear: It is better for the United States to intervene unilaterally to stop the killing than not to intervene just because the appropriate multilateral authorization could not be obtained in time. In effect, he believes that Americans have the *duty* to intervene because they have the *ability* to do so. "Can" implies "must." Michael Ignatieff would attach a stipulation to Hoffmann's argument. He poses the question this way: "[W]hen foreigners are being massacred overseas, interests say 'stay out.' Values cry, 'go in.' What does a president do then?" According to Ignatieff, "[V]alues trump interests. When innocent civilians are dying, America may have to intervene."[102] However, he would limit unilateral U.S. interventions to those involving probable genocide, which the 1948 Convention on the Prevention and Punishment of the Crime of Genocide defines as "acts committed with intent to destroy, in whole or in part, a national, ethnical, racial or religious group, as such."[103] Ignatieff believes that this "sets the bar for intervention very high," and in any case intervention should only be attempted in situations "where force can actually turn the situation around."[104] This last caveat is one we accept but which many human rights advocates reject.

The human rights–based argument for American *unilateral last resort* is seductive, but we are not convinced by it. Many who hold this position argue that U.S. unilateralism is not like the unilateralism of other countries, countries with imperial pasts and perhaps ongoing imperial ambitions. They imply that the United States will take better care of those in whose affairs it might choose to intervene.

But while this argument may appeal to European or American advocates, we cannot conceive it being made by Cubans, Filipinos, Grenadans, Panamanians, Vietnamese, Dominicans, Mexicans, or others who have felt the sting of what they regard as U.S. imperialism. Consider, for example, the testimony of a former U.S. chief of mission in Cuba, who recalled (perhaps with some exaggeration), "Before Castro came to power, the president of Cuba sat by a red telephone and waited for the U.S. ambassador to call. And when the ambassador called, the

Cuban president understood that the only words he was permitted to utter were 'yes sir,' and he knew he was to utter them in English."[105] Human rights advocates who are comfortable with the United States as a unilateral last resort should recognize that those who take it upon themselves to intervene unilaterally in the affairs of other nations, for whatever reason, are, ipso facto, "imperialists," in the view of many of those whose sovereign borders are transgressed.

Whether or not the United States has imperialist proclivities, other considerations prevent us from endorsing a policy of unilateral U.S. intervention, even with the caveat restricting the commitment to cases of probable genocide. First, what kind of "intervention" can be expected from a nation that requires, to use Stanley Hoffmann's phrase, "combatant immunity"? Probably one in which a great many bombs are dropped in an effort to stop the killing. But as we saw in Kosovo, the bombing speeded up the Serbs' forced removal of the ethnic Albanian Kosovars. NATO's high-tech weapons were overmatched on the ground in Kosovo by the Serbs' mobility and their ability to camouflage their weapons and troops.[106] Did we, via our bombing campaign, make life better for the Kosovars? The answer may well turn out to be no. If so, it will add empirical force to a moral point made by Carl Kaysen: "You can't justify killing for something you aren't willing to die for."[107]

Second, it is unclear whether the United States would be willing to stay the course and actually leave the situation better off than we found it when we went in, and with less risk of a recurrence of communal violence and killing. This is the other side of the fickleness of U.S. interventions: Sometimes we stay, but sometimes we leave in a hurry. Stanley Hoffmann and others have argued persuasively that such interventions must not be aimed only at "rescue" but at a "restoration of the peace," so as to avoid reentry into the cycle of more killings, more revenge, another intervention, etc.[108]

A restoration of the peace might involve some sort of partition that U.S. military forces would have to impose on the local warring factions. But of course such action would likely require taking casualties. An even more daunting task is the one recommended by the last U.S. ambassador to Yugoslavia, Warren Zimmermann: the construction of a fully functioning multiethnic society in places like Bosnia, Kosovo, Rwanda, and other areas torn by communal violence and killing. "The challenge to the world community," he says, "is not to break up multi-ethnic states, but to make them more civil. It's the borders in the mind . . . that are most in need of changing."[109] While this is an admirable objective, the question is whether the United States or any other nation has the commitment to accomplish this where the will to succeed is lacking among the groups involved.

Human rights activists make a valuable contribution when they ask what is to be done to stop the communal killing, as cases arise often with little warning, perhaps with insufficient time to assemble a multilateral "coalition of the willing" to deal with it. But from the standpoint of the United States, the proper question is not "Must the United States stand idly by while vast numbers of people are killed?" but rather the following: "Since the probability of an effective, unilateral American intervention to stop intrastate communal killing is low (based on recent experience in Somalia, Bosnia, Rwanda, East Timor, Kosovo, and elsewhere), how should U.S. policy be changed to raise the odds of more successful multilateral interventions in the future?" Human rights advocates for unilateral U.S. interventions should ask not who will intervene if the UN Security Council does not sanction multilateral action. They should instead ask whether the United States can expect to intervene *successfully* in most such situations. If it cannot then it should not.

While it is true that the United States has the military might to intervene in these cases, a successful intervention involves far more than adequate military might. As the experience of the 1990s shows unequivocally, success also involves just those intangibles that are especially difficult for Americans to grasp. Reinhold Niebuhr put the point in the context of our unique historical experience:

We can understand the neat logic of either economic reciprocity or the show of pure power. But we are mystified by the endless complexities of human motives and the varied compounds of ethnic loyalties, cultural traditions, social hopes, envies and fears which enter into the policies of nations, and which lie at the foundation of their political cohesion.[110]

For all our economic, political, and military power, the United States lacks almost completely any meaningful experience of those characteristics of human communities that, when they unravel, can lead to communal killing. The ancestors of most Americans came to the United States to help ensure that their descendants did *not* have that sort of experience. And by and large, we have remained strangers to it. America's success in promoting liberal, cosmopolitan views among its own people has led, ironically, to a pronounced lack of empathy and comprehension of the sorts of furies that have been unleashed in the Chechnyas, Kosovos, East Timors, and Afghanistans of the world. That is why, finally, any decision to intervene must include not only representatives of the state that can provide the money, guns, and planes but also representatives of states with more experience of the sort of communal life that Americans do not have.

Leadership Without Unilateralism: Talking Points for the Next U.S. President

A new American administration had taken office in 2001. What should be its policy regarding attempts to stop communal killing? Former *New York Times* columnist Karl E. Meyer recently argued that the new U.S. president will have three options:

1. *All-out Wilsonianism.* Declare an all-out war on tyrants who cause massacres, and use all the force at his disposal to right the wrongs of the world;

2. *Anti-Wilsonianism.* Take George Kennan's advice, stop trying to tell others how to run their affairs, and lead by moral example; or

3. *"Zero-tolerance" Multilateral Wilsonianism.* For the first time, make a serious commitment to a multilateral approach to solving the problem, thereby giving substance to what is currently a myth—the so-called "international community."[111]

The first two options are not in the cards for Americans. We often say we do not wish to rule the world, and we don't. But we tend to think we could do so effectively, so we often feel compelled to tell the other nations of the world what to do and how to do it. These are undeniable facts of America's past, present, and, in all probability, future.

Meyer's third way, the zero-tolerance multilateralist way, is his and our preferred option. Its viability, though, is subject to whether sufficient courage can be mustered. Meyer concludes by providing what are, in essence, "talking points" for a major address by the new U.S. president, George W. Bush, to the American people on the necessity for a multilateral approach to intervention:

> How refreshing it would be if the next chief executive reported to the Americans on the world as it really is, warned human rights activists that frustration and disappointments were unavoidable, acknowledged that double standards exist and that the "international community" has yet to be created, added that the most likely threats to peace and human rights will arise from civil strife within sovereign frontiers, that to deal with this threat the world needed both regional and international standby reserves, that Washington would do what it could to help, and that as a first step he or she would seek to persuade Americans that it was in their interest to pay the dues owed an organization inspired by American ideals and located in the world's most ethnically diverse city. How refreshing, and how necessary.[112]

Meyer's "third way" goes to the heart of what is required: not a retreat to haphazard, episodic, and ineffective American unilateral intervention, but a bottom-up reinvestment in the UN, in the Security Council, in a standing UN police capability for intervention, in regional organizations that may be involved—in short, in a commitment to the one way, the only way, that the problem of communal killing in the 21st century can be dealt with successfully: multilaterally, with U.S. leadership but with very significant input from those equally concerned nations that have the relevant historical experience.

If communal killing in the 21st century is to be prevented and managed successfully, three qualities, in equal measure, will be required from the American people and their leaders: (1) leadership; (2) the courage to face the inevitable moral blind alleys that will confront all who intervene to stop communal killing; and (3) an ironclad commitment to zero-tolerance multilateralism, what Clinton administration UN ambassador Richard Holbrooke has called "leadership without unilateralism."[113] The next president, were he to embrace this program, will require adroit political moves and much political will to convince the Congress, the American people, and the international community of its necessity. But as Stanley Hoffmann has written: "Statesmen should remember that they have been elected to persuade and to lead, and not just to accept as fixed the momentary moods and pernicious prejudices of the public."[114] It is up to all of us remind our leaders of their responsibilities.

Self-Determination and Wilson's Ghost

Richard Holbrooke recently laid the blame for the conflicts in the Balkans at Woodrow Wilson's doorstep. Wilson, according to Holbrooke, is "the guy who gave us this mess. In the name of self-determination he created boundaries in south-central Europe that violated reason."[115] This assessment is a bit unfair to Wilson, who after all did not draw all those borders by himself in Paris. But it is true that Wilson's enthusiasm for universal self-determination was unwise and that his promotion of American-style democracy was fitful, uneven, and generally unsuccessful.

Why, in light of Wilson's failure to solve the issue of self-determination, do so many enter the 21st century in awe of him? Ronald Steel has proposed a hypothesis: "In his idealism, his moralizing, and in his insatiable tinkering to make everything better for everyone's good, he is America's inner self."[116] Steel means this as a criticism of both Wilson and the mentality he embodies. The irony is that this is exactly how Wilson liked to describe himself. "Sometimes people call me an idealist," he said on September 8, 1919. "Well, that is the way I know I am an American. America is the only idealistic nation in the world."[117]

Yet a curious amnesia afflicts those idealists who find Wilson's enthusiasm for self-determination contagious, who believe that America has a special mission, and the ability, to make the world over in its image. They conveniently, but remarkably, forget that Wilson *failed*. Though they pursue Wilson's dream, they ignore the entreaties of Wilson's ghost. To believe in universal self-determination is to subscribe to an illusion. To believe in the sanctity of all nationalist fantasies, to pretend that claims to self-determination can be made compatible with a little tinkering is what made Woodrow Wilson so dangerous. As Holbrooke recognizes, we are still paying the price, still trying unsuccessfully to grapple with Wilson's ghost in the Balkans.

Wilson's most recent biographer, Louis Auchincloss, reminds us of something so simple, so basic, that we wonder how a man as brilliant as Wilson could have failed to understand its significance:

> It might be noted here that the principle of self-determination is as difficult to apply in our day as it was in Wilson's. Will it stop short of splitting our planet into an impossible number of small bickering nations? It may be well to remember of our two most revered presidents that Washington fought a war to affirm the doctrine, and Lincoln one to deny it.[118]

Alas, for Wilson and for us as we enter the 21st century, the international arena is sufficiently complex to fully verify the views of both Washington and Lincoln—at least to their contemporary partisans. Because the world is so complex, because self-determination can be both a supreme good for some and a supreme evil for so many, those who deal with this problem must prepare to encounter great discomfort in moral blind alleys. They (and we) need to seek the opinions and assistance of others, as we deal with self-determination and its operational twin, intervention.

Wilson was not prepared because, in his arrogance, he did not feel the need. We should not make the same mistake.

Liberalism must be more liberal than ever before, it must even be *radical,* if civilization is to escape the typhoon. . . . I do not hesitate to say that the war we have just been through, though it was shot through with terror of every kind, is not to be compared with the war we would have to face the next time.

Woodrow Wilson, January 1919[1]

Nuclear weapons pose an intolerable threat to all humanity and its habitat, yet tens of thousands remain in arsenals built up at an extraordinary time of deep antagonism. That time has passed, yet assertions of their utility continue. . . . *The proposition that nuclear weapons can be retained in perpetuity and never used—accidentally or by decision—defies credibility.* The only complete defence is the elimination of nuclear weapons and assurance that they will never be produced again.

The Canberra Commission on the Elimination of Nuclear Weapons, 1996[2]

4

Avoiding Nuclear Catastrophe

Moving Steadily and Safely to a Nuclear-Weapons-Free World

The Cold War is over, yet tens of thousands of nuclear weapons that were developed to support nuclear deterrence remain in arsenals around the world. Together, the United States and Russia possess more than 95 percent of the world's nuclear weapons. Their command and control systems are still tuned to permit immediate launch. In addition, Russia's forces are in deep trouble. Its nuclear infrastructure—both technical and human—continues to deteriorate, raising the specter of increased risk of accidental and inadvertent nuclear launches.

Enough nuclear firepower exists in each arsenal to kill tens of millions of human beings in each other's societies, to destroy enemy nations and—through the effects of wind-blown radiation—nonbelligerent nations as well. Any nuclear event of this kind would likely result in the worst catastrophe in human history.

Moreover, the clear intent of Russia and the United States to maintain indefinitely their nuclear forces and contingency plans for their use will surely lead to further proliferation of the weapons. When Robert McNamara stated in Moscow in 1989 that the indefinite combination of human fallibility and nuclear weapons would lead inevitably to their use and to the destruction of nations, the statement shocked many.[3] Today, its inclusion in the 1996 Report of the Canberra Commission on the Elimination of Nuclear Weapons has met wide acceptance.

We propose a program of moving steadily and safely to a nuclear-weapons-free world, which can lead to the removal of this post–Cold War nuclear danger.[4]

Wilson's "Typhoon," Our Nuclear Holocaust

As the Paris peace conference proceeded, Woodrow Wilson came by degrees to the conclusion that the next war involving the Great Powers would destroy whole nations. He began to urge on his British, French, and Italian counterparts preventive *radical* measures to secure the peace that called into question the centuries-old European tradition of "balancing power." Not incidentally, the radicalization of Wilson's views began to accelerate after he arrived in Paris in December 1918—after he had seen firsthand some of the catastrophic damage that had been done by what he began to call the "Great War for Civilization," especially in France, where much of it was fought.[5] In addition, all over Europe, monarchies and empires that had ruled for centuries were collapsing. Millions of citizens in Europe's most advanced nations were destitute and starving. Revolutionary slogans calling for the destruction of liberal Western institutions were being shouted in the streets from Moscow to London. As Wilson saw it, the situation was desperate; the dogs of chaos were barking just beyond the doors at Versailles. That Western civilization would survive seemed far from guaranteed. Wilson came to see, as he put it in January 1919, that, "Liberalism must be more liberal than ever before, it must even be *radical*, if civilization is to escape the typhoon."[6]

Because of the unprecedented nature of this threat, according to Wilson, *radical* solutions, such as a "peace without victors" and his League of Nations, were required to insure that nothing like it ever occurred again. They were needed to destroy the "balance of power" system whose built-in paranoia and mistrust had, in Wilson's view, caused the war.

In this sense, Wilson's famous statement that the war had been fought "to make the world safe for democracy" was not the slogan of an idealistic dreamer, but rather represented what he took to be one of the absolutely necessary preconditions for the survival of civilized life on earth. It derived less from Wilson's dreams than from his nightmares. True to his roots in the Presbyterian tradition, Wilson proposed not a scheme of certain perfection, but a strategy of possible survival.

In this way, as the historian Frank Ninkovich has written, "Wilsonianism became an internationalism of fear," the grasp of which required "an abstract sensibility rather than something that was automatically felt in the pit of one's stomach."[7] If a nonpunitive peace treaty could be crafted, Wilson argued, the Allies need no longer fear the Germans, nor vice versa. Wilson was, in effect, asking the delegates in Paris, and by extension the citizens they represented, to imagine a far greater threat than Germany—an abstract threat, a dark vision of future conflict on the order of that foretold in one of Wilson's favorite sections of the Bible, the Book of Revelation. If humanity did not act decisively at Versailles to prevent this "typhoon" from being realized, Wilson believed, the world would be visited in due course by an incomparably more destructive war than the one just concluded.

Wilson's analysis proved to be eerily correct. The world had changed; past experience was no longer, therefore, a reliable guide to coping with the new circumstances. Portentous events would soon take place in Europe that would be driven by German motives of revenge and conquest, which would be made possible by the Germans' technological capacity to act on these motives. Something similar would occur in Japan. The failure to recognize the nascent reality of these threats, however abstract and incredible they may have seemed to many of Wilson's listeners at the time, did in fact lead to the catastrophic "typhoon" we know as the Second World War, and its nearly 50-year aftermath, the Cold War.

In retrospect, we can now understand these catastrophes for what they were: essentially the products of a failure of imagination, a failure to consider seriously the possibility that new threats might differ qualitatively from those experienced in the past, and thus may require solutions that are, in the description Wilson disliked but to which he ultimately found no suitable alternative—*radical*.

Why was Wilson so unpersuasive to so many, particularly his fellow Americans? Why was he unable to communicate successfully the mortal fear of the potential destruction of civilization that he felt so keenly? According to Frank Ninkovich, it was because "Wilsonianism was altogether too radical a departure for the American people to support" because "most people prefer to lead their lives on the basis of experience rather than imagination," and "nations are no different."[8] America had entered the war and won it. It could do so again if it should prove necessary. In any case, the war was over. The threat that had brought America into the war—the aggressiveness of imperial Germany—had been vanquished. Having made their sacrifice in the Great War, Americans were thereafter in no mood to consider Wilson's apocalyptic projections and radical solutions. America sought most of all to return to "normalcy," the term popularized by Wilson's successor, Warren G. Harding.

The end of the Second World War produced the same kind of dichotomy, the same splitting of American leaders, scholars, and citizens into two principal camps. On one side were those who felt, as Wilson had, that the threat to civilization had grown exponentially during the course of the war and that radical measures had to be undertaken to prevent a catastrophe. Those holding this view tended to be deeply affected by what they perceived as the disparity between the destructive power of conventional weapons and the two atomic bombs dropped by the United States on Japan in August 1945. On the other hand, there were those who considered atomic bombs to be, more or less, just big bombs and, in any case, nothing to worry about because the United States was the sole possessor of them. Here again, with the benefit of hindsight, we can observe the growth of a "radical" point of view, which viewed the future as threatened by factors that are discontinuous with the past, and a fundamentally "conservative" point of view that saw the future as threatened, if at all, by more and bigger versions of the same threats faced in the immediate past.

The post–World War II Wilsonian radicals believed the advent of nuclear weapons changed nearly everything about warfare. One of the earliest and most eloquent exponents of the new paradigm was the American political scientist and strategist Bernard Brodie, who wrote in his path-breaking 1946 book, *The Absolute Weapon,* that he was "not for the moment concerned about who will *win* the next war in which atomic bombs are used. Thus far the chief purpose of our military establishment has been to win wars. From now on its chief purpose must be to avert them. It can have almost no other purpose."[9] In 1946, this was a stunning and controversial position. Brodie was no ivory-tower scientist; he was a military strategist in the employ of the U.S. Army Air Corps. In *The Absolute Weapon,* he was in effect explaining to his colleagues why they should forget everything they thought they knew about war. From now on, in the nuclear age, they must be in the business of preventing war.

Anti-nuclear Wilsonianism also included efforts to bring nuclear weapons and nuclear energy under international control. In 1946, the United States proposed what came to be called the Baruch Plan, which would have created an International Atomic Development Authority that would have been given sole control over all aspects of nuclear development, including the power to punish any who might seek an independent nuclear capability. In a Wilsonian touch, the plan would have been made immune from a UN Security Council veto. But by this time, the Cold War was well underway, and the Soviet Union regarded the Baruch Plan as merely a way of ratifying the U.S. monopoly on nuclear knowledge protecting its nuclear secrets. The Soviets proposed instead the creation of an international agency that would oversee the destruction of all existing nuclear materials, and would share equally among nations any new knowledge that might emerge.[10] Neither plan had much chance of succeeding. East and West were already hunkered down for a Cold War in the course of which more than 100,000 nuclear warheads would be built by the United States and Soviet Union (roughly equivalent to two million bombs of the size dropped on Hiroshima), along with ballistic missiles, bombers, and submarines with which to launch them in the event of war.[11] Each side's arsenal was built to deter the other, yet each addition added to the magnitude of the potential catastrophe, should deterrence fail.

From roughly the early 1960s until the present, Washington and Moscow have each possessed many times the nuclear firepower required to destroy each other as functioning societies, and much of life on earth with them. This is in spite of the fact that leaders who have had ultimate responsibility for nuclear weapons have almost uniformly believed that any use of nuclear weapons would be suicidal. Dwight Eisenhower said, for example, that "no [nuclear] war can be *won,* for war in the nuclear age would entail destruction of the enemy and suicide for ourselves."[12] And according to Charles de Gaulle, "After a nuclear war, the two sides would have neither powers, nor laws, nor cities, nor cultures, nor cradles, nor tombs."[13] Nikita Khrushchev put it this way: "When I . . . learned all the facts about nuclear power, I couldn't sleep for several days. Then I became convinced that we could never possibly use these weapons, and I was able to sleep again."[14] To these men, the paradigm had shifted. Great Power war, with which each had been involved virtually all his adult life, was now believed to be equivalent to suicide. The ultimate solution to the threat would be to abolish nuclear weapons. Yet because of the ideological Cold War between East and West, nuclear arsenals continued to grow and threaten, by their very existence, everything that they were designed and built to protect. As Khrushchev put it paradoxically but truly, even though "we could never possibly use these weapons . . . all the same, we must be prepared."[15] In other words, we must continue to prepare to do that which it would be insane and evil actually to do.

Wilson's "typhoon" was metaphorical and, in his lifetime, hypothetical. Hitler and the Nazis made it real. The possibility of our nuclear extinction is already real and has been real for decades. It is a fact, now, today, this minute—even in the absence of the Cold War. It is true that the United States and Russia have substantially reduced their arsenals since the late 1980s—between 1987 and 1998, the United States has reduced its nuclear force from 13,655 strategic warheads (with a total yield of nearly three and a half million kilotons) to 7,256 strategic warheads (with a yield of just under two million kilotons), and the Soviet Union and then Russia have moved from 8,619 strategic warheads (with a combined yield of nearly five million kilotons) to 6,340 strategic warheads (just under three million kilotons).[16] Yet in terms of the security of the human race from nuclear holocaust, these reductions still leave the United States with the capacity to kill approximately 67 million Russians using only one-third of its forces, while the Russians can kill about 75 million Americans, using 40 percent of its weapons, assuming that each side's weapons are directed at military targets.[17] Many more people could be killed with far fewer weapons, if population centers were made the principal objective of an attack. This is so even though the United States and Russia are, at the political level, no longer enemies. Moreover, it is widely accepted by both Western and Russian security experts that the present arsenal of Russia is increasingly at risk for nuclear accidents, nuclear theft, and serious malfunctions in its command and control systems, due to lack of resources.

Some readers of the previous paragraph will have encountered this frightening information for the first time. Perhaps you had assumed that these matters had been dealt with decisively, that nuclear danger is now small and shrinking fast, in the absence of the Cold War. Alas, the reverse is true, in many respects. And so we find ourselves looking over our shoulders at Wilson's ghost yet again as we try to articulate an effective response to this crisis. Like Wilson, we base our response on *fear*—we believe realistic fear—of a possible event: a set of developments leading to the use of part or all of the nuclear arsenals of the United States and Russia. Wilson's "typhoon"—the Second World War—took four years to wreak its havoc. And despite its horrors, it was mostly reversible. A nuclear catastrophe on the order suggested above would take a few hours to do its immediate damage—something Wilson could never have imagined. And its effects might well be irreversible. It could result in the extinction of whole nations and groups of nations—belligerents and nonbelligerents alike—along with hundreds of millions of their human inhabitants.

In the 21st century, in the absence of the Cold War, we are not satisfied that the risk of such a nuclear catastrophe is "improbable." The 1996 Canberra Commission *Report on the Elimination of Nuclear Weapons* gave what we regard as the appropriate response to this misplaced and dangerous confidence in "probabilities."[18] It said that sooner or later, nuclear weapons will be used, whether or not we can currently imagine how that use might come to pass. Moreover, the stakes are too high to assume otherwise because the extent of the possible disaster is too great. We therefore advocate a process leading ultimately to the elimination of nuclear weapons, beginning with very, very large reductions in the sources of greatest danger by far: the U.S. and Russian arsenals. We also urge that the initial steps toward elimination be taken quickly, along with the development of procedures for the verifiable removal and destruction of all the weapons.

In this chapter we will briefly describe the nature of the nuclear threat, examine it from the standpoint of our moral values, review the consensus view that nuclear weapons are militarily useless, discuss the pros and cons of deploying antiballistic missile systems, and describe a road to abolishing nuclear weapons that we believe is verifiable and multilaterally feasible—a safe road to a nuclear-weapons-free world.

The Nuclear Threat in the 21st Century

The nuclear threat differs from those we have previously discussed in this book in that it strikes many people, if it strikes them at all, as entirely *abstract*. The average American's conception of the issue seems to us something like this:

> Our missiles are pointed at Russia's missiles, so they cancel each other out. This results in a situation that, while perhaps not ideal, is not all that bad or dangerous. Of course, maintaining "deterrence" in this way may be a little costly, but we can afford it. Besides, you never know who else might develop nuclear weapons, and we need ours to deter such development or respond to it. All of these considerations mean that it is probably a good idea to maintain our U.S. nuclear arsenal pretty much as is, on "automatic pilot," making the kinds of reductions that Presidents Bush and Yeltsin agreed to in 1992—reductions not yet ratified by Congress and the Russian Parliament. Now I can stop thinking about the problem and focus on threats that seem more likely to affect me than the alleged risk of blowing up the world.

This is, more or less, the current attitude of many people toward the nuclear threat in the 21st century. We understand the inclination, in the public and even among political leaders, to downplay that threat or ignore it. It is just too bizarre, too apocalyptic, too unimaginable to believe that it is real, in the absence of the Cold War. And yet this is precisely the wrong attitude to take—and it is dangerous in its own right.

The widespread perception of the remoteness of the nuclear threat in the 21st century leads us to believe that it would be useful, in an introductory way, to make the threat as concrete as possible, more vivid than it may seem when we think of all those missiles and warheads as canceling each other out. It is important for us all to understand the effects of the weapons themselves—what they might do, and what they have done—and then let you, the reader, decide if you think this is or is not a problem requiring urgent attention.

The International Physicians for the Prevention of Nuclear War

(IPPNW), a group that won the Nobel Peace Prize in 1985, asked in a 1992 report: What are the likely effects of *a one megaton explosion? (The explosive power of current U.S. and Russian nuclear inventories would be four thousand times as great.)*[19] This is what the U.S. and Russia threaten to use against each other even as you read the following:

General effects. The immediate human casualties stem from three different sources of injury: the blast effects of the explosion itself; the burns resulting both from direct exposure to the intense heat generated by the explosion itself and from the resulting massive fires; and the radiation released by a nuclear detonation, delivered in the form of fallout of radioactive material down wind from the explosion.

Ground Zero. At ground zero, the explosion creates a crater 300 feet deep and 1200 feet in diameter. All life and structures are obliterated.

0–1 Mile. Within one second, the atmosphere itself ignites into a fireball more than a half mile in diameter. The surface of the fireball (cooler than its center) radiates nearly three times the light and heat of a comparable area of the surface of the sun. The fireball rises to a height of six miles or more. All life below is extinguished in seconds.

1–3 Miles. The flash and heat from the explosion radiate outward at the speed of light, causing instantaneous severe burns. A blast wave of compressed air follows slightly more slowly, reaching a distance of 3 miles in about 12 seconds. From the blast wave alone, most factories and commercial buildings collapse, and small frame and brick residences are destroyed. Debris carried by winds of 250 mph inflict lethal injuries throughout this area. At least 50 percent of the people in the area die immediately, prior to any injuries from radiation or the developing firestorm.

3–6 Miles. The direct heat radiating from the explosion causes immediate third-degree burns to exposed skin, and the exploding blast wave destroys many small buildings. The combination of heat and blast causes fuel tanks to explode. A firestorm begins to develop, as winds and intense heat sweep individual fires together into a single raging conflagration. The firestorm consumes all nearby oxygen, sucking it out of any underground stations and asphyxiating the occupants. Shelters become ovens and, over the ensuing minutes to hours, fatalities are likely to approach 100 percent.

6–12 Miles. The shock wave reaches a distance of 8 miles approximately 40 seconds after the immediate explosion. People directly exposed to the electromagnetic radiation (in the form of intense light) generated by the exploding warhead suffer second-degree burns. Depending on the ability of protective structures to withstand blast and resist fire, total early casualties (killed and injured) may range from 5 to 50 percent.

Radiation Casualties. In the immediate proximity of the explosion (6 miles or less) injuries resulting from radiation exposure have little significance, because most (perhaps all) susceptible individuals will have died from the more rapidly fatal burn and blast injuries. At greater distances, radioactive fallout becomes a major source of short-term and medium-term health problems.

Medical Care in the Aftermath of Nuclear Explosion. The barriers to effective medical care will be enormous. The most important of these are the sheer numbers of casualties and the fact that the explosion itself will have destroyed hospitals and other medical facilities [including drug supply warehouses] and killed or injured most medical personnel. . . . In the United States burn injuries alone would require 142 times as many intensive care units as would be available. Even for most of those with less severe injuries, however, effective medical care will likely be impossible.[20]

This is what nuclear weapons *do:* They blast, burn, and irradiate at a level and with a speed and finality that is almost incomprehensible. This is exactly what the U.S. and Russia continue to threaten to do to one another with their nuclear weapons every minute of every day in this new 21st century.

While admirably documented and helpfully concrete, the IPPNW report still deals in abstract numbers, derived from a hypothetical exploded nuclear weapon somewhere over the United States or Russia. It is thus useful to recall that our knowledge of the effects of nuclear war are not entirely hypothetical, and that we have real-world evidence of what happened when the United States dropped atomic bombs on Hiroshima and Nagasaki in August 1945. In Hiroshima, nearly 140,000 people died immediately; approximately 200,000 died overall. In Nagasaki, approximately 74,000 people died within four months; and 108,000 died overall. On November 7, 1996, in testimony to the International Court of Justice, the mayor of Nagasaki recalled his memory of the attack:

> Nagasaki became a city of death where not even the sound of insects could be heard. After a while, countless men, women and children began to gather for a drink of water at the banks of nearby Urakami River. Their hair and clothing scorched and their burnt skin hanging off in sheets like rags. Begging for help they died one after another in the water or in heaps on the banks. Then radiation began to take its toll, killing people like the scourge of death expanding in concentric circles from the hypocenter. Four months after the atomic bombing, 74,000 people were dead and 75,000 had suffered injuries, that is, two-thirds of the city population had fallen victim to this calamity that came upon Nagasaki like a preview of the Apocalypse.[21]

Why did so many civilians have to die? The United States was seeking to end the war without having to fight its way to Tokyo, island by island, and the civilians, who made up nearly all of the victims in Hiroshima and Nagasaki, were unfortunately "co-located" with military targets. While the annihilation of humans was not precisely the objective of those targeting the bombs, it was an inevitable result of the choice of those targets. It is worth noting, in this regard, that at one point during the Cold War, it is said that the United States had more than 200 nuclear warheads targeted on Moscow, because it contained so many military targets and so much "industrial capacity." Presumably, the Soviets likewise targeted many U.S. cities, because of their connection to the U.S. "military-industrial capacity."[22] The statement that our nuclear weapons do not target populations is totally misleading in the sense that the so-called collateral damage of our strikes would include tens of millions of Russian dead.

For decades, U.S. nuclear forces have been designed to absorb a Soviet or Russian nuclear attack and respond with sufficient strength to inflict "unacceptable" damage on the Russians. This has been, and must always be, the foundation of our nuclear deterrent. But we have also maintained a capability to "launch on warning" in order to reduce the number of our weapons that would be destroyed by a Russian first strike. Our force would thus be launched while the Russian warheads were in flight. No more than 15 minutes could be allowed to receive the warning of the Russian attack, determine the response, and respond.

To make that possible, the commander-in-chief of the U.S. Strategic Air Command (CINCSAC), carried with him a secure telephone, no matter where he went, 24 hours a day, seven days a week, 365 days a year. This CINCSAC telephone was linked at all times to the underground nuclear command post of the North American Aerospace Defense Command (NORAD), deep inside Cheyenne Mountain, in Colorado, and to the president. (The president, wherever he happens to be, always has at hand nuclear release codes in the "football," a briefcase carried for him at all times by a U.S. military officer.) CINCSAC's standing orders were to be able to answer the telephone by the end of the third ring. If it rang, and if he was informed that a nuclear attack of enemy ballistic missiles (presumably Russian) appeared to be underway, he was allowed between two and three minutes to decide whether the warning was valid (over the years, we have received many false warnings) and if so, how we should respond. He was then given approximately ten minutes to locate the president, inform him of his recommendations, permit him to discuss the situation with two or three of his closest advisers (presumably the secretary of defense and the chairman of the Joint Chiefs of Staff) and transmit his decision to CINCSAC, to be passed immediately, along with the codes, to the launch sites. The president's options would essentially be these: He could decide to ride out the attack and defer until later any decision to launch a retaliatory strike. Or he could order an immediate retaliatory strike, thereby launching U.S. weapons that were targeted on military-industrial assets in Russia. The Russians presumably have analogous facilities and arrangements.[23] The whole situation was so bizarre as to be beyond belief. But that is what we lived with for 40 years.

The situation has changed somewhat since the end of the Cold War. The United States and Russia no longer target specific missiles or other specific sites (although retargeting can be done in less than five minutes). Yet in other respects, very little has changed. Therein lies great danger, one exacerbated by the lack of public awareness of it. For example, Bruce G. Blair, a former U.S. Air Force nuclear missile launch officer who is now president of the Center for Defense Information in Washington, D.C., recently conducted in-depth interviews with officials at all levels of the U.S. nuclear command structure. From these interviews, Blair concludes that, in June 2000, there were approximately 2,260 so-called vital Russian targets on the U.S. target list. About 1,100 of these are nuclear weapons sites. The others are a miscellaneous array of secondary assets, including bases for the Russian army—an army that is in total disarray and on the verge of disintegration. In addition, Blair was told that China has been put back on the target list, after being absent for 20 years, and that the target list has, in fact, been growing since 1993, when the last arms control treaty (START-2) was signed by the United States and Russia.

Blair also addresses a second issue, one that makes the situation especially dangerous from moment to moment and day to day. He observes that more than a decade after the end of the Cold War:

> The United States has about 2,200 strategic warheads on alert, according to Strategic Command Officers. Virtually all missiles on land are ready for launch in two minutes, and those on four submarines, two in the Atlantic and two in the Pacific, are ready to launch on 15 minutes' notice, officers say.[24]

Blair concludes: "It is clear that leaders are clinging to outdated planning that helps keep large numbers of American and Russian missiles on hair-trigger alert."[25]

The U.S. and Russian nuclear arsenals constitute what the strategist Herman Kahn long ago called the "doomsday machine."[26] And as John Steinbruner has pointed out, "because of the magnitude and imminence of the threat entailed, the pattern of nuclear weapons deployment [of the United States and Russia] is the single most objective determinant of security for all countries whether or not they participate directly in the activities involved."[27] The risk of nuclear catastrophe derives from the combination of the *magnitude* and the *imminence* of the threat: too many lethal weapons, too little time to decide. That is the current situation. The United States and Russia have the capacity to destroy much of civilized life on earth and, in a crisis, their leaders may not have enough time to sort out rationally how to avoid doing so.

Two other categories of nuclear threat at the outset of the 21st century deserve special attention.

1. *Risk of nuclear proliferation.* Until the principal custodians of nuclear weapons—the United States and Russia—renounce them, other nations will continue to believe that such weapons will add to their security and will confer membership in the club of Great Powers. India and Pakistan officially joined the nuclear club in 1998. North Korea may have the bomb. Israel has long had it. Iraq is surely working toward it and Iran may be as well. The world has become a very dangerous place in the past decade. And as Jonathan Schell recently wrote, "Ten years after the collapse of the Soviet Union, the startling fact is that nuclear arms control is faring worse in the first days of the twenty-first century than it did in the last days of the Cold War."[28]

2. *Risk of nuclear terrorism.* This risk, sometimes called "loose nukes," has increased since the collapse of the Soviet Union.[29] The problem is this: that a terrorist group will steal or buy a nuclear weapon and use it to extort concessions from Western countries or to destroy an enemy. This problem led former U.S. secretary of defense William Perry and Ashton Carter, a former assistant secretary of defense, to recommend recently that the United States continue to assist the Russians to account for and dispose of their nuclear materials *even in the absence of arms control agreements.*[30]

Even taking account of these dangers, the risk of a single nuclear detonation, or several, leading to nuclear holocaust is low; and the risk of a nuclear detonation in anger of any kind is very low. After all, there has been none since August 1945. This was the argument made by the United States before the International Court of Justice in 1996, when it gathered to address the question: "Is the threat or use of nuclear weapons in any circumstance permitted under international law?"[31] Lawyers for the United States. argued that the risk was vanishingly small, especially when compared to what they said had been the demonstrated capacity of nuclear deterrence to deter Great Power war since the Second World War.

Several of the judges turned the likelihood question on its head, asking, in effect, whether *any* likelihood of the near destruction of human civilization is justified if it can be avoided? Judge Shahabuddeen answered as follows:

> Once it is shown that the use of a nuclear weapon could annihilate mankind, its repugnance to the conscience of the international community is not materially diminished by showing that it need not have that result in every case; it is not reasonable to expect that the conscience of the international community will, both strangely and impossibly, wait on the event to see if the result of any particular use is the destruction of the human species. The operative consideration is the risk of annihilation.[32]

This is, we believe, the correct way to consider the problem: begin at the end, at the possible catastrophe; ask whether anything—anything at all—could justify such an outcome; if the answer is no, then you have your marching orders: the capacity to destroy nations must be *eliminated*. Since the possible outcome is absolute, action to prevent it must be absolute.

The Moral Implications of the Use of Nuclear Weapons

From the moment on July 16, 1945, when the first atomic bomb was successfully exploded in Alamogordo, New Mexico, it was clear to many that the phenomenon thus unleashed was different not just in degree, but in kind, from anything that had come before. The physicist I. I. Rabi later said that every military and political leader in the world with responsibility for nuclear weapons ought to observe in person at least one atmospheric test of a nuclear weapon. Rabi believed the effect would be so overpowering, so utterly frightening, that a sane person could draw only one conclusion: that these weapons must never be used and the only way to ensure that is to abolish them. The scientific chief of the Manhattan Project, J. Robert Oppenheimer, later wrote of that explosion: "At that moment . . . there flashed through my mind a passage from the Bhagavad-Gita, the sacred book of the Hindus: 'I am become Death, the Shatterer of Worlds.'"[33] Then came, a month later, the holocausts in Hiroshima and Nagasaki.

Ever since 1945, the awful destructive power of nuclear weapons has stimulated a torrent of discussion regarding their moral justification. Many have argued that nothing morally justifies either the use or the possession of nuclear weapons and that until all nuclear weapons are eliminated, such weapons as exist be held and controlled by an authorized international agency in association with the United Nations. But the Cold War intervened almost immediately, the nuclear arms race heated up, threats and counterthreats ensued, and what might be called the "radical" position came to be regarded by many in the West as unrealistic. We in the West could not give up our nuclear weapons, it was argued, because they were needed to deter a Warsaw Pact attack with conventional weapons. Eventually, citizens in the West ceased even to worry about "the bomb" and were encouraged to do so by those who emphasized the stability of nuclear deterrence. With a few episodic exceptions such as the Cuban missile crisis, this embrace of "safety via deterrence" was paradigmatic from the 1950s through the end of the Cold War. But opposition voices raising the moral issue were beginning to be heard.

The theory of nuclear deterrence, while in some respects arcane and exceedingly complex, boils down to this: Two nuclear-armed nations, each unable to *defend* themselves against a nuclear attack by the other, seek to *deter* such an attack by possessing a credible threat of retaliation with a nuclear attack of its own. This is the core of what Bernard Brodie called "strategy in the missile age."[34] If they strike us first, we must possess enough firepower after the attack to inflict unacceptable damage on them. Therefore, they will not ever try to do so, if they remain sane. This is sometimes called the "theory" of mutual assured destruction. In reality, it is not a *theory* but a *condition* in which the United States and Soviet Union found themselves during the Cold War. The condition generated both arms races and efforts at arms control throughout the period. It was that condition which, in 1983, the U.S. Catholic bishops chose to examine from a moral point of view.

The bishops of the U.S. Catholic Conference embarked on what must surely be the most exhaustive, informed, and balanced *moral* examination of nuclear deterrence ever undertaken. Rereading the preamble of their Pastoral Letter on War and Peace, *The Challenge of Peace*, we are struck by the intensity of their commitment:

> We cannot avoid our responsibility to lift up the moral dimensions of the choices before our world and nation. The nuclear age is an age of moral as well as physical danger. *We are the first generation since Genesis with the power to threaten the created order.* We cannot remain silent in the face of such danger. . . . We need a moral about face. The whole world must summon the moral courage and technical means to say no to nuclear conflict; no to weapons of mass destruction; no to an arms race which robs the poor and the vulnerable; and no to the moral danger of a nuclear age which places before humankind indefensible choices of constant terror or surrender.[35]

One need not be a Catholic, or even a Christian, to appreciate the seriousness of the bishops' endeavor. Their statement of the problem is arresting: What should we say, think, or do about the brutal fact that we now have the physical capability to destroy all that exists on earth, beginning with ourselves, the human race? *The Challenge of Peace* has become the most widely read and discussed analysis ever written of the morality of nuclear weapons and nuclear deterrence.

The bishops analyzed the problem of nuclear deterrence within the established parameters of Just War Doctrine. J. Bryan Hehir, now dean of Harvard Divinity School, was the coordinator of the research and drafting of *The Challenge of Peace* in his capacity as director of the

Office of International Justice and Peace of the U.S. Catholic Conference.[36] He points out that in the bishops' analysis, nuclear deterrence failed the moral test on two key points, noncombatant immunity (or discrimination) and proportionality, each of which would require leaders to be able to control the direction, duration, and extent of any war involving nuclear weapons.[37] The bishops didn't believe a nuclear war could be, or would be, limited so as to conform to the Just War principles of noncombatant immunity and proportionality, and they left no doubt about their conclusion: "The danger of escalation is so great," they wrote, "that it would be morally unjustifiable to initiate nuclear war in any form."[38]

During the period that they were doing their research, the Bishops were told by a wide array of specialists that if either or both of the principal nuclear powers admitted that a nuclear war could not be limited or controlled, this would have greatly weakened the regime of deterrence that linked them, thereby raising the risk of nuclear war. How then, the bishops were asked, did they intend to square their belief in the inherent nondiscrimination and nonproportionality of nuclear weapons with their belief that a nuclear war should never occur, under any circumstances?[39] They advocated a two-phase solution:

1. No *use* of nuclear weapons which would violate the principles of discrimination or proportionality may be *intended* in a strategy of deterrence.

2. Deterrence is not an adequate strategy as a long-term basis for peace; it is a transitional strategy justifiable only in conjunction with resolute determination to pursue arms control and disarmament.[40]

According to the first principle, the United States and Russia are currently trapped in what is essentially an insoluble moral dilemma. They cannot morally intend to do that upon which the credibility of deterrence is said to depend: retaliate massively in response to a nuclear attack. But according to the second principle, the nuclear powers should not try to square the circle, but rather to move as urgently as feasible to eliminate the nuclear weapons themselves, which are the source of the

conundrum. It is on this basis that the bishops advocated a "strictly con-
ditioned"—that is, temporary—acceptance of nuclear deterrence. It is
morally defensible only to the extent that nuclear weapons are in the
process of being abolished.

The Challenge of Peace went through several drafts that were subjected
to public scrutiny. The bishops and their staff consulted with scientists,
politicians, military commanders, strategists, historians, political scientists, and philosophers—including critics and defenders of the current
deterrence regime. Well into their inquiry, they crashed head-on into the
main obstacle to moral simplicity on nuclear matters: the fact of a Cold
War between two nuclear-armed superpowers, each of which considered the other an "evil empire." The bishops had become convinced by
the arguments they heard that unilateral disarmament, which was conceptually the simplest way to "say no" to nuclear war, would likely result
in disaster: nuclear blackmail, the subjugation of the West, or worse,
nuclear annihilation. This is why, as they ruefully concluded, "the danger of the situation is clear; but how to prevent the use of nuclear
weapons, how to assess deterrence, and how to delineate moral responsibility in the nuclear age are less clearly seen."[41]

In the context of 1983, when the Pastoral Letter was published, J.
Bryan Hehir characterized the bishops' approach to the problem of
eventually transcending deterrence as the "political option," meaning
that they sought to restart an arms control process that many believed
the United States had given up altogether.[42] That was a bare minimum
for conformity to the bishops' moral standard. But the bishops also envisioned a possibility few saw clearly, if at all, in the dark days of the early
1980s. They saw the possibility of transcending deterrence by *ending the
Cold War,* which they described as caused fundamentally by "the radical
distrust which marks international politics."[43] As the Reverend Hehir
summarizes the argument, "Deterrence has one basic role: the prevention of nuclear war long enough to move beyond deterrence."[44]

Herein lies the great opportunity regarding nuclear weapons from a
moral point of view as we enter the 21st century. While the conditions
required (and to an extent foreseen) by the bishops for moving beyond
nuclear deterrence now exist, and have existed for a decade, we are no
less reliant on deterrence now than we were in 1983. We are *conceptually*

no closer to abolishing nuclear weapons because the United States and Russia continue to act and to deploy the weapons within the confines of the old Cold War paradigm of deterrence. Even though the size of the nuclear arsenals has been halved, roughly speaking, in the past decade, the inability of the U.S. and Russian leaders to break out of deterrence-based thinking makes it almost inconceivable to many that we will move to the elimination of the weapons on each side. Our nuclear establishment has been incapable so far of thinking in these terms on their own. The Cold War is gone, but deterrence is not. This is morally unacceptable, militarily unnecessary, and extremely dangerous.

❖

Robert McNamara: Too often, nuclear deterrence is discussed in the abstract. Strategies are concocted to fight hypothetical wars. It all seems so rational, as long as it is hypothetical and we believe we can control the outcome. In this way, we convince ourselves that nuclear wars can be avoided or limited or perhaps even won. My experience as a decision maker in the Cuban missile crisis, and subsequently as a researcher of the crisis, leads me to the opposite conclusion: In a deep crisis, things often spin out of control, and, no matter what started the crisis, it is the very existence of the nuclear weapons themselves—the possibility they will be used and that the conflict will escalate—that becomes the biggest threat. I believe the Cuban missile crisis showed that nothing short of the elimination of nuclear weapons can change this. Nothing short of elimination, therefore, is morally defensible.

I want now to summarize what I have learned about the missile crisis from my experience in the event, and from the series of five conferences on the crisis in which I participated from 1987 to 1992.

The crisis began when the Soviets moved nuclear missiles and bombers to Cuba—secretly and with the clear intent to deceive—in the summer and early fall of 1962. The missiles were to be targeted against cities along America's East Coast, putting 90 million Americans at risk. Photographs taken by a U-2 reconnaissance aircraft on Sunday, October 14, 1962, brought the deployments to President John F. Kennedy's attention. He and his military and civilian security advisers believed that the Soviets' action posed a threat to the West. Kennedy therefore authorized a naval quarantine of Cuba, to be effective Wednesday, October 24. Preparations also began for air strikes and an amphibious invasion. The contingency plans called for a first-day air attack of 1,080 sorties—a huge attack. An invasion force of 180,000 troops was assembled in southeastern U.S. ports. The crisis came to a head on the weekend of October 27–28. Had Soviet leader Nikita Khrushchev not publicly announced on that Sunday, October 28th, that he was removing the missiles, I believe that on Monday, a majority of Kennedy's military and civilian advisers would have recommended launching the attacks.

By the conclusion of the third Cuban missile crisis conference in Moscow, in January 1989, it had become clear that the decisions of each of the three nations before, during, and after the crisis had been distorted by misinformation, miscalculation, and misjudgment. At the time, some of us—particularly President Kennedy and I—believed that the United States faced great danger.[45] The Moscow meeting confirmed that judgment. But during a subsequent conference in Havana, in January 1992—almost 30 years after the event—we learned that we had seriously underestimated those dangers. While in Havana, we were told by the former Warsaw Pact chief of staff, General Anatoly Gribkov, that in 1962 the Soviet forces in Cuba possessed not only nuclear warheads for their intermediate-range missiles targeted on U.S. cities, but nuclear bombs and tactical nuclear warheads as well.[46] The tactical warheads were to be used against U.S. invasion forces. At the time the CIA was reporting no warheads on the island—they believed the first batch was to be delivered by a Russian ship named the Poltava.

In November 1992, we learned more. An article in the Russian press stated that, at the height of the missile crisis, Soviet forces on Cuba possessed a total of 162 nuclear warheads, including at least 90 tactical warheads. Moreover it was reported that, on October 26, 1962—a moment of great tension—warheads were moved from their storage sites to positions closer to their delivery vehicles in anticipation of a U.S. invasion.[47] The next day, Soviet Defense Minister Rodion Malinovsky received a cable from General Issa Pliyev, the Soviet commander in Cuba, informing him of this action. Malinovsky sent it to Khrushchev. Khrushchev returned it to Malinovsky with "Approved" scrawled across the document. Clearly, there was a high risk that in the face of a U.S. attack—which, as I have said, many in the U.S. government, military and civilian alike, were prepared to recommend to President Kennedy—the Soviet forces in Cuba would have decided to use their nuclear weapons rather than lose them.[48]

We need not speculate about what would have happened in that event. We can predict the results with certainty. Although a U.S. invasion force would not have been equipped with tactical nuclear warheads—President Kennedy and I had specifically prohibited that—no one should believe that had American troops been attacked with nuclear weapons, the United States would have refrained from a nuclear response. And where would it have ended? In utter disaster.[49]

What lesson should we draw from these stunning data, which suggest that our brush with nuclear catastrophe in October 1962 was extraordinarily close? The lesson, if it had not been clear before, was made so in Havana when we first began to learn, from General Gribkov, about Soviet preparations for nuclear war in the event of a U.S. invasion. Near the conclusion of that session, I asked Cuban President Fidel Castro, the host of the conference, two questions:

(a) Were you aware of it [the Soviet deployment of tactical nuclear warheads, and plans for their use]; and

(b) What was your interpretation or expectation of the possible effect on Cuba? How did you think the U.S. would respond, and what might the implications have been for your nation and the world?[50]

Castro's answer sent a chill down my spine. He replied:

Now, we started from the assumption that if there was an invasion of Cuba, nuclear war would erupt. We were certain of that. . . . We would be forced to pay the price, that we would disappear.[51]. . . Would I have been ready to use nuclear weapons? Yes, I would have agreed to the use of nuclear weapons. . . . I would have agreed, in the event of the invasion you are talking about, with the use of tactical nuclear weapons. . . . If Mr. McNamara or Mr. Kennedy had been in our place, and had their country been invaded, or their country was going to be occupied . . . I believe they would have used tactical nuclear weapons.[52]

I hope that President Kennedy and I would not have behaved as Castro suggested we would have. His decision would have destroyed his country. Had we responded in a similar way, the damage to our own would have been disastrous. But human beings are fallible. We know we all make mistakes. In our daily lives, mistakes are costly, but we try to learn from them. In conventional war, they cost lives, sometimes thousands of lives. But if mistakes were to affect decisions related to the use of nuclear forces, there would be no learning period. They would result in the destruction of entire nations. Therefore, I strongly believe that the indefinite combination of human fallibility and nuclear weapons carries a very high risk of a potential nuclear catastrophe.[53]

❖

Threatening to commit mass murder may have been morally acceptable—at least conditionally—during the Cold War. But in the absence of the Cold War, as we have indicated, nuclear deterrence is militarily unnecessary, morally repugnant, and extremely dangerous. In 1983, the bishops framed the key moral choice with regard to nuclear weapons by quoting the Old Testament book of Deuteronomy:

> I set before you life or death, a blessing or a curse. Choose life then, so that you and your descendants may live in the love of God, obeying His voice, clinging to him; for in this your life consists, and on this depends your long stay in the land.[54]

With regard to nuclear danger, during the Cold War most felt that we could "choose life" only conditionally, partially, by trying to avoid situations in which initiation of nuclear war became alarmingly high. The use of nuclear weapons was clearly unacceptable, but without a deterrent strategy—based on the threat of their use—the West believed it faced communist domination. That was the dilemma.

In the 21st century, there is no such dilemma. The worldwide communist movement—formerly a threat to our security—is dead, a thing of the past. And although J. Robert Oppenheimer was right to equate nuclear weapons with death and the shattering of worlds, we now have an opportunity to choose life by eliminating those instruments of death. What was conditionally moral in 1983—nuclear deterrence—should no longer be morally acceptable. The conditions of world politics have been revolutionized, but our thinking about nuclear weapons and nuclear deterrence has not. It is time—past time—for a paradigm shift in our thinking.

Antiballistic Missile Systems: The Pros and Cons of Their Deployment

Some would argue that we can avoid such a shift in strategy by the deployment of an impenetrable antiballistic missile system. But the cure is certain to be worse than the disease.

Of all the manifestations of U.S. unilateralist tendencies, potentially the most dangerous in the long run may be the stubborn conviction, held by several generations of Americans, that technology can solve any problem, including the problem of defending against a massive nuclear attack. The debate over the possibilities and limits of missile defense has occurred in essentially identical form in the 1960s (when it was called ballistic missile defense, or BMD); in the 1970s (antiballistic missile systems, or ABM); in the 1980s (Strategic Defense Initiative, SDI, or "Star Wars"); and in the 1990s (National Missile Defense, or NMD).

Missile defense advocates throughout this period have typically argued that a unilateral deployment of U.S. missile defense is more moral, and will provide more security to Americans, than reliance on "mutual assured destruction." The most famous advocate of missile defense was President Ronald Reagan, who sought to make his Strategic Defense Initiative a cornerstone of U.S. national security policy. Reagan's thinking on the issue is instructive, as it contains all the elements of a peculiarly American point of view characteristic of advocates of missile defense: (1) shock at learning that the fate of America actually rests with the leaders in the Kremlin, upon whose nuclear restraint we are dependent (just as they are dependent upon ours!); (2) a leap to the conclusion that it would be more ethical, more moral, to defend the United States in the traditional sense, rather than to deter a nuclear attack by threatening to kill tens of millions of people in a retaliatory strike; (3) the confidence that American ingenuity and scientific acumen can overcome any technical difficulties that some say make missile defense against a massive attack infeasible; and (4) the belief that our action will be seen by others as so rational that they will take no action to counter it.

The story of Reagan's (and America's) mindset with regard to missile defense has been brilliantly told by Frances FitzGerald in her recent book, *Way Out There in the Blue*.[55] She states that on July 31, 1979, Reagan visited the headquarters of the NORAD, whose principal function is to alert the military and political leadership in the event of a nuclear attack on the United States. After touring the facility, Reagan, a prospective presidential candidate, had a personal discussion with General James Hill, the NORAD commander. It was in the course of that conversation that the idea of missile defense began to take shape in Reagan's mind. According to FitzGerald, Reagan asked Hill "what could be done if the Soviets fired just one missile at an American city. Hill replied that they could track the missile, but that nothing could be done to stop it." On the flight back to Los Angeles, Reagan told an aide, "We have spent all that money and have all that equipment, and there is nothing we can do to prevent a nuclear missile from hitting us. We should have some way to defend ourselves against nuclear missiles."[56] This revelation—that our strategy is to deter nuclear attacks rather than defend against them—is something that is repeatedly rediscovered by the American people and American politicians.

On March 8, 1983, President Reagan gave his famous speech to the National Association of Evangelicals, proclaiming Moscow to be the center of an "evil empire." The evil men in Moscow were capable, at any moment, of deciding for their own reasons to destroy the United States, and there was absolutely nothing the American president or anyone else could do about it, he said. Thus the stage was set, a little more than two weeks later, for one of the most remarkable events of Reagan's presidency: his March 23, 1983, "Star Wars" speech to the nation over television and radio.

As FitzGerald indicates, the conception and the language in that speech came almost exclusively from Reagan himself. These were the words drafted personally by Reagan that shocked his scientific adviser, George Keyworth, and his own staff, including his speech writers:

Would it not be better to embark upon a path that will eventually let us and our allies use *defensive* measures—not the threat of retaliation—to deter aggression in the free world? . . . In short, how much better it would be if we could begin to shift from a strategy of deterrence with offensive weapons to a strategy of forward strategic defense. . . . But is it not worth every investment to free the world from the threat of nuclear war? . . . Wouldn't it be better to save lives than to avenge them?

I call upon the scientific community in this country, who gave us nuclear weapons, to turn their great talents to the cause of mankind and world peace; to give us the means of rendering these weapons impotent and obsolete.[57]

Four days later, Reagan returned to the apocalyptic vision he had experienced on his 1979 tour of NORAD headquarters. In an interview he said, "To look down to an endless future with both of us sitting here with these horrible missiles aimed at each other and the only thing preventing a holocaust is just so long as no one pulls the trigger—this is unthinkable."[58] And if the missile defense of America could become a reality, Reagan was also inclined, as he often said, to share it with the Soviets. As FitzGerald shows, Reagan's views were deeply felt and, as we know, they resonated with a significant portion of the American people.

What is wrong with this wish, this feeling that nuclear vulnerability should be escaped via a new incarnation of old-fashioned defensive systems? First, as to feasibility: In none of its incarnations has a missile defense shield been shown to be feasible against a large, determined offense. "Hitting a large number of bullets with other bullets" turns out to be technically very challenging. In large part, the lack of feasibility derives from the need for the performance of such a system not only to be both perfect—it must allow zero nuclear missiles through its "shield"—but to be perfect without ever having been fully tested. It cannot be fully tested because to do so would alarm the rest of the world, as a full-blown test of such a system—especially if it were space-based, as an impenetrable shield would have to be—would appear indistinguishable, in important respects, from preparation to attack.

Second, paradoxically, pursuit of a large-scale missile defense leads to offensive arms races. From the 1960s to the present, scientists have shown that it is much easier to respond to an adversary's missile defense system, should one ever be developed, with an offensive buildup, and means to overcome the opponent's defenses, rather than with one's own analogous defensive shield.[59] Thus the deployment of large-scale defensive systems, or the threat to do so, will stimulate arms races of offensive weapons (including weapons with penetration aids), thereby increasing the nuclear threat, rather than decreasing it.

Third, the technology involved in any missile defense shield would be among the most advanced, tightly guarded national secrets. Giving this technology, should it ever exist, to a potential nuclear adversary, knowing that the technology could also be put to offensive military uses (and to commercial uses as well), is highly unlikely.

It is understandable that Americans look to missile defense as a solution to the dilemmas of mutual assured destruction. Yet an "escape clause" from nuclear vulnerability via missile defense is simply a denial of the singular features of nuclear weapons: first, that they are different from conventional weapons and thus they cannot be used as conventional weapons are used; and second, that they cannot be defended against in the usual fashion. Joseph Nye has warned against what he calls "stunted moral reasoning" about missile defenses, noting that "the morality of such an initiative will depend on the consequences, not the motives. It may be 'better to defend than to avenge,' but only if the consequences of trying to defend do not increase the risk of nuclear conflict in the meantime."[60] But this is exactly what is accomplished by the pursuit of large-scale missile defenses: an increased risk of arms races, instability, and even nuclear war.

❖

Robert McNamara: During the latter part of my tenure as Secretary of Defense, I had considerable experience with the supreme paradox of missile defense: that efforts to defend one's citizens against a large-scale missile attack, which seem to some to be superior to efforts to deter via a capacity for mutual assured destruction, are actually counterproductive. It was during this period—1966–67—that I began to think seriously about the benefit that might accrue from seeking a formal agreement with the Russians limiting missile defenses, so that we could constrain dangerous offensive arms races and the instability that goes with them.

In November 1966, Deputy Secretary of Defense Cyrus Vance and I were in Austin, Texas, to meet with President Lyndon Johnson to go over the defense budget for the next fiscal year. At the time, we had reconnaissance photographs showing that the Russians had begun to deploy an antiballistic missile defense (ABM) system around Moscow. Now, we assumed that while Moscow might receive the first deployment, the Russians must intend this as a first step toward a nationwide system. (I am now inclined to believe that assumption was incorrect.) In response, without support from the executive branch, the Congress authorized and appropriated funds for the deployment of a U.S. defensive missile system. I was opposed to this because it seemed obvious that the proper response to the deployment of a Soviet ABM system, given the reality of nuclear deterrence, would be a further buildup of U.S. offensive nuclear forces to compensate for any potential losses (due to the Soviet defenses) in our ability to penetrate through to our targets.

But it was a tough sell, because some nuclear scientists, especially Edward Teller—the "father of the H-bomb"—had convinced some of the Joint Chiefs and some in Congress that "you won't put any [nuclear] genie back into the bottle. All you can do is to create new genies, and hope that they will be better and more benevolent ones."[61] I persuaded President Johnson to hold off on authorizing an ABM system until we had a chance to explore with the Russians whether they would be amenable to a multilateral approach—to an agreement on mutual restraints with regard to both ABMs and offensive nuclear systems.

Our preliminary contacts with the Russians suggested that they were deeply reluctant to consider any limits on defense of the motherland. We pushed for talks as soon as possible, but the Soviets refused to move. Finally, in June 1967, a meeting was scheduled between President Johnson and the Soviet Prime Minister Alexei Kosygin in the college town of Glassboro, New Jersey, which happened to be located about halfway between Washington and New York, where Kosygin was attending a session of the UN General Assembly. The president took up the matter of missile defense with Kosygin during the morning of June 23, and at one point in the discussion, he became so frustrated and angry with Kosygin for stonewalling all his attempts to describe the need to develop mutual restraints on missile defenses that he finally said, "Bob, for God's sake, you tell Kosygin what's wrong with their plan." So I told the Soviet prime minister, "If you proceed with the antiballistic missile system deployment our response will not, should not, be to deploy a similar system. That would be the reverse of what is required. We will not do that. Our response will be to expand our offensive weapons in order to maintain deterrent stability— strategic stability. Now," I continued, "it's not in our interest or in your interest to do that. The way to stop that is for both of us to agree today that we will engage in talks leading to a treaty that will prohibit deployment of large-scale antiballistic missile systems." Now Kosygin really became angry. The blood rose in the face of this normally taciturn Russian leader, his veins swelled, and he pounded the table and said: *"Defense is moral, offense is immoral!"* That is what he really believed.[62]

Eventually, however, the Russians came around to our point of view. On May 26, 1972, the ABM Treaty was signed, leading a short time later to the first limit on offensive nuclear weapons. The "historic essence" of the treaty, as the journalist John Newhouse notes, was that "each side surrendered any meaningful right to defend its society and territory against the other's nuclear weapons." I also agree with Newhouse's assessment that "the ABM Treaty is the backbone of today's arms control regime and, as such, is relied upon by the world."[63] Years later, we learned that the talks in Glassboro were a useful, even a necessary preparation for the ABM Treaty. At the time, the Politburo itself was divided on the issue of missile defenses. Kosygin reported when he got back to Moscow that the Johnson administration was not only favorably disposed to an agreement on ABMs, but that some such agreement might open the door to bilateral treaties limiting offensive arms as well.[64]

This only serves to emphasize the point: Much can be accomplished by agreeing *multilaterally* to deal with missile defenses, by limiting or prohibiting them; while nothing but suspicion and instability will arise from seeking unilateral escape via missile defense from the condition of nuclear vulnerability. This was learned by both the Russians and by the United States more than a quarter century ago.

As we enter the 21st century, we seem to have cycled back into another loop of arguing over fundamentals regarding missile defense. In 1997, the United States adopted a plan known as "three-plus-three." According to this arrangement, the administration would spend three years designing and testing a missile defense system that could be deployed in another three years, in 2003, if approval was given. This would consist of some dozens of ground-based interceptors presumed to be capable of blocking missiles launched at the United States from so-called rogue states (for example, North Korea or Iraq), or accidental launches from Russia or China.[65] Not satisfied with this proposal, presidential candidate George W. Bush declared in May 2000: "As president, I intend to develop and deploy an effective missile defense system at the earliest possible date to protect American citizens from accidental launches or blackmail by rogue nations."[66] Later he referred to a system that would defend all 50 states and our allies as well.[67] After a failed test on July 8, 2000, President Bill Clinton announced that all plans for missile defense had been put on hold, to be decided by the next administration. Now that George W. Bush is president, he must decide on the core question: whether or not to pursue a national missile defense—and if so, what kind?—that could, in effect, nullify the 1972 ABM Treaty. As part of that discussion, he must consider the likelihood that even a rogue state could overcome such a defense by penetration aids.

The reaction around the world to recent U.S. activity on the missile defense front has been deeply skeptical. The Russians see the United States as heading toward an abrogation of the ABM Treaty, which they regard, in the words of Russian Foreign Minister Igor Ivanov, as "the cornerstone of strategic stability."[68] What alarms the Russians is U.S. unilateralism on the issue. According to Ivanov, "if the United States *unilaterally* withdraws from the ABM Treaty, Russia will no longer be bound by its obligations to reduce strategic armaments, and the very process of nuclear disarmament will be inevitably terminated, if not reversed."[69] Even stronger condemnation comes from Russia's military. Defense Minister Igor Sergeyev has described U.S. missile defense plans as part of a quest for "strategic domination."[70] And General Leonid Ivashov, the Russian Defense Ministry spokesman, has referred to the U.S. claim of being at risk of nuclear attack from "rogue states" as "fairy tales" meant to justify a quest for global hegemony.[71] The Russians have proposed instead a limited missile defense system that would not abrogate an amended ABM Treaty.[72] And initial steps have been taken to establish in Moscow a Joint Data Exchange Center for giving joint advance warning of missile launches to both Washington and Moscow.[73]

The Chinese have been even stronger in their condemnation of the U.S. pursuit of even a limited missile shield. Even a small deployment, ostensibly to guard against attacks by "rogue states" would be sufficient to negate the entire Chinese deterrent of approximately 20 missiles capable of reaching the United States. Sha Zukang, director general of the Department of Arms Control and Disarmament at the Ministry of Foreign Affairs, has warned that such a U.S. deployment would lead to an expansion of China's nuclear forces, and it could even force China to reconsider existing arms control agreements that it has signed, such as the Non-Proliferation Treaty.[74]

U.S. allies are also unenthusiastic. The Canadian foreign minister, Lloyd Axworthy, has said that "we have expressed very strong concerns that any movement of the National Missile Defense that abrogates the ABM Treaty would be wrong. We don't like anything that would further expand acceleration of missile capacity."[75] And French foreign minister Hubert Védrine has urged the Americans "not to be disproportionate between the threat and destabilizing possibilities."[76]

William Perry, a former U.S. secretary of defense, has offered the following critique of the unilateralist tunnel vision characteristic of U.S. quests for a large-scale missile defense shield. Perry believes that while it is not unreasonable to ask whether missile defense might be useful as an insurance policy against a "rogue state," we must also ask "two fundamental questions: (1) Will the insurance be collectible—that is, will the defense work? And (2) how much does the policy cost—considering both dollar costs and geopolitical costs?"[77] Perry's answers to these questions focus not on Russia's reaction, which he anticipates will be strongly negative but perhaps manageable, but on China's. He identifies the unintended but probable consequences of such a U.S. deployment: First, China will expand its strategic weapons program, using the missile defense deployment as the reason. Second, tensions in the Taiwan Strait will greatly increase, along with pressure on the United States to provide

Taiwan with the capability to deploy theater missile defenses. Third, India, alarmed at the Chinese buildup, will increase its own nuclear forces, as will Pakistan, responding to India. "This is not a worst-case scenario," Perry warns. "Indeed, I believe it is the *likely* consequence in the Asia-Pacific region of a national missile defense deployment."[78] He recommends that we do nothing unilaterally on missile defense but instead work cooperatively with the Russians and Chinese if we believe that "rogue states" really do pose a nuclear threat. Even if such cooperative efforts were to fail, the United States could still organize a multilateral effort to destroy the offensive weapons, by conventional means, before they became operational.

Sigmund Freud wrote that the defining characteristic of an illusion is not that it is unlikely, but rather that it is the product of an unfulfilled wish.[79] So it is with America and its periodic pursuit of a "shield" behind which it might escape the fate of all other nations on earth: vulnerability to nuclear devastation. The more powerful the wish, according to Freud, the greater the tendency to subscribe to the illusion. And it is clear that many Americans, unscathed in the 20th century by the carnage that has ravaged other parts of the world, are deeply offended at their vulnerability and wish it were otherwise.

As Frances FitzGerald has emphasized, this particular illusion of safety from large-scale nuclear missile attacks interacts powerfully with the idea of "American exceptionalism"—the notion that America is somehow different from the other nations of the world.[80] The pursuit of this illusion results, however, in yet another instance of the United States acting as a "rogue superpower": a unilateralist, triumphalist America intent on pursuing its illusions at the expense of the security of the greater global community. But there is no unilateral escape from nuclear vulnerability. Nuclear elimination is the only way out of the box.

The Emperor Has No Clothes:
The Military Uselessness of Nuclear Weapons

❖

Robert McNamara: Very soon after becoming secretary of defense in 1961, I concluded that nuclear weapons were militarily useless, other than to deter one's opponent from their use. Although I believe Presidents Kennedy and Johnson agreed with my conclusion, it was impossible for any one of us to state such views publicly because they were totally contrary to established U.S. and NATO policy.

After leaving the Defense Department, I became president of the World Bank. During that period from 1968 to 1981 I was prohibited, as an employee of a international institution, from commenting publicly on issues of U.S. national security. After my retirement from the bank, I began to reflect on how I, with my seven years' experience as secretary of defense, might contribute to an understanding of the issues with which I began my public service career.

At that time, much was being said and written regarding how the United States could, and why it should be able to, "fight and win a nuclear war" with the Soviets. This implied, of course, that nuclear weapons had military utility: that they could be used in battle with ultimate net gain to whomever had the largest force or used them with the greatest acumen, and adhered to the strictures of nuclear war-fighting strategy. Having studied these views, I decided to go public with some information that I knew would be controversial, but that I felt was needed to inject reality into these increasingly unreal discussions about the ostensible military utility of nuclear weapons.

And so in 1983, I published an article in *Foreign Affairs* magazine that concluded, in part, as follows:

> Having spent seven years as secretary of defense dealing with the problems unleashed by the initial nuclear chain reaction 40 years ago, I do not believe we can avoid serious and unacceptable risk of nuclear war until we recognize—until we base all our military plans, defense budgets,

weapons deployments, and arms negotiations on this recognition—that *nuclear weapons serve no military purpose whatsoever. They are totally useless—except only to deter one's opponent from using them.*

That is my view today. It was my view in the 1960s.

At that time, in long private conversations with successive Presidents—Kennedy and Johnson—I recommended, without qualification, that they never initiate, under any circumstances, the use of nuclear weapons. I believe they accepted my recommendation.[81]

The article turned out to be not just controversial, but downright inflammatory! I was accused in print and in person—especially in Europe—of single-handedly destroying the West's nuclear deterrent. In reality, what I was destroying—at least this was my intention—was the *illusion* of nuclear deterrence. I had indicated that while I was secretary of defense (and I believed during all subsequent U.S. administrations), at no time was an American president under any conceivable circumstance going to authorize the use of NATO nuclear forces in response to a conventional attack by Warsaw Pact forces in Europe. Why? Because it would have been totally irresponsible! Contrary to all the talk about fighting and winning nuclear wars, no president could have the slightest confidence that escalation could be controlled. And so he was just not going to authorize initiation of the use of nuclear weapons, when a very likely effect would be the catastrophic destruction of the United States.

In truth, for nearly 40 years, with respect to our stated nuclear policy, it could be said that *the emperor had no clothes. I do not believe that after 1960, by which time the Soviets had acquired a survivable retaliatory force, any one of our ten presidents—Dwight Eisenhower, John Kennedy, Lyndon Johnson, Richard Nixon, Gerald Ford, Jimmy Carter, Ronald Reagan, George Bush, Bill Clinton, and George W. Bush—would ever have initiated the use of nuclear weapons.* Nor would our allies have wished them to do so. To initiate a nuclear strike against a comparably equipped opponent would have been tantamount to committing suicide. To initiate use against a nonnuclear opponent would have been militarily unnecessary, politically indefensible, and morally repugnant.

In 1983 this view struck many in the United States and the West as perverse and idiosyncratic. But that was because so many who had served in the West's nuclear chain of command had not revealed their true beliefs regarding the utility of nuclear weapons because of their institutional commitment to the standing NATO policy of potential first use of nuclear weapons against a Warsaw Pact conventional force attack in Europe.

In order to appreciate why "the emperor has no clothes"—why no sane Western leader was going to initiate nuclear war—it is useful to describe the views of military officers responsible for dealing with the *operational* reality of nuclear deterrence, not its theory or "theology," as it is sometimes called. General G. Lee Butler, a former commander of the U.S. Strategic Forces (the top U.S. military official with regard to nuclear weapons), has eloquently described his understanding of how nuclear deterrence becomes something like Frankenstein's monster in moments of crisis:

[I]t is absolutely fair to conclude that the presence of nuclear weapons introduced great caution. It is equally true, however, to say that deterrence had this further peculiar quality: it worked best when you needed it least. In periods of relative calm, you could point with pride to deterrence and say, "Look how splendidly it's working!" It was in moments of deep crisis that not only did it become irrelevant but all the baggage that came with it—the buildup of forces, the high states of alert—turned the picture absolutely upside down. As you entered the crisis, thoughts of deterrence vanished and you were simply trying to deal with the classic imponderables of crises. . . . It is miraculous that we escaped this period without a nuclear conflict. . . . I would like to ask you to reflect on the very singular human experience of being engaged in decisions that could have led to nuclear war. . . . I have arrived at the conclusion that it is simply wrong, morally speaking, for any mortal to be invested with the authority to call into question the survival of the planet. . . . There is no security to be found in nuclear weapons. It's a fool's game.[82]

Butler was severely chastened by his experience. He could not square the enormity of his responsibilities with the minuscule control, at best, he could expect to exercise over any process leading to nuclear war. As Butler looked back on his experience, he drew the conclusion that this situation, known to the world by the bland term "deterrence," was actually a mutual national suicide pact between the United States and Russia. What has made him an activist for nuclear elimination is that, unaccountably, the situation he used to confront every day as commander of U.S. Strategic Forces still exists today, even though the Cold War conditions that generated it have disappeared.

This is the core reason—the supreme irrationality and danger of nuclear deterrence—that so many other former military and civilian leaders have endorsed, as an ultimate objective, returning to a nuclear-weapons-free world. For example, four recent unclassified (but not widely disseminated) reports, by influential security experts, all recommend major changes in nuclear strategies and drastic reductions in force levels.

- The Spring 1993 issue of *Foreign Affairs* carried an article, co-authored by the retired chairman of the Joint Chiefs of Staff, Admiral William J. Crowe, Jr., which concluded that by the time of our entry into the 21st century, the United States and Russia could reduce their strategic nuclear forces to 1,000–1,500 each. The article was later expanded into a book co-authored with McGeorge Bundy and Sidney Drell, *Reducing Nuclear Danger: The Road Away From the Brink,* in which the authors added: "Nor is 1,000–1,500 the lowest level obtainable in the early 21st century."[83]

- In December 1995, the Stimson Center in Washington, D.C., issued a report, *An Evolving Nuclear Posture,* signed by four recently retired U.S. four-star officers, including General Andrew Goodpaster, President's Eisenhower's military aide and later the supreme Allied commander in Europe. The report recommended moving through a series of four steps to the "goal of elimination" of nuclear weapons.[84]

- In August 1996, the Canberra Commission, appointed by Australian Prime Minister Paul Keating, issued its *Report on the Elimination of Nuclear Weapons.* The *Report* recommended "a program to achieve a world totally free of nuclear weapons."[85] The commission members included, among others: Michel Rocard, former prime minister of France; Joseph Rotblat, winner of the 1995 Nobel Peace Prize, and one of the designers of the original atomic bombs dropped on Japan; Field Marshall Lord Michael Carver, former chief of the British defense Staff; General G. Lee Butler, former commander of the U.S. Strategic Air Command; and Robert McNamara. The Canberra Commission's recommendations were unanimous.

• In 1997, the U.S. National Academy of Sciences issued a report stating that reductions by the United States and Russia, within a few years, to a level of 2,000 warheads each "should be easily accommodated within the existing and anticipated strategic force structures of both sides."[86] It recommended moving subsequently to 1,000 warheads each, and then to "roughly 300 each."[87]

It should be emphasized that these reports were drafted by main-stream specialists: politicians, military commanders, civilian defense leaders, scientists and academics from all over the world.

Moreover, the conclusion reached by these prestigious commissions should not come as a surprise. For the past 20 years, more and more Western military and civilian security experts have expressed doubts about the military utility of nuclear weapons. This is what they have said:

• By 1982, five of the seven retired chiefs of the British defense staff expressed their belief that initiating the use of nuclear weapons, in accordance with NATO policy, would lead to disaster. Lord Louis Mountbatten, chief of staff from 1959 to 1965, said shortly before he was assassinated in 1979, "As a military man I can see no use for nuclear weapons."[88] And Field Marshall Lord Michael Carver, chief of staff from 1973 to 1976, wrote in 1982 that he was totally opposed to NATO ever initiating the use of nuclear weapons.[89]

• Henry Kissinger, speaking in Brussels in 1979, made clear that he believed the United States would never initiate a nuclear strike against the Soviet Union, no matter what the provocation. "Our European allies," he said, "should not keep asking us to multiply strategic assurances that we cannot possibly mean or if we do mean, we should not execute because if we execute them we risk the destruction of civilization."[90]

- Melvin Laird, secretary of defense under President Nixon, said in 1982 that "a worldwide zero nuclear option with adequate verification should be our goal. . . . These weapons . . . are useless for military purposes."[91]

- Former West German Chancellor Helmut Schmidt told the British Broadcasting Company in 1987: "Flexible Response [NATO's strategy calling for the use of nuclear weapons in response to a Warsaw Pact attack by nonnuclear forces] is nonsense. Not out of date, but nonsense. . . . The Western idea, which was created in the 1950s, that we should be willing to use nuclear weapons first, in order to make up for our so-called conventional deficiency, has never convinced me."[92]

- Admiral Noel Gayler, former commander in chief of all U.S. forces in the Pacific, remarked in 1987: "There is no sensible use of any of our nuclear forces. The only reasonable use is to deter our opponents from using nuclear forces."[93]

- General Larry Welch, former U.S. Air Force chief of staff and a former commander of the Strategic Air Command, put a similar thought in these words: "Nuclear deterrence depended on someone believing that you would commit an act that is totally irrational, if done."[94]

- In July 1994, General Charles A. Horner, then chief of the U.S. Space Command, stated: "The nuclear weapon is obsolete. I want to get rid of them all."[95]

- In December 1996, 19 retired U.S. military officers and 42 senior admirals and generals from other nations across the world stated their support for complete elimination of nuclear weapons.[96]

- In February 1998, 119 present and former heads of state and other senior civilian leaders—including Helmut Schmidt, Michel Rocard, former British Prime Minister James Callaghan, and Jimmy Carter—stated their support for the elimination of nuclear weapons.

Many former civilian and military leaders have thus come forward, declaring that during and since their days of nuclear responsibility, they never considered nuclear weapons to be "weapons" at all, recognizing that their use would almost surely have led to uncontrollable escalation, resulting in a nuclear catastrophe for civilization. As responsible decision makers, they would not have initiated the use of the weapons. Yet they are perplexed and dismayed because, in the absence of the Cold War, the nuclear arsenals and strategies of the United States and Russia still bear all too close a resemblance to their Cold War counterparts. What seems to be operating now is simple inertia and an unconscionable dual failure of imagination: a failure to imagine the catastrophe that might happen, due to misunderstanding, misperception, or miscalculation; and a failure to imagine safe and feasible paths to a nuclear-weapons-free world.

The Road to a Nuclear-Weapons-Free World

In the early 1980s, during the tumult in the United States over nuclear arms control, "Star Wars," nuclear war fighting, and the like, a popular bumper sticker read: "One nuclear bomb can ruin your whole day." The irony of juxtaposing nuclear finality with childish frivolity drew rueful smiles back then. It seemed to be the ultimate understatement, primarily because most of those who displayed this particular bumper sticker were inclined to deny the possibility of just "one nuclear bomb." Yet if taken literally, that bumper sticker speaks a basic truth about nuclear weapons: It only takes one, just one, to create an unprecedented human tragedy.

This is the fear that lies behind much of the skepticism among specialists over the years about the possibility of moving to a nuclear-weapons-free world.[97] While it is readily admitted that there are dangers associated with holding large numbers of nuclear weapons and ballistic missiles, especially with the command-and-control systems continually on alert, there are also problems to be surmounted if we are to move to very low numbers of nuclear weapons. These problems include the following:

- *Cheating.* Suppose that the United States has eliminated its nuclear arsenal, in accordance with some international regime that is in place. What happens if another country, say, Iraq or Libya or even a nationalist government in Russia, has hidden a few bombs and delivery vehicles and that, at a moment of high international tension, it announces that it has such weapons and uses the threat of their deployment to blackmail part or all of the rest of the world. Or suppose it is thought that the country in question is bluffing, the bluff is called, and nuclear war is the result. This is a concern even when the big nuclear powers have redundant "overkill" capability. But many consider this an enormous danger as the verified numbers of nuclear weapons approach zero.

- *Breakout.* Suppose, again, that the nuclear arsenals have been eliminated and nuclear production forsworn by all nuclear-capable countries. But suppose also that a secret program of development is undertaken by another country or group and that, again at a moment of crisis, or merely in pursuit of a long-standing political objective— for example, territory—this country or group now threatens nuclear annihilation of another, if its demands are not met. What can a disarmed world do but cave in to the newly armed (or rearmed) nuclear bully that has managed to break out of the international constraints presumably placed upon it?

These have been the principal arguments against moving to a nuclear-weapons-free world. Even if the country that has cheated, or broken out, has but one nuclear bomb, it could cause ruin for an enemy.

During the Cold War, these discussions of cheating and breakout had little relevance because of the huge numbers of weapons held by the major adversaries. And deep cuts in the superpowers' arsenals seemed politically out of the question, given the global ideological competition between East and West. Now that this competition no longer exists, these questions have become more meaningful. The United States and Russia have destroyed thousands of nuclear weapons since the end of the Cold

War. The question now is whether they will—or should—find ways to resolve the difficult issues associated with further deep cuts and movement toward a nuclear-weapons-free world?

Many skeptics believe that as the United States and Russia reduce their nuclear capabilities below certain thresholds, the world will become more dangerous. What if we drop to, say, 1,000 on each side, they ask, which is far less than U.S. military targeters say is needed for full "coverage" of Russian targets? Then they ask, what if a brutal Russian regime takes over and, declares that it seeks to reannex the Baltic republics and dares the United States and the West to do something about it? The Russians may believe that Russia will survive. And then what if the United States and Russia reduce to, say, 400–500, or roughly the size of the arsenals of China, France, and Britain? Would the United States then be at risk for nuclear blackmail by China, perhaps over the Taiwan issue? And as the nuclear arsenals of all the declared and undeclared nuclear powers approach zero, the difficult problems of cheating and breakout must be addressed.

The answer to this litany of fears is obvious, but, for some reason, it is obscure to many people. John Holdren of Harvard's John F. Kennedy School of Government calls this the "compared to what?" problem. According to Holdren:

> There are real difficulties on the road to a NWFW [nuclear-weapons-free world], and real dangers at the destination. But these are to be compared not to the perfection of a hypothetical hazard-free world, but rather to the risks and difficulties of continuing to live in a world from which nuclear weapons in the possession of states has not been banned and nuclear weapons in the possession of sub-national groups cannot be ruled out.[98]

Will there be more nuclear weapons states in the absence of movement toward zero? Almost certainly, the answer is yes. Will the dangerous nuclear stockpiles of the nuclear weapons states become increasingly at risk for nuclear theft? Yes, again. These are the kinds of tradeoffs that are involved in comparing the risks of moving toward, and arriving at, a nuclear-weapons-free world. A decade, or two or three down the road, a nuclear-weapons-free world will be far less risky that any kind of nuclearized world.

Many others who favor large reductions are concerned that, while the United States and Russia may have persuaded themselves of the wisdom of deep reductions, moving to zero nuclear weapons might be unwise, because others—perhaps countries like Pakistan or Israel—simply would not eliminate their nuclear arsenals, in the belief that their nuclear capability is all that prevents aggression by a large adversary.[99] But this is no reason not to begin movement toward deep reductions now in the arsenals of the largest nuclear weapons powers—the United States and Russia—and later in those of Britain, France, and China. It might take a decade or more, for example, to put in place the verification system that would permit reduction in their nuclear arsenals to, say 100 weapons each. If and when we get to that much lower level, then discussions could be initiated about security guarantees to certain states to lead these other states to embrace zero.

It is worth noting that much progress has been made in the past decade on the two primary dimensions of risk, and therefore of concern: First is the *vertical* dimension, along which each side monitors the proliferation or elimination of the weapons of the other side. This is sometimes called the revolution in "transparency" in the Russian-American nuclear relationship. Second, is the *horizontal* dimension, which is concerned with what is sometimes called "the length of the fuse"—in essence, the alerting procedures, including how long it might take to reassemble nuclear warheads and launch vehicles that have been separated under the terms of some future international agreement (the separate parts having been placed in different physical locations). That is the good news: Progress has been made since the end of the Cold War that was unthinkable before. Cuts are continuing in absolute numbers in each arsenal; dealerting is being discussed by the two sides and is recognized as a necessary component of any comprehensive effort to move toward zero; material necessary for making nuclear bombs is being protected with more care than previously; improved schemes for cutoffs of fissile materials continue to be developed; and the transparency of the monitoring schemes continues to improve.[100] So much for the feasibility of what might be called the "physics" of the effort to move safely to a nuclear-weapons-free world.

But there is also an important "psychological" component to the effort. This has been especially emphasized by Lord Michael Carver, the former chief of the British defense staff, who has argued that we must not be distracted from *zero* as the ultimate number of acceptable nuclear weapons on earth:

> [T]he most important thing at this moment is to persuade everyone, even those not inclined to accept it, that the target has got to be total elimination. If you start peddling solutions which are not perhaps quite total elimination but something that comes close to it, you lose the whole force of the argument. Until you've dramatically fixed zero as the target, you'll just get the sort of silly thing you get now. Of course, when you come to actual details and a verification system, you've got to face all these problems; and of course you have to have steps along the way. But don't let's say that a target less than the absolute target would be acceptable.[101]

There is no need for hedging about the ultimate destination, which is a nuclear-weapons-free world. To get there, nuclear weapons must be eliminated, prohibited—whatever one's favorite verb may be to convey the absence of even one nuclear bomb—everywhere.

In the past decade, several thoughtful efforts have been made to articulate a feasible and detailed plan for proceeding urgently but safely to a nuclear-weapons-free world. All of them have at their core what John Steinbruner has called "a program of progressive restraint."[102] No one envisions reaching the goal overnight, or next year, or even within a decade. The point is to get serious, and to remain serious, about reducing the size and usability of the U.S. and Russian nuclear arsenals, to allow sufficient time along the way to establish procedures for verification and for confidence-building.

The program of the Canberra Commission on the Elimination of Nuclear Weapons is especially well thought out. The commission envisions a basic four-phase process in reaching a nuclear-weapons-free world:

The Commitment. The basic requirement is "for the five [now seven] declared nuclear weapon states to commit themselves unequivocally to proceed with all deliberate speed to a world without nuclear weapons."[103] In fact, in May 2000, as part of the Non-Proliferation Treaty Review Conference, the five original nuclear powers—which are also the five permanent members of the UN Security Council—agreed to the "unequivocal" elimination of nuclear weapons.[104] But none—and certainly not the United States—has yet made specific plans to fulfill the commitment. Such a commitment, according to the Canberra Commission, can be fulfilled whether or not any other profound changes may occur in the international security environment.

The Immediate U.S.-Russian Program. Most of the world's nuclear weapons reside in the arsenals of the United States and Russia. The Canberra Commission thus recommends that the following program commence immediately: (a) all nuclear forces should be taken off alert; (b) all warheads should be removed from delivery vehicles; (c) all deployments of nonstrategic nuclear weapons should cease; (d) all nuclear testing should cease; (e) negotiations should begin toward further reductions (START-2 and START-3) in the arsenals; and (f) the United States and Russia should sign an agreement of reciprocal no-first-use of nuclear weapons, and of nonuse against nonnuclear weapons states. None of these tasks are simple. But none are impossible, given the requisite commitment of political leaders in Washington and Moscow.[105]

Other Nuclear Weapons States. As the size of the U.S. and Russian arsenals approaches that of the other declared nuclear powers—roughly 100–500—the smaller nuclear powers must participate formally in all agreements and arrangements. The Canberra Commission recommends, in fact, that these nations be brought into the process much earlier, to get comfortable with the proceedings. The commission also suggests that negotiations be extended to all other nuclear nations not later than discussions concerning the reduction of *all*—not just the U.S. and Russian—arsenals to 100 warheads each.[106]

Getting to Zero. The Canberra Commission is particularly concerned that the Non-proliferation Treaty, the Anti-Ballistic Missile Treaty, and other traditional cornerstones of arms control be preserved. It is possible, they say, that a new international legal framework will be necessary, including a comprehensive treaty eliminating and prohibiting nuclear weapons. In any case, the commission also points out that while necessary, the legal framework will not by itself move the process toward a nuclear-weapons-free world. Only political will can make that happen, beginning in Moscow and Washington, but expanding across the globe by the time zero is reached, verified, and ratified by the nations of the world.[107]

A world without nuclear weapons, as envisioned by the Canberra Commission, would in certain respects be a far different one from either the world of the present or that of the past. For example, it was once said that in the late 1970s, more than 95 percent of the relationship between the United States and Soviet Union was tied up in arms control negotiations. That number would move to zero, excluding verification mechanisms. India and Pakistan would surely relate differently. Israel and the Middle East would be quite different. And so on. On the other hand, it is easy to see why we must keep our eye firmly on zero as the required number of nuclear weapons. For a world that will consent to relinquishing its nuclear weapons, and its right to make them, is a world in which many countries are made to feel more secure *without* them than they feel at present *with* them.

And so we return to our original question: If we are able to return to a nuclear-weapons-free world, will it be a better world? While a nuclear-weapons-free world will not be a world without risks, the regime thus established will be more robust, with regard to the ability of fallible human beings to manage the risks without catastrophic failure—without, that is, the risk of the entire planet being blown sky-high. In addition, on the day nuclear deterrence comes to an end, we will truly be able to say, at last, that the Cold War has ended. That would be something to celebrate.[108]

The 21st Century's Nuclear Crisis in Slow Motion

Several decades ago, the Princeton theologian Paul Ramsey made an effort to awaken his fellow Americans to the immorality of nuclear deterrence. He proposed the following analogy to support his case:

Suppose that one Labor Day weekend no one was killed or maimed on the highways; and that the reason for this remarkable restraint placed on the recklessness of drivers was that suddenly everyone of them discovered he was driving with a baby tied to his front bumper! That would be no way to regulate traffic *even if it succeeds* in regulating it perfectly, since such a system makes innocent human lives the *direct object* of attack and uses them as a mere means for restraining the drivers of automobiles.[109]

The political philosopher Michael Walzer, who quotes Ramsey in his own discussion of nuclear deterrence, rejects the analogy for the following reason: "Though deterrence turns American and Russian civilians into a mere means for the prevention of war, it does so without restraining any of us in any way."[110] As Walzer rightly says, "We are hostages who lead normal lives. . . . That is why deterrence, while in principle so frightening, is so easy to live with . . . [and] we have come to live with it casually—as Ramsey's babies, traumatized for life in all probability, could never do, and as hostages in conventional wars have never done."[111]

We may know intellectually that we are hostages, and periodically we may think about it, regret it, become frightened about it, and perhaps even try to do something about it. But most of the time most of us do not, because we are not required to do so by the immediate circumstances of our daily existence. And in this lies the deeply insidious nature of the 21st century's nuclear "crisis in slow motion."[112] Because we are hostages at a distance, we grow apathetic, inattentive to what can and should be done to eliminate our hostage relationship to nuclear weapons. We conveniently forget what could happen.

In the 1960s, the nuclear strategist Herman Kahn speculated on the conditions necessary for returning to a nuclear-weapons-free world. Kahn concluded that following a U.S.-Soviet nuclear war of considerable magnitude, resulting in the greatest single catastrophe in human history, leaders of the nuclear states (assuming they have survived, of course) would have to agree immediately to a pact banning nuclear weapons forever. But Kahn cautioned that they must do so before the living have time to bury the dead. If they do not move this swiftly, mistrust and suspicion, of the sort that doubtless triggered the nuclear war in the first place, will return with a vengeance, and overwhelm the memory of simple horror, which is the only stimulus that might induce mankind to renounce what Bernard Brodie had first called "the ultimate weapon."[113]

Will we continue to sleepwalk into a potential nuclear catastrophe? And will only such a catastrophe serve to move us toward a nuclear-weapons-free world? We hope not. Instead, it is our hope that Wilson's ghost, in its nuclear guise, can be kept at bay until the work is accomplished—until nuclear weapons no longer exist.

Yet we should keep in mind that Wilson failed to convince the United States and the world of the need for a radical solution "if civilization is to escape the typhoon."[114] Can we?

You are betrayed. You fought for something you did not get. And the glories of the armies and the navies of the United States is gone like a dream in the night, and there ensues upon it, in the suitable darkness of the night, the nightmare of dread which lay upon the nations before this war came; and there will come some time, in the vengeful Providence of God, another war, in which not a few hundred thousand . . . will have to die, but . . . many millions. . . .

Woodrow Wilson, speech in St. Louis, September 1919[1]

Wilsonianism did have a starry-eyed side but . . . its image of the world was utterly terrifying.

Frank Ninkovich, 1999[2]

If we cannot learn to accommodate each other respectfully in the twenty-first century, we could destroy each other at such a rate that humanity will have little to cherish.

Carnegie Commission on Preventing Deadly Conflict, 1997[3]

5

Reducing Human Carnage

An Agenda for the 21st Century

This chapter is a kind of "executive summary" of the actions we believe are necessary to prevent the 21st century from becoming as bloody as or even bloodier than the 20th—actions to avoid the killing of another 160 million human beings by violence inflicted by other human beings. It is a radical agenda, even a revolutionary agenda, in that it requires an unprecedented moral commitment to avoid killing, in addition to an equally unprecedented commitment to "zero-tolerance multilateralism." Our agenda consists of three linked arguments, each of which rests on the premise that far too little has been done to ensure that the 21st century is not haunted by Wilson's ghost. First, since the end of the Cold War we have failed to take the necessary steps to prevent Great Power conflict—to bring Russia and China in from the cold. Our message: *Empathy now!* Second, since the end of the Cold War we have failed to enact a credible plan for reducing communal killing. Our message: *Resolve conflict without violence now!* Third, since the end of the Cold War we have failed to move decisively to reduce nuclear danger. Our message: *Radical reductions—and ultimate elimination—beginning now!* This is our call to action.

The Imperatives: Moral and Multilateral

We have written this book in an attempt to address two fundamental questions: (1) Why, in essence, did 160 million people die in violent conflict in the 20th century? and (2) What must be done to prevent the 21st century from becoming as lethal—or worse—than the 20th? We have relied on a historical analogy to enrich and to enlarge on the situation we face today, comparing the challenges of our era to the immediate aftermath of the First World War—especially the implications of Woodrow Wilson's failure to establish international relations on a moral foundation and his failure to anchor it in his multilateral creation, the League of Nations. Wilson's ghost still haunts us, for his failures are also our own failures.

We have argued throughout this book that Wilson's ghost has two fundamental messages for us now, as we confront the 21st century. We have expressed them in the form of two "imperatives":

- *The Moral Imperative.* Establish as a major goal of U.S. foreign policy, and indeed of foreign policies across the globe, the avoidance in the 21st century of the carnage—160 million dead—caused by conflict in the 20th century.

- *The Multilateral Imperative.* Recognize that the United States must provide leadership to achieve the objective of reduced carnage, but, in doing so, it will not apply its economic, political, or military power unilaterally, other than in the unlikely circumstances of a defense of the continental United States, Hawaii and Alaska.

Our emphasis on the moral imperative is driven by two factors: (1) what we believe is the arrogance exhibited by many international relations scholars and practitioners, past and present, in excluding from their professional vocabulary all mention of morality; and (2) our concomitant belief that the carnage of the 20th century has been immoral, by any reasonable definition of "morality." Similarly, our emphasis on the multilateral imperative is driven by our belief that the United States, past and present, has often been arrogantly unilateralist in its approach to the rest of the world, and that unilateralism has contributed to the tragedy of the 20th century.

In short, a U.S. foreign policy that is both insensitive to morality and unilateralist will fail to achieve what should be one of the most basic objectives of any foreign policy, especially the foreign policy of a nation as moralistic as the United States: to prevent the killing of other human beings. To fail in this task is downright dangerous at the outset of the 21st century.

In this brief chapter, we offer a synopsis of what is to be done, based on our analysis of the three issues we have addressed: the prevention of Great Power conflict, especially as regards Russia and China; reducing communal killing; and avoiding nuclear catastrophe. There are no algorithms in this chapter, for the road to hell in foreign policy is often paved with adherence to algorithms and with the unimaginative and thoughtless nature of much that passed for U.S. foreign policy in the 20th century.

What follows are foreign policy positions and measures that build on our moral and multilateral imperatives. In this way, we take seriously the several messages we believed are being conveyed to us across decades of brutal carnage by Wilson's ghost.

Preventing Great Power Conflict: Bringing Russia and China in from the Cold

For much of the 20th century, Russia and China constituted the bulk of what was called in the West the "East bloc"—the communist bloc of nations whose ideology we found noxious, whose international behavior we often found reprehensible, and whose leaders seemed at times bent on world domination. That era is finished. Never in world history has an international alliance of this magnitude disappeared so completely and unexpectedly, yet relatively peacefully, as did the communist bloc at the end of the Cold War.

Russia and China remain nuclear powers with hegemonic ambitions in their respective regions, and they are also deeply suspicious of the West. Both Russia and China seem to have formed the impression that the West, and particularly the United States, still behaves toward them as it did during the Cold War, when it was their sworn enemy.[4] We noted in Chapter Two four common features of the Russian and Chinese view:

- *U.S. "Arrogance."* To Moscow and Beijing, U.S. actions on NATO expansion and Taiwan epitomized an arrogant refusal by the United States to accord Great Power status to any country other than the United States itself.

- *U.S. "Betrayal."* Both the Russians and Chinese interpret U.S. actions as fundamental betrayals of previous U.S. pledges and commitments.

- *U.S. "Threat."* These ostensible betrayals threaten the legitimacy of the Moscow and Beijing governments.

- *U.S. "Flashpoint."* Each issue could become a "flashpoint" in which the current testy relationships explode into dangerous crises. Indeed, we have seen recent evidence of this danger.

As mentioned, we do not claim that these impressions are "true" in any absolute sense. But we do believe that U.S. behavior since the end of the Cold War can be interpreted, not irrationally, as the Russians and Chinese have done.

The *moral* directive as regards bringing Russia and China "in from the cold" is this: Develop a much deeper sense of *empathy* with the stated and implied views of the Russian and Chinese leaders. Do not discount these as propaganda, at least not without a serious analysis. If their views are not credited—if U.S. officials continue to act as if the Russians and Chinese "should" understand that the United States is a benign super-power—things could get out of hand and relations could get caught in a downward spiral that could prove dangerous, even catastrophic.

We also emphasized the *multilateral* corollary: the United States must learn to think more imaginatively about the paths that might lead inad-vertently to conflict with both Russia and China. In particular, we urge that U.S. officials not be limited to considerations of "probable" crises or clashes. Instead, they should consider, as they begin their deliberations, what is *possible*, not just what seems probable at the moment. Few, if any, Great Power wars have developed according to anyone's plan. Most have had important unintended aspects, and it is often that which is unintended that has led to disaster. When the stakes are so high, as they are when Great Powers—now nuclear powers—have strained relations and conflicting interests mixed with misperceptions and misunderstandings, then it pays to examine even scenarios that may seem improbable at the moment.

What is most needed in the West, especially in the United States, is a conceptual shift from deterrence—or even "competition"—to reassurance.[5] Officials from the West must be especially concerned not to discount as fake or ephemeral the outbursts of nationalism—what Isaiah Berlin called the "inflamed desire of the insufficiently regarded to count for something among the cultures of the world"—which potentially contain the seeds of conflict.[6] In emphasizing the importance of empathy and inadvertent paths to possible conflict, we emphatically warn those who may wish to approach the Russians and Chinese in the roles of oblivious victors, complacent rationalists, or pugnacious realists that these views are counterproductive and uninformed about the true nature of the issues now dividing Russia and China from the West.

Reducing Communal Killing: Intervention in "Dangerous, Troubled, Failed, Murderous States"

In Chapter Three, we asserted that self-determination was Woodrow Wilson's dream but our nightmare. In the euphoria of the immediate aftermath of the First World War, Wilson incautiously declared on several occasions that the right of national self-determination is an inalienable right of all "peoples." Taking Wilson at his word, from that day to our own, "nations" have declared themselves sovereign states, or declared the intention to make such a declaration, in great numbers. This has been the greatest single contributor to the periodic outbreak of communal violence and killing throughout the 20th century: the intention to secede, conquer, or expand in the name of self-determination of "peoples." But what is a "people"? Who adjudicates competing, often incompatible, claims to statehood made by different "peoples"? Wilson's inability to resolve this issue led to communal conflict on a wide scale in his own day in the Balkans, in Africa, and elsewhere, sowing the seeds of continuing ethnic tension.

The key questions to be faced by the international community, represented by the United Nations, are concerned with *intervention* to stop (or prevent) communal killing: when, how, with whom, and for what objective? In deciding to intervene, leaders must confront what the political philosopher Thomas Nagel calls "moral blind alleys"—situations that may not have a morally satisfactory solution, and thus for which intervention may exacerbate, rather than ameliorate, instances of communal violence and killing.[7] The Protestant theologian Reinhold Niebuhr put it another way: "How much evil must we do in order to do good?"[8] Posing the question in this way will be painful at times, because *not* to intervene will seem to many like an endorsement of the killing that is in progress. It need not be. It may rather be an honest acknowledgment of the limitations on the international community to intervene successfully in these sorts of conflicts. As difficult as it is to accept, we may have to admit that at times some of these conflicts have no solution, at least no solution achievable by the application of external military force.

Our multilateral corollary we call "zero-tolerance multilateralism." This means that in no case should the United States intervene on its own: via a unilateral decision, using U.S. forces, for U.S. motives alone, and on behalf of U.S. interests, without consultation with others who have similar values and interests, and some capacity to participate constructively in the decision of whether to intervene and in the intervention itself. Arguments can be made, and often are made, by human rights activists that in cases such as Bosnia and Rwanda, the United States must be the "unilateral last resort." But even in these instances, if the United States cannot convince others of the need to intervene, and thus is unable to demonstrate to others that the intervention will probably accomplish whatever its objective may be, it should not intervene unilaterally.

All significant interventions to stop communal killing will have difficult problems to overcome if they are to succeed. Among the most difficult and pervasive are: (1) dealing with the longstanding bias in favor of state sovereignty, for interventions will nearly always involve, to one degree or another, a failed state; (2) assuring popular support for the intervention in the countries that make up the coalition that is intervening, by appealing to common human values (a foundation for support that is often difficult to sustain, especially if things go wrong); (3) assembling coalitions quickly and acting decisively, two attributes one seldom finds in international coalitions of any kind; (4) recognizing that the ferocity and extent of the killing will be shocking to outsiders, and will act as a brake on the enthusiasm of many for intervening; and (5) avoiding what Michael Ignatieff has called "the seductiveness of moral disgust"—the tendency, before, during, or after an intervention to lapse into the point of view that, if warring ethnic or religious groups really want to destroy one another, then maybe they should just be permitted to do it and get it over with.[9] During the Cold War, it was seldom necessary to confront such problems directly. Now they have become the central issues for those contemplating an intervention with the objective of stopping communal killing.

Avoiding Nuclear Catastrophe: Moving Steadily and Safely to a Nuclear-Weapons–Free World

The risk of nuclear catastrophe continues to threaten our planet, and our view of what is to be done with nuclear weapons is simple: "Say no to nuclear weapons, arms races, and nuclear danger." With the Cold War over, nuclear weapons can and must now be eliminated. This is the safe and sensible way forward, rather than trying—as many in the United States urge yet again—to construct a defensive "shield" over the United States to protect against nuclear missiles of adversaries or rogue states.

In moving in the direction of a nuclear-weapons-free world, we are particularly impressed by the approach taken in the *Report of the Canberra Commission on the Elimination of Nuclear Weapons* (1996).[10] Its essential elements are as follows:

The Commitment. The political will must be found to undertake a process of radical, rapid denuclearization leading ultimately to the elimination of nuclear weapons. The United States must lead the way in this effort.

The Immediate U.S.-Russian Program. Momentum must be established first between the United States and Russia to: (a) resume serious discussions about further cuts in nuclear arms until the number of weapons, now in the thousands, can be reduced to roughly the number held by China, France, and Britain—around 500 or so; and (b) reduce the risk of use of nuclear weapons in the interim by a series of actions, including de-alerting those still in existence.

Other Nuclear Weapons States. Once the United States and Russia have only about 500 or so weapons, multilateral talks should begin working toward zero nuclear weapons on all sides.

Getting to Zero. The negotiations should include immediate discussion of a verification regime far more transparent than any now in existence, to prevent possible effects of cheating and breakout. We believe that problems along these lines can be solved if the states involved really want to solve them.

Will We Tend to the Details in Time?

As Woodrow Wilson looked out on the 20th century, in 1919, he saw a terrifying specter of unprecedented war, chaos, killing, and destruction. Skeptics believed that Wilson argued the truth of this vision only to raise the odds of getting the League of Nations approved as a kind of first installment on what they took to be the supremely idealistic idea of world government. Wilson, for his part, often said that he was a realist, not a starry-eyed idealist. Wilson was right about the 20th century; his predictions about it were tragically correct.

We are of the first generation of the human race that conceivably can destroy human civilization quickly and completely, and we have attempted to provide an outline of the issues needing urgent attention if the 21st century is not to exceed the 20th in horror. The actions recommended in this book can be accomplished if we set out to do so. But the first step is to stimulate public debate—of which there has been very little—on the problems and possible solutions.

Sometimes people call me an idealist. Well, that is the way I know that I am an American. America is the only idealistic nation in the world.

Woodrow Wilson, September 8, 1919[1]

Wilson was not merely a dreamer, but a man, who found moral reasons, as he said, for "leading others into our ways of thinking and enlisting them in our purposes." He has never been more relevant.

Ronald Steel, 2000[2]

Listening to Wilson's Ghost

THE BRITISH HISTORIAN and philosopher R. G. Collingwood wrote in his autobiography: "The chief business of twentieth-century philosophy is to reckon with twentieth-century history."[3] But how do we "reckon" with a century in which human beings killed 160 million other human beings in violent conflict? How do we explain that? And if we believe we have some semblance of understanding as to why the century was such an uninterrupted, man-made tragedy, how can we transform such an understanding into lessons we can apply in the 21st century? Is such an undertaking even feasible? Or is just wishful thinking to believe that we can actually learn enough? Much seems to be at stake, for human beings now have the capacity to kill one another much more efficiently and much more rapidly than was the case throughout much of the 20th century. Not only *must* find a way to reduce the risk of conflict, killing, and catastrophe, but we *can* find a way.

But can we really? Some believe the problem is primarily psychological, or perhaps biological. That is, in order to significantly reduce such risks, human nature will have to change. And while gene research continues to unravel the genetic code, the transformation of Homo sapiens into a pacific creature seems a bit too far in the future to be relevant. Others believe the problem is political. That is, until a fully functioning world government is in place, we should not expect to reduce these risks much, if at all. Still others take the view that runaway technology is the culprit. But what can be done to reverse the course of technology, and who would even want to do such a thing, should it be possible? The advance of technology, after all, has given many of us longer, easier, more fulfilling lives.

All of these views lead to skepticism regarding our ability to change the course of our own history in the one very basic way that is the focus of this book: by reducing the killing of human beings by other human beings. Yet the skeptics are left, as we see it, with this choice: Either become fatalists who believe that we are set on a course on which we could, as the Carnegie Commission stated, "destroy each other at such a rate that humanity will have little to cherish"; or become pollyannas who deny that the danger exists. Both views evince powerlessness. It is remarkable how many people appear to hold a view that seems to run counter to all available evidence. We can learn from the past, and we do so all the time.

We believe, contrary to the skeptics, that the past can be made to yield lessons that are relevant to the future. We have devoted much of the past 15 years of our lives to studying conflict in the 20th century, delving in particular into the histories of the Cuban missile crisis and of the Vietnam war in search of lessons that, if learned and applied, can help us reduce the risk of making the kind of mistakes that took the world to the brink of nuclear war in October 1962, or that led to the tragedy of the war in Vietnam.[4] We are convinced, moreover, that the lessons we have drawn are both valid and valuable. But while we assert the possibility of learning and applying such lessons, we cannot prove our case to those who refuse to consider it.

For such people, we extend the following invitation: *Listen carefully, and with an open mind, to Wilson's ghost.* Listen for hints as to how we might avoid future conflicts between Great Powers, from one who saw the problem on the horizon in 1919, but failed to implement action that might have prevented it. Listen, too, to Wilson's voice of experience—of he who inadvertently set the 20th century on its chaotic and violent course of communal killing, by failing to grapple successfully with problems of self-determination and ethnic and religious conflict. And listen, finally, to the message of one who saw indistinctly but powerfully the possibility that civilization itself might be gravely damaged in some future war. Listen to Wilson's ghost in its various guises and ask yourself whether it is speaking to you, to your epoch, to your dangers. Ask yourself whether you hear its voice, echoing down the decades at you, amplified by events Wilson sensed might occur, but which he did not live to experience.

And if its fateful encounters with conflict, killing, and catastrophe resonate with your analysis of the situation we face in the 21st century, then listen further to what we take to be its two principal lessons: first, that we must seek to build a foreign policy on a foundation of basic morality, asking at every juncture how we might reduce the number of people who could conceivably be killed because of our decisions, our policies; and second, that in international affairs, very little good is possible in the long run from unilateral action by any Great Powers—including the United States—but much can be done multilaterally to ameliorate the conditions that lead to mistrust in international affairs, thence to conflict. We think that if you listen hard, and with an open mind, there is much to learn. Does this make us idealists? Only in the sense that Wilson was an idealist: He believed in the power of human beings to change the course of their history for the better. As Ronald Steel has recently written, while Wilson may have been an idealist, he was no dreamer. He was a doer.[5]

So we return to Collingwood's exhortation: to "reckon" somehow with the 20th century. In the end, we must return to what we believe are basic human values in any attempt at reckoning with 160 million people killed in violent conflict. In the end, we must ask ourselves, for what purpose did so many die? Was it just meaningless? If not, what was the meaning of it? We like the American poet Archibald MacLeish's answer:

> *They say: Our deaths are not ours; they are yours; they*
> *will mean what you make them.*
> *They say: Whether our lives and our deaths were for peace*
> *and a new hope or for nothing we cannot say; it is*
> *you who must say this.*
> *They say: We leave you our deaths. Give them their*
> *meaning. . . .*[6]

Don't we have a responsibility to redeem, in some measure, the lives of those who died violently in the 20th century? And how do we discharge our responsibility, if not to learn the lessons of past generations, and apply them to a future that will be not only ours, but that of the yet unborn?

NOTES

Book Epigraphs

1. Woodrow Wilson, quoted in Frank Ninkovich, *The Wilsonian Century: American Foreign Policy Since 1900* (Chicago: University of Chicago Press, 1999), p. 72 (emphasis added).
2. Ninkovich, *Wilsonian Century*, pp. 48–49.

Prologue

1. Woodrow Wilson, speech to a plenary session of the Paris Peace Conference, February 14, 1919. Quoted in Herbert Hoover, *The Ordeal of Woodrow Wilson* (Washington, DC: Woodrow Wilson Center Press, 1992; first published in 1958), pp. 185–186.
2. Ibid., pp. 300, 303.
3. Woodrow Wilson, speech in Sioux Falls, South Dakota, September 8, 1919. Quoted in ibid., p. ix.
4. A policy-oriented but still fundamentally historical approach to Wilson and some of the events alluded to in this book may be found in Robert A. Pastor, ed., *A Century's Journey: How the Great Powers Shape the World* (New York: Basic Books, 1999). See especially two of the chapters written by Pastor: Chapter Six, "The Great Powers in the Twentieth Century: From Dawn to Dusk"; and Chapter Nine, "Looking Back and Forward: The Trajectories of the Great Powers."
5. See Chapter One of this book for details on casualty figures.
6. Senator Frank Brandegee (R-Conn.), quoted in Walter A. McDougall, *Promised Land, Crusader State: The American Encounter with the World Since 1776* (Boston: Houghton Mifflin, 1997), p. 141.
7. David Lloyd George, quoted in Hoover, *Ordeal of Woodrow Wilson*, p. 254.
8. Article X of the Covenant of the League of Nations. Quoted in ibid., p. 266.
9. Woodrow Wilson, testimony before the Senate Foreign Relations Committee, August 20, 1919. Quoted in ibid., p. 266.
10. Woodrow Wilson, quoted in ibid., p. 74.
11. Redraft of Article X of the Covenant of the League of Nations, by Sen. Henry Cabot Lodge (R-Mass.), with assistance from Sen. Porter J. McCumber, August 1919. Quoted in Louis Auchincloss, *Woodrow Wilson* (New York: Viking Penguin, 2000), p. 115.
12. Woodrow Wilson, quoted in Ninkovich, *Wilsonian Century*, p. 75.
13. Woodrow Wilson, quoted in Auchincloss, *Woodrow Wilson*, p. 116.

14. See Niall Ferguson, *The Pity of War: Explaining World War I*, pp. 458–462, for an analysis of what might have happened if Germany had won a very different war, one in which Britain and the United States did not participate. Ferguson speculates that something like a German-led European Union might have developed, with Hitler becoming a mediocre postcard painter in Vienna.

15. George F. Kennan, quoted in Arthur S. Link, "The Higher Realism of Woodrow Wilson." In Cathal J. Nolan, ed., *Ethics and Statecraft: The Moral Dimension of International Affairs* (Westport, CT: Praeger, 1995), pp. 95–107, p. 106.

16. See Ninkovich, *Wilsonian Century,* pp. 48–77.

17. The phrase comes from McGeorge Bundy, *Danger and Survival: Choices About the Bomb in the First Fifty Years* (New York: Random House, 1988), p. 462.

18. See Thomas J. Knock, *To End All Wars: Woodrow Wilson and the Quest for a New World Order* (New York: Oxford, 1992), pp. 3–14 and 246–276.

19. John Keegan, *The First World War* (New York: Knopf, 1998), p. 3.

20. See James G. Blight and David A. Welch, *On the Brink: Americans and Soviets Reexamine the Cuban Missile Crisis,* rev. ed. (New York: Hill and Wang, 1990).

21. Hoover, *Ordeal of Woodrow Wilson,* pp. 300, 303.

22. Robert Conquest, *Reflections on a Ravaged Century* (New York: Norton, 2000).

23. George F. Kennan, "The War to End War," *New York Times,* November 11, 1984. Reprinted in Kennan, *At a Century's Ending: Reflections, 1982–1995* (New York: Norton, 1996), pp. 17–19. The passage quoted is on pp. 17 and 19.

Chapter One: A Radical Agenda

1. Woodrow Wilson, speech to the U.S. Senate, July 10, 1919. Quoted in John Morton Blum, *Woodrow Wilson and the Politics of Morality* (New York: HarperCollins, 1956), p. 181.

2. Stanley Hoffmann, *World Disorders: Troubled Peace in the Post-Cold War Era* (Lanham, MD: Rowman & Littlefield, 1998), pp. 77–78.

3. George Bush, speech to the United Nations, October 1, 1990. Quoted in Henry Kissinger, *Diplomacy* (New York: Simon & Schuster, 1994), p. 805.

4. Bill Clinton, speech to the United Nations, September 27, 1993. Quoted in ibid., p. 805.

5. Niall Ferguson, *The Pity of War: Explaining World War I* (New York: Basic Books, 1999), p. 462.

6. Norman Angell, *The Great Illusion* (1910). Quoted in Ferguson, *Pity of War,* p. 21.

7. Angell, *Great Illusion.* Quoted in ibid., p. 22.

8. Angell, *Great Illusion.* Quoted in John Keegan, *The First World War* (New York: Knopf, 1999), p. 10.

9. David Starr Jordan, in *New York World,* December 13, 1910. Quoted in Joseph S. Nye, Jr., *Understanding International Conflicts,* 2nd ed. (New York: Longman, 1997), p. 5.

10. William James, "The Moral Equivalent of War." In Bruce Kuklick, ed., *The Library of America Edition of the Writings of William James, 1902–1910* (New York: Literary Classics, 1987), pp. 1281–1293, p. 1281.

11. Dan Smith, ed., *The State of War and Peace Atlas,* 3rd ed. (New York: Penguin, 1997), p. 100.

12. Ibid., p. 13.

13. Frank Whelon Waymon, J. David Singer, and Meredith Sarkees, "Interstate, Intrastate, and Extra-Systemic Wars 1816–1995." Paper presented at the annual meeting of the International Studies Association, April 1996, Table 1, p. 10. Cited in Graham Allison and Hisashi Owada, "The Responsibilities of Democracies in Preventing Deadly Conflict: Reflections and Recommendations," a discussion paper of the Carnegie Commission on Preventing Deadly Conflict, July 1999, p. 32.

14. Ruth Leger Sivard, *World Military and Social Expenditures 1996* (Washington, DC: World Priorities, 1996), p. 7. Quoted in John D. Steinbruner, *Principles of Global Security* (Washington, DC: Brookings, 2000), p. 232.

15. Sivard, *World Military and Social Expenditures 1996,* p. 7. Quoted Steinbruner, *Principles of Global Security,* p. 232. This number is also used by Allison and Owada, "Responsibilities of Democracies," p. 34.

16. Lewis H. Lapham, "War Movie," *Harper's Magazine* (July, 1999), pp. 12–15, p. 12.

17. Smith, *State of War and Peace,* p. 14.

18. Josef Joffe, "The Worst of Times," *New York Times Book Review,* November 21, 1999, p. 22.

19. As of 1996, the official death toll from the bombing of Hiroshima was 197,045. The official death toll of the Nagasaki bombing, also by 1996, was 108,039. See Charles J. Moxley, Jr., *Nuclear Weapons and International Law in the Post–Cold War World* (Lanham, MD: Austin & Winfield, 2000), p. 433. Moxley cites official Japanese government figures published on the 50th anniversary of the bombings.

20. Carnegie Commission on Preventing Deadly Conflict, *Preventing Deadly Conflict: Final Report with Executive Summary* (Washington, DC: Carnegie Commission, 1997), p. 13.

21. "Catastrophe in Congo," editorial in the *International Herald Tribune,* June 26, 2000, p. 8.

22. Arnold Isaacs, *Vietnam Shadows: The War, Its Ghosts and Its Legacy* (Baltimore: Johns Hopkins University Press, 1997), p. 157.

23. William Styron, *Sophie's Choice* (New York: Bantam, 1979), p. 589.

24. Dante Alghieri, *Inferno,* trans. by James Nachtwey (New York: Hyperion, 2000).

25. Immanuel Kant, *The Critique of Practical Reason,* trans. by Thomas Kingsmill Abbott (Chicago: Encyclopedia Britannica, 1952).

26. *Preventing Deadly Conflict: Final Report with Executive Summary,* p. xii. The membership of the Commission included, for example, Gro Harlem Brundtland (former prime minister of Norway); David Owen (former foreign minister of Great Britain); Garreth Evans (the Australian foreign minister); and Sir Brian Urquhart (former undersecretary general of the United Nations).

27. Robert S. McNamara, James G. Blight, and Robert K. Brigham, with contributions by Thomas J. Biersteker and Col. Herbert Y. Schandler, *Argument Without End: In Search of Answers to the Vietnam Tragedy* (New York: PublicAffairs, 1999), pp. 396–397.

28. Ibid., Chapter 5, "Escalation," pp. 151–217.

29. United Nations demographers estimate that the world population grew from approx-

imately 2.3 billion in 1945 to approximately 6 billion by the end of the 20th century. In 1982, they predicted that the world's population would reach 10.2 billion by the end of the 21st century, with an essentially zero growth rate. They also predict that 94 percent of population growth in the 21st century will occur in the poorest countries. See Commission on Global Governance, *Our Global Neighborhood* (New York: Oxford University Press, 1998), pp. 27–28, 139.

30. Smith, *State of War and Peace,* p. 13. See also pp. 90–95, "Table of Wars, 1990–1995."

31. Ibid., pp. 14–15.

32. Robert D. Kaplan, "The Coming Anarchy," *Atlantic Monthly,* February 1994.

33. Robert D. Kaplan, *The Ends of the Earth: A Journey to the Frontiers of Anarchy* (New York: Vintage, 1996), p. 4.

34. Ibid., p. 3.

35. Ibid., p. 8.

36. Ibid., p. 436 (emphasis in the original).

37. Ibid., p. 437.

38. Michael Ignatieff, *The Warrior's Honor: Ethnic War and the Modern Conscience* (New York: Metropolitan, 1997), p. 108.

39. Ibid., p. 108.

40. Kant, *Critique of Practical Reason,* p. 348.

41. Immanuel Kant, *Fundamental Principles of the Metaphysic of Morals,* trans. by Thomas Kingsmill Abbott (Chicago: Encyclopedia Britannica, 1952), p. 260 (emphasis in the original).

42. Ibid., p. 260.

43. At the time, Robert McNamara was a lieutenant colonel assigned to the 20th Air Force, which dropped the nuclear bombs on Japan. A few months earlier, in March 1945, he had been on the island of Guam when B-29 bombers of the 20th Bomber Command, headquartered on Guam, fire-bombed Tokyo, burning to death 80,000 human beings—almost all civilians—in a single night.

44. St. Augustine, quoted in United States Conference of Catholic Bishops, *The Harvest of Justice Is Sown in Peace* (Washington, DC: U.S. Catholic Conference, 1993), p. 16.

45. Michael Sandel, editorial in *New York Times,* December 31, 1989.

46. Kissinger, *Diplomacy,* p. 810.

47. Ibid., p. 805.

48. Ibid., pp. 810–811.

49. Carl Kaysen, "Is War Obsolete," *International Security,* Vol. 14, No. 4 (Spring 1990), pp. 441–463, p. 462.

50. These and similar maxims are cited, with reference to the original sources, in Jonathan Granoff, "Nuclear Weapons, Ethics, Morals and Law," *Brigham Young University Law Review,* 2000, pp. 1413–1442, pp. 1421–1422.

51. Hans Küng, "The Principles of a Global Ethic." In Küng, ed., *Yes to a Global Ethic* (New York: Continuum, 1996), pp. 12–26. Cited in *Preventing Deadly Conflict: Final Report with Executive Summary,* p. 118.

52. Alexander Hamilton, quoted in Stanley Hoffmann, *Duties Beyond Borders: On the Limits and Possibilities of Ethical International Politics* (Syracuse, NY: Syracuse University Press, 1982), p. 18.

53. Niccolò Machiavelli, *The Prince.* Quoted in Hoffmann, *Duties Beyond Borders,* p. 24.

54. The phrases are Stanley Hoffmann's: See *Duties Beyond Borders,* p. 25 ("philosophy of emergency"); and p. 36 ("philosophy of public safety").

55. Reinhold Niebuhr, "The Children of Light and the Children of Darkness." In Robert McAfee Brown, ed., *The Essential Reinhold Niebuhr: Selected Essays and Addresses* (New Haven, CT: Yale University Press, 1986), pp. 160–181, 165.

56. Ibid., p. 165.

57. Ibid., p. 166.

58. Ibid.

59. Ibid., p. 181.

60. Robert S. McNamara, *In Retrospect: The Tragedy and Lessons of Vietnam,* rev. ed. (New York: Vintage, 1996), p. 216.

61. Ibid., p. 217.

62. McNamara et al., *Argument Without End,* pp. 292–301.

63. By the end of 1967, there were 15,979 Americans and several hundred thousand Vietnamese killed in the war. By January 1973, when the Paris Peace Accords were signed and the United States officially withdrew from the war, 59,191 Americans had been killed in action. See McNamara, *In Retrospect,* , p. 321; see also Maurice Isserman, *Witness to War in Vietnam* (New York: Perigree, 1995), pp. 114–146.

64. See Ibid., chapters 3–6.

65. Hoffmann, *Duties Beyond Borders,* p. 26.

66. Ibid., p. 41.

67. See James G. Blight and David A. Welch, *On the Brink: Americans and Soviets Reexamine the Cuban Missile Crisis,* rev. ed. (New York: Hill & Wang, 1990); and James G. Blight, Bruce J. Allyn, and David A. Welch, *Cuba on the Brink: Castro, the Missile Crisis and the Soviet Collapse* (New York: Pantheon, 1993).

68. Ibid., p. 143.

69. Ernest R. May and Philip D. Zelikow, eds., *The Kennedy Tapes: Inside the White House During the Cuban Missile Crisis* (Cambridge, MA: Harvard University Press, 1997), p. 149.

70. Ibid., p. 233–34.

71. Robert F. Kennedy, *Thirteen Days: A Memoir of the Cuban Missile Crisis,* afterword by Richard E. Neustadt and Graham T. Allison (New York: Norton, 1971), p. 106. This passage is contained in a note added to the text by its editor, Kennedy White House special assistant Theodore C. Sorensen.

72. McGeorge Bundy, *Danger and Survival: Choices About the Bomb in the First Fifty Years* (New York: Random House, 1988), p. 457.

73. Hoffmann, *Duties Beyond Borders,* p. 43.

74. Raymond Robins, quoted in H. W. Brands, *What America Owes the World: The Struggle for the Soul of Foreign Policy* (New York: Cambridge University Press, 1998), p. 245.

75. Madeleine K. Albright, quoted in Samuel P. Huntington, "The Lonely Superpower," *Foreign Affairs,* Vol. 78, No. 2 (March/April, 1999), p. 37.

76. Strobe Talbott, quoted in ibid., p. 38 (emphases are Talbott's).

77. Ibid.

78. Ibid.

79. John Lewis Gaddis, *The United States and the End of the Cold War* (New York: Oxford, 1992), p. 208.

80. David E. Sanger, "All Pumped Up and Nowhere to Go," *New York Times,* July 9, 2000, section 4, pp. 1, 5.

81. Ibid., pp. 42–3.

82. George W. Ball, *The Past Has Another Pattern: Memoirs* (New York: Norton, 1982), p. 378.

83. Arthur Schlesinger, Jr., quoted in Gaddis, *The United States and the End of the Cold War,* p. 47.

84. Richard N. Haass, "What to Do with American Primacy," *Foreign Affairs,* Vol. 78, No. 5 (September/October 1999), pp. 37–49.

85. Hoffmann, *World Disorders,* pp. 77–8.

86. Woodrow Wilson, Speech to the U.S. Senate, July 10, 1919. Quoted in Blum, *Woodrow Wilson and the Politics of Morality,* p. 181.

Chapter 2: Preventing Great Power Conflict

1. Woodrow Wilson, cable to Col. Edward House (Paris), October 29, 1918. Quoted in Herbert Hoover, *The Ordeal of Woodrow Wilson* (Washington, DC: Wilson Center Press, 1992), p. 40. (Originally published in 1958.)

2. George F. Kennan, "The New Russia as a Neighbor," in *At a Century's Ending* (New York: Norton, 1996), pp. 320–333, p. 333.

3. Sam Nunn, "Address to the American Assembly." In Ezra F. Vogel, ed., *Living with China: U.S.-Chinese Relations in the Twenty-first Century* (New York: Norton, 1997), pp. 277–287, p. 287.

4. Woodrow Wilson, quoted in Frank Ninkovich, *The Wilsonian Century: U.S. Foreign Policy since 1900* (Chicago: University of Chicago Press, 1999), p. 75.

5. This account follows the fine narrative of Donald Kagan in his *On the Origins of War and the Preservation of Peace* (New York: Doubleday, 1995), pp. 281–297.

6. Ibid., p. 285.

7. Ibid., p. 288.

8. Ibid., p. 297.

9. Ralph K. White, *Fearful Warriors: A Psychological Profile of U.S.-Soviet Relations* (New York: Free Press, 1984), p. 160.

10. Ibid., p. 161, emphasis in the original.

11. Ibid., pp. 162–163.

12. Robert S. McNamara, James G. Blight, and Robert K. Brigham, with contributions by Thomas Biersteker and Col. Herbert Schandler, *Argument Without End: In Search of Answers to the Vietnam Tragedy* (New York: PublicAffairs, 1999), pp. 40–57.

13. McGeorge Bundy, transcriber, and James G. Blight, editor, "October 27, 1962: Transcripts of the Meetings of the EXCOMM," *International Security,* Vol. 12, No. 3 (Winter 1987/88), pp. 30–92, 59.

14. Ibid., p. 31.

15. Isaiah Berlin, quoted in Michael Ignatieff, "The Ends of Empathy," *The New Republic,*

April 29, 1991, pp. 31–37, 33–34. See also Isaiah Berlin's classic essay on the significance of empathy, "Herder and the Enlightenment," in Henry Hardy and Roger Hausheer, eds., *The Proper Study of Mankind: An Anthology of Essays by Isaiah Berlin* (New York: Farrar, Straus, and Giroux, 1998), pp. 359–435, especially pp. 389–405.

16. Michael Ignatieff, *The Warrior's Honor: Ethnic War and the Modern Conscience* (New York: Metropolitan Books, 1997), p. 60.

17. Woodrow Wilson, quoted in Hoover, *Ordeal of Woodrow Wilson,* p. 20.

18. Thomas C. Schelling, *Arms and Influence* (New Haven, CT: Yale University Press, 1966), p. 109.

19. Ibid., pp. 121–122.

20. Richard E. Neustadt and Graham T. Allison, "Afterword" to Robert F. Kennedy, *Thirteen Days: A Memoir of the Cuban Missile Crisis* (New York: Norton, 1971), pp. 107–150, p. 118 (emphasis added).

21. Ibid., p. 112.

22. John F. Kennedy, "Statement on Cuba, September 4, 1962." In David L. Larsen, *The "Cuban Crisis" of 1962: Selected Documents, Chronology and Bibliography,* 2nd ed. (Lanham, MD: University Press of America, 1988), pp. 17–18, p. 17.

23. Bundy and Blight, "October 27, 1962," pp. 74–75 (all emphases in the original).

24. Sergei Khrushchev, now a U.S. citizen and a research fellow at Brown University's Watson Institute for International Studies, has discussed this with us on many occasions.

25. Robert S. McNamara, *In Retrospect: The Tragedy and Lessons of Vietnam,* rev. ed. (New York: Vintage, 1996), p. 203.

26. See McNamara et al., *Argument Without End,* pp. 396–397, for a discussion of "crises in slow motion."

27. John D. Steinbruner, *Principles of Global Security* (Washington, DC: Brookings, 2000), p. 196.

28. Ibid., pp. 197–198.

29. Ibid., p. 198.

30. Reported in *The New York Times,* September 3, 2000, p. 1.

31. Boris N. Yeltsin, statement of December 5, 1994 in Budapest, at a meeting of the Conference on Security and Cooperation in Europe (CSCE)—now the Organization of Security and Cooperation in Europe (OSCE). Quoted in William G. Hyland, *Clinton's World: Remaking American Foreign Policy* (Westport, CT: Praeger, 1999), p. 99.

32. Steinbruner, *Principles of Global Security,* p. 212.

33. Strobe Talbott, "The Crooked Timber: A Carpenter's Perspective." A speech given at All Souls College, Oxford University, January 21, 2000, p. 9. (Manuscript available from the author.)

34. Michael R. Beschloss and Strobe Talbott, *At the Highest Levels: The Inside Story of the End of the Cold War* (Boston: Little, Brown, 1993), pp. 185–186 (emphasis added).

35. Baker's own account of the discussions with Gorbachev does not contradict the account by Beschloss and Talbott. Baker says that Gorbachev told him pointedly that "certainly, any extension of NATO is unacceptable." At the same meeting, Soviet Foreign Minister Eduard Shevardnadze told Baker that German "unification does raise the question of whether NATO is going to exist as it has," prompting Baker to comment: "Both of them seemed to envision a Europe in which CSCE was strengthened

and NATO and the Warsaw Pact just faded away or melded into one another." See James A. Baker, III, with Thomas M. DeFrank, *The Politics of Diplomacy: Revolution, War & Peace, 1989–1992* (New York: Putnam, 1995), p. 235. Strange though this may have seemed to Baker, it does seem to have been the view of the Soviet leadership. After all, NATO was formed to oppose Soviet expansion. The Soviet Union and Warsaw Pact were dissolving. So, to the Soviets, why wouldn't NATO also dissolve?

36. Sergey Rogov, "The Challenges to Russia's Foreign Policy." In Michael Mandelbaum, ed., *U.S.-Russia Relations* (Washington, DC: Aspen Institute, 1999), pp. 11–19, p. 14.

37. Charles Krauthammer, April 17, 1998. Quoted in Hyland, *Clinton's World,* p. 104.

38. Sen. Dale Bumpers, April 29, 1998. Quoted in ibid.

39. *New York Times* editorial, April 29, 1994. Quoted in ibid.

40. Celeste Wallander, "Russian Foreign Policy in the Wake of the Kosovo Crisis." In Mandelbaum, ed., *U.S.-Russia Relations,* pp. 5–10, p. 6.

41. Ibid., p. 7.

42. Ibid.

43. Marshall Igor Sergeev, in *Krasnaya Zvezda,* July 10, 1999, trans. by Svetlana Savranskaya.

44. Vladimir Putin, quoted in William Pfaff, "Nothing Very Romantic About Putin's Nationalism," *International Herald Tribune,* February 28, 2000, p. 10.

45. Daniel Williams, "Russia to Rebuild Conventional Forces," *International Herald Tribune,* August 14, 2000, pp. 1, 6.

46. Leonid Ivashov, quoted in *Krasnaya Zvezda,* October 27, 1999 (trans. by Svetlana Savranskaya).

47. Vladimir Putin, *First Person,* trans. by Catherine A. Fitzpatrick (New York: PublicAffairs, 2000), pp. 174–177. (Four interviews with Nataliya Gevorkyan, Natalya Timakova, and Andrei Kolesnikov.)

48. Sir Isaiah Berlin, quoted in Pfaff, "Nothing Very Romantic About Putin's Nationalism," p. 10.

49. Rogov, "Challenges to Russia's Foreign Policy," p. 16.

50. Samuel P. Huntington, *The Clash of Civilizations and the Remaking of World Order* (New York: Simon & Schuster, 1996), pp. 183–206.

51. Jack F. Matlock, Jr., "Russia and the CIS." In David L. Boren and Edward J. Perkins, eds., *Preparing America's Foreign Policy for the 21st Century* (Norman: University of Oklahoma Press, 1999), pp. 25–29, p. 26.

52. George F. Kennan, quoted in James M. Goldgeier, "The U.S. Decision to Enlarge NATO: How, When, Why, and What Next?" *Brookings Review,* Vol. 17, No. 3 (Summer 1999), pp. 18–21, p. 18.

53. George F. Kennan, "The New Russia as a Neighbor." In *At a Century's Ending* (New York: Norton, 1996), pp. 320–333, p. 330.

54. Ibid., p. 330.

55. Steinbruner, *Principles of Global Security,* p. 214.

56. For accounts of the 1995–1996 Taiwan crisis, see Richard Bernstein and Ross H. Munro, *The Coming Conflict with China* (New York: Vintage, 1998), pp. 152–157; and Patrick Tyler, *A Great Wall: Six Presidents and China, An Investigative History* (New York: PublicAffairs, 1999), pp. 5–17.

57. Ashton B. Carter and William J. Perry, *Preventive Defense: A New Security Strategy for America* (Washington, DC: Brookings, 1999), p. 99.

58. Li Peng, quoted in Bernstein and Munro, *The Coming Conflict with China,* p. 154.

59. See Ibid., p. 153.

60. Carter and Perry, *Preventive Defense,* pp. 106–107.

61. See Tyler, *A Great Wall,* p. 7.

62. Ibid., p. 6.

63. James A. Kelly, "What Is Beijing's Policy Paper Trying to Convey?" *International Herald Tribune,* March 13, 2000, p. 8.

64. Elisabeth Rosenthal, "China Stiffens Warning to Taiwan." *International Herald Tribune,* March 16, 2000, pp. 1, 6, p. 6.

65. Ibid., pp. 1, 6.

66. Joseph Fitchett, "Europe Fears Fallout From Taiwan Tensions." *International Herald Tribune,* March 17, 2000, pp. 1, 4.

67. Li Daoyu, "The View From China." In Boren and Perkins, *Preparing America's Foreign Policy for the 21st Century,* pp. 43–48, p. 47.

68. Steinbruner, *Principles of Global Security,* p. 218.

69. Text of the Shanghai Communiqué quoted in Tyler, *A Great Wall,* p. 142.

70. Text of the Taiwan Relations Act quoted in ibid., p. 6.

71. Henry Kissinger, quoted in Bernstein and Ross, *The Coming Conflict with China,* p. 151.

72. Ibid.

73. Wang Jisi, quoted in Tyler, *A Great Wall,* pp. 36–37.

74. For an analysis of the impact of the embassy bombing, see Robert A. Pastor, "Is China a Threat or a Partner?: The Logic of the Downward Spiral," *Brown Journal of Foreign Affairs,* Vol. 6, No. 2 (Summer/Fall 1999), pp. 3–13.

75. On "crises in slow motion," see McNamara et al., *Argument Without End,* pp. 396–397.

76. Michel Oksenberg, "The American View of China." In Boren and Perkins, *Preparing America's Foreign Policy for the 21st Century,* pp. 61–66, p. 64.

77. Michel Oksenberg, "China: A Tortuous Path Onto the World's Stage." In Robert A. Pastor, ed., *A Century's Journey: How the Great Powers Shape the World* (New York: Basic Books, 1999), pp. 291–331, p. 294–295.

78. According to Therese Delpech of the Centre d'Etudes et Recherches Internationales, at the Fondation Nationale des Sciences Politiques in Paris, this was the conclusion of French leaders, following 17 hours of intense discussion with Chinese President Jiang Zemin during a state visit to Paris in the fall of 1999. See Fitchett, "Europe Fears Fallout from Taiwan Tensions," pp. 1, 4.

79. Joseph S. Nye, Jr., "Clear Up the Dangerous Ambiguity About Taiwan," *International Herald Tribune,* March 12, 1998, p. 8. See also Robert A. Pastor, "The Paradox of the Double Triangle," *World Policy Journal,* Spring, 2000, pp. 19–30, especially 23–24.

80. We are grateful to China specialist Harry Harding, dean of the Elliott School of International Affairs, George Washington University, for suggesting this possibility.

81. Anders Aslund, "Russia's Collapse," *Foreign Affairs,* Vol. 78, No. 5 (September/October 1999), pp. 64–77, p. 73.

82. Ibid., p. 74.

83. Ibid., p. 73.

84. George Soros, *The Crisis of Global Capitalism: Open Society Endangered* (New York: PublicAffairs, 1998), p. xv.

85. Gerald Segal, "Does China Matter?" *Foreign Affairs,* Vol. 78, No. 5 (September/October 1999), pp. 24–36, p. 24.

86. Michael Howard, *The Causes of Wars, and Other Essays* (Cambridge, MA: Harvard University Press, 1983), pp. 25, 47.

87. Ibid., p. 26.

88. John J. Mearsheimer, "Disorder Restored." In Graham Allison and Gregory F. Treverton, eds., *Rethinking America's Security: Beyond Cold War to New World Order* (New York: Norton, 1992), pp. 213–237, p. 214 (emphasis added).

89. Kenneth Waltz, *Man, the State and War* (New York: Columbia, 1959).

90. Paul Kennedy, "Conclusions." In Lundestad, ed., *The Fall of Great Powers,* pp. 371–381, p. 376.

91. Ibid., pp. 380–381.

92. Immanuel Wallerstein, "Peace, Stability, and Legitimacy, 1990–2025/2050." In Lundestad, ed., *The Fall of Great Powers,* pp. 331–349.

93. Mearsheimer, "Disorder Restored," p. 236.

94. We argue in Chapter Four that such a policy is both dangerous and irresponsible.

95. Gaddis, *The United States and the End of the Cold War,* p. 171.

96. Gilpin, "The Cycle of Great Powers," p. 323.

97. Ibid., p. 324.

98. Henry A. Kissinger, "The Architecture of an American Foreign Policy for the Twenty-first Century." In Boren and Perkins, eds., *Preparing America's Foreign Policy for the 21st Century,* pp. 299–308, p. 302.

99. Ibid., p. 302.

100. Zbigniew Brzezinski, "A Geostrategy for Eurasia." In Boren and Perkins, eds., *Preparing America's Foreign Policy for the 21st Century,* pp. 309–318, pp. 311, 309. (The chapter is reprinted from the October 1997 issue of *Foreign Affairs.*)

101. Ibid., p. 312.

102. Ibid., p. 313.

103. Ibid., p. 312.

104. Ibid., p. 313.

105. Joseph S. Nye, Jr., *Bound to Lead* (New York: Basic Books, 1990).

106. Isaiah Berlin, "The Bent Twig: On the Rise of Nationalism." In Berlin, *The Crooked Timber of Humanity*, ed. by Henry Hardy (New York: Knopf, 1991), pp. 238–261, pp. 260–261.

107. Steinbruner, *Principles of Global Security,* p. 2.

108. Ibid., p. 230.

109. See Therese Delpech, "Is the Violent Century of Wars and Revolutions Really Over?" *International Herald Tribune,* February 3, 2000, p. 8.

110. John F. Kennedy, "Commencement Address at American University, June 10, 1963." In *Public Papers of the Presidents, 1963* (Washington, DC: U.S. Government Printing Office, 1962), pp. 459–464, p. 462.

111. Ignatieff, *The Warriors' Honor,* p. 60.

Chapter 3: Reducing Communal Killing

1. Woodrow Wilson, speech in Paris, May 19, 1919. Quoted in Herbert Hoover, *The Ordeal of Woodrow Wilson* (Washington, DC: Woodrow Wilson Center Press, 1992), p. 263 (originally published in 1958).

2. Stanley Hoffmann, *World Disorders: Troubled Peace in the Post-Cold War Era* (Lanham, MD: Rowman & Littlefield, 1998), p. 152.

3. David Rieff, "A New Age of Liberal Imperialism?" *World Policy Journal*, Vol. 16, No. 2 (Summer 1999), pp. 1–10, p. 10.

4. Michael Ignatieff, *Blood and Belonging: Journeys into the New Nationalism* (New York: Farrar, Straus, and Giroux, 1993), pp. 4–5.

5. See Hoover, *Ordeal of Woodrow Wilson*, pp. 61–81.

6. Ibid., p. 263.

7. Woodrow Wilson, quoted in David Fromkin, *Kosovo Crossing: American Ideals Meet Reality on the Balkan Battlefields* (New York: Free Press, 1999), p. 128.

8. Hoover, *Ordeal of Woodrow Wilson*, pp. 70–74.

9. Ibid., p. 75.

10. John Morton Blum, *Woodrow Wilson and the Politics of Morality* (New York: Harper-Collins, 1956), p. 163.

11. See Scott R. Feil, *Preventing Genocide: How the Early Use of Force Might Have Succeeded in Rwanda* (Washington, DC: Carnegie Commission on Preventing Deadly Conflict, 1998). The chronology at the end is especially useful on the "pre-history" of the genocide. See also William Shawcross, *Deliver Us from Evil: Peacekeepers, Warlords and a World of Endless Conflict* (New York: Simon & Schuster, 2000), pp. 124–145.

12. Harold Nicolson, quoted in Michael Ignatieff, *Virtual War: Kosovo and Beyond* (New York: Metropolitan Books, 2000), p. 20.

13. Woodrow Wilson, quoted in Fromkin, *Kosovo Crossing*, p. 131.

14. Woodrow Wilson, quoted in ibid.

15. Samuel P. Huntington, "The Lonely Superpower," *Foreign Affairs*, Vol. 78, No. 2 (March/April 1999), pp. 35–49, pp. 40–44.

16. Michael Hirsh, "At War with Ourselves," *Harper's Magazine*, Vol. 299, No. 1790 (July 1999), pp. 60–69, p. 62.

17. Anne-Marie Slaughter Burley and Carl Kaysen, "Introductory Note: Emerging Norms of Justified Intervention." In Laura W. Reed and Carl Kaysen, eds., *Emerging Norms of Justified Intervention* (Cambridge, MA: American Academy of Arts and Sciences, 1993), pp. 7–14, p. 9.

18. Reinhold Niebuhr to James B. Conant, March 6, 1946. Quoted in Richard Fox, *Reinhold Niebuhr: A Biography* (New York: Pantheon, 1985), p. 225. We have taken Niebuhr's declarative statement—"how much evil we must do in order to do good"—and turned it into a question.

19. Reinhold Niebuhr, *The Irony of American History* (New York: Scribner's, 1952), p. 39.

20. Thomas Nagel, *Mortal Questions* (New York: Cambridge University Press, 1979), pp. 54–55 (emphasis in the original).

21. Ibid., p. 74.

22. Ignatieff, *Virtual War,* pp. 96–97.

23. Ibid., pp. 95–96. See also William Pfaff, "Now They Tell Us: NATO Missed Most of Its Targets in Kosovo," *Boston Globe,* May 15, 2000, p. A11.

24. Human Rights Watch, *WorldReport 2000* (New York: Human Rights Watch, 2000), pp. xvii–xviii.

25. Paul Ramsey, quoted in James Turner Johnson, *Morality and Contemporary Warfare* (New Haven: Yale University Press, 1999), p. 76.

26. Nagel, *Mortal Questions,* p. 73.

27. See William Pfaff, "Luck Enabled NATO to Win Its Anti-Heroic War," *International Herald Tribune,* July 8, 1999, p. 8.

28. United States Conference of Catholic Bishops, *The Harvest of Justice Is Sown in Peace* (Washington, DC: U.S. Catholic Conference, 1993).

29. Ibid., p. 16.

30. See Michael Walzer, *Just and Unjust Wars: A Moral Argument with Historical Illustrations,* 2nd ed. (New York: Basic Books, 1992), pp. 44–50.

31. Pope John Paul II, quoted in U.S. Bishops, *Harvest of Justice Is Sown in Peace,* p. 15.

32. Canadian General Romeo Dallaire, who commanded UN forces in Rwanda at the time, believes the timely imposition of as few as 5,000 troops could have effectively prevented or ended the killing in Rwanda at any time between April 7 and April 21, 1994. His conclusions are supported in the analysis of Feil, *Preventing Genocide.* Alan J. Kuperman disagrees. His detailed analysis is "Rwanda in Retrospect," *Foreign Affairs,* Vol. 79, No. 1 (January/February 2000), pp. 94–118. Kuperman believes that, at most, perhaps 20–25 percent of the nearly one million killed in Rwanda might have been spared by timely military intervention. The view of Dallaire and Feil is defended by Alison Des Forges of Human Rights Watch in *Foreign Affairs,* Vol. 79, No. 3 (May/June 2000), pp. 141–142, with a response from Kuperman (pp. 142–144).

33. Nagel, *Mortal Questions,* pp. 54–55.

34. Ibid., p. 74.

35. Niebuhr, *Irony of American History,* p. 37.

36. General William T. Sherman, quoted in Michael Howard, "Managing Conflict—The Role of Intervention: Lessons from the Past." In *Managing Conflict in the Post-Cold War World: The Role of Intervention* (a report of the Aspen Institute, Aspen, CO, 1996), pp. 35–43, p. 43.

37. Walzer, *Just and Unjust Wars,* p. 325.

38. Ibid., p. 326.

39. Timothy Garton Ash, "Kosovo: Was It Worth It?" *New York Review of Books,* Vol. 47, No. 14 (September 21, 2000), pp. 50–60, p. 52.

40. Ibid., p. 58.

41. Ibid., p. 57. Garton Ash adapts a comment attributed to Karl Kraus, the great satirist of fin-de-siècle Vienna, regarding psychoanalysis.

42. McNamara et al., *Argument Without End,* p. 394.

43. John Lewis Gaddis, *The United States and the End of the Cold War* (New York: Oxford, 1992), p. 212 (emphasis in the original).

44. See Hoffmann, *World Disorders,* p. 70.

45. Michael J. Smith, "Humanitarian Intervention: An Overview of the Ethical Issues." In

Joel H. Rosenthal, ed., *Ethics and International Affairs,* 2nd ed. (Washington, DC: Georgetown University Press, 1999), pp. 271–295, p. 274.

46. David Rieff, "The Necessity of War," *Los Angeles Times Book Review,* September 3, 2000, p. 7.

47. Jim Hoagland, "Who Wants Peacekeeping? Put Up or Shut Up," *International Herald Tribune,* August 3, 2000, p. 8.

48. Rieff, "Necessity of War," p. 7.

49. Michael Ignatieff, *The Warrior's Honor: Ethnic War and the Modern Conscience* (New York: Metropolitan Books, 1997), pp. 96–97.

50. Ibid., p. 96.

51. Hoffmann, *World Disorders,* p. 151.

52. Ibid., p. 176.

53. We are grateful to Michael Ignatieff for suggesting these characterizations to us.

54. Article 2(7) of the United Nations Charter. Quoted in Lori Fisler Damrosch, "Changing Conceptions of Intervention in International Law." In Reed and Kaysen, eds., *Emerging Norms of Justified Intervention,* pp. 91–110, p. 94 (emphasis added).

55. Chapter VII of the United Nations Charter. Quoted in ibid., p. 94.

56. Ibid., p. 97.

57. Anne Marie Slaughter Burley, "Commentary" (on Lori Fisler Damrosch, "Changing Conceptions of Intervention in International Law"). In Reed and Kaysen, eds., *Emerging Norms of Justified Intervention,* pp. 11–112, p. 111.

58. Boutros-Boutros Ghali, quoted in Ignatieff, *Warrior's Honor,* p. 75.

59. Boutros-Boutros Ghali, quoted in ibid., p. 73.

60. Kofi Annan, "Two Concepts of Sovereignty," *The Economist,* September 18, 1999, pp. 49–50, p. 49.

61. Ibid., p. 50.

62. Stanley Hoffmann, "Commentary" (on Ernst B. Haas, "Beware the Slippery Slope: Notes Toward the Definition of Justifiable Intervention"). In Reed and Kaysen, eds., *Emerging Norms of Justifiable Intervention,* pp. 88–89, p. 89.

63. Huntington, "Lonely Superpower," pp. 40–44.

64. Thucydides, *History of the Peloponnesian War.* Quoted in Joseph S. Nye, Jr., *Understanding International Conflicts,* 2nd ed. (New York: Longman, 1997), p. 17.

65. See Joseph S. Nye, Jr., *Bound to Lead: The Changing Nature of American Power* (New York: Basic Books, 1990).

66. Hubert Védrine, quoted in Gwyn Prins, "The Politics of Intervention." In Jeffrey Boutwell, ed., *Intervention, Sovereignty and International Security* (Cambridge, MA: Pugwash Conferences on Science and World Affairs, 2000), pp. 46–59, p. 47.

67. Boris Yeltsin and Jiang Zemin, "Communiqué" of Summit Conference, December 9–10, 1999. Quoted in ibid., p. 46.

68. Ibid.

69. See Robert Jervis, "Introduction: Approach and Assumptions." In Robert Jervis, Janice Gross Stein, and Richard Ned Lebow, eds., *Psychology and Deterrence* (Baltimore: Johns Hopkins, 1985), pp. 1–12, especially pp. 4–5.

70. Sam Keen, "To Create an Enemy." Quoted in Aaron T. Beck, *Prisoners of Hate: The Cognitive Basis of Anger, Hostility, and Violence* (New York: HarperCollins, 1999), p. 170.

71. Erik H. Erikson, "Reflections on Ethos and War," *Yale Review,* 1984, pp. 481–486.

72. Slaughter Burley, "Commentary," p. 111.

73. Michael Ignatieff, "A Bungling UN Is Undermining Itself," *International Herald Tribune,* May 16, 2000, p. 6. Ignatieff urges the abandonment of UN peacekeeping altogether.

74. Chaim Kaufmann, "Intervention in Ethnic and Ideological Wars: Why One Can Be Done and the Other Can't," *Security Studies,* Vol. 6, No. 1 (Autumn 1996), pp. 62–102, p. 88.

75. Ibid., p. 91.

76. Robert S. McNamara, *In Retrospect: The Tragedy and Lessons of Vietnam,* rev. ed. (New York: Vintage, 1996).

77. See McNamara, et al., *Argument Without End,* pp. 99–150.

78. Averell Harriman, "Memorandum of Conversation with Secretary McNamara," August 22, 1967. Quoted in McNamara, *In Retrospect,* p. 300.

79. See McNamara, et al., *Argument Without End,* pp. 111–115.

80. Charles de Gaulle, "News Conference of July 23, 1964." In Marcus G. Raskin and Bernard B. Fall, eds., *The Viet-Nam Reader: Articles and Documents on American Foreign Policy and the Viet-Nam Crisis* (New York: Random House, 1965), pp. 268–271, pp. 270–271.

81. Dean Rusk (as told to Richard Rusk; ed. by Daniel S. Papp), *As I Saw It* (New York: Norton, 1990), p. 268.

82. Hoffmann, *World Disorders,* p. 152.

83. Ignatieff, *Warrior's Honor,* pp. 189–190.

84. David Rohde, "Kosovo Seething," *Foreign Affairs,* Vol. 79, No. 3 (May/June 2000), pp. 66–79, p. 69.

85. Ibid., p. 76.

86. General Douglas MacArthur, quoted in Ian Buruma, "MacArthur's Children," *New York Review of Books,* Vol. 46, No. 16 (October 21, 1999), pp. 33–37, p. 33.

87. Rieff, "A New Age of Liberal Imperialism?" p. 10.

88. Rieff, "New Age of Liberal Imperialism?"

89. Stanley Hoffmann, *World Disorders: Troubled Peace in the Post-Cold War Era* (Lanham, MD: Rowman & Littlefield, 1998), p. 233.

90. See Michael Ignatieff, "The Reluctant Imperialist," *New York Times Magazine,* August 10, 2000, pp. 42–47, especially p. 44.

91. Bernard Kouchner, quoted in ibid., p. 45.

92. Rohde, "Kosovo Seething," p. 66.

93. Smith, "Humanitarian Intervention," pp. 289–290.

94. Ibid., p. 290.

95. Walzer, *Just and Unjust Wars,* p. 107.

96. I. William Zartman, "Intervening to Prevent State Collapse." In James P. Muldoon, JoAnn Fagot Aviel, Richard Reitano, and Earl Sullivan, eds., *Multilateral Diplomacy and the United Nations Today* (Boulder, CO: Westview, 1999), pp. 68–77, p. 75.

97. Ignatieff, *Warrior's Honor,* p. 4. See pp. 9–33 generally on ethical issues associated with television coverage of "man-made" humanitarian disasters.

98. "Human Rights Ideals," editorial (from the *New York Times*) in the *International Her-*

ald Tribune, December 9, 1999, p. 8; Michael Ignatieff, "Human Rights: The Midlife Crisis," *New York Review of Books,* May 20, 1999, pp. 58–62.

99. Stephen Lewis, "After Rwanda, the World Doesn't Look the Same," *International Herald Tribune,* July 10, 2000, p. 8.

100. Hoffmann, *World Disorders,* pp. 65–66.

101. Ibid., p. 172.

102. Michael Ignatieff, "The Next President's Duty to Intervene," *New York Times,* February 13, 2000, Section 4, p. 17.

103. Convention on the Prevention and Punishment of the Crime of Genocide (1948). Quoted in Diane F. Orentlicher, "Genocide." In Roy Gutman and David Rieff, eds., *Crimes of War: What the Public Should Know* (New York: Norton, 1999), pp. 153–157, pp. 153–154.

104. Ignatieff, "Next President's Duty to Intervene," p. 17.

105. Wayne S. Smith, interview with James G. Blight, Miami, Florida, January 8, 1991. Smith's first posting in the foreign service was in the Havana embassy in 1957. Later, during the Carter administration, he was chief of the U.S. Interests Section in Havana.

106. See Ignatieff, *Virtual War,* pp. 91–112; see also Michael Mandelbaum, "A Perfect Failure: NATO's War Against Yugoslavia," *Foreign Affairs,* Vol. 78, No. 5 (September/October 1999), pp. 2–8.

107. Carl Kaysen suggested this to the authors at a conference held at the American Academy of Arts and Sciences, Cambridge, MA, at which the first draft of the manuscript for this book was reviewed.

108. Stanley Hoffmann, quoted in Smith, "Humanitarian Intervention," p. 286.

109. Warren Zimmermann, *Origins of a Catastrophe* (New York: Times Books, 1999), p. 237.

110. Niebuhr, *Irony of American History,* p. 41.

111. Karl E. Meyer, "Enforcing Human Rights," *World Policy Journal,* Vol. 16, No. 3 (Fall 1999), pp. 45–50. The three headings are ours, not Meyer's.

112. Ibid., p. 50.

113. Richard Holbrooke, *To End a War* (New York: Random House, 1998), p. 365.

114. Hoffmann, *World Disorders,* p. 176.

115. Richard Holbrooke, quoted in Hirsh, "At War with Ourselves," pp. 66–67.

116. Ronald Steel, "Mr. Fix-It," *New York Review of Books,* Vol. 47, No. 15 (October 5, 2000), pp. 19–21, p. 19.

117. Woodrow Wilson, quoted in Hoover, *Ordeal of Woodrow Wilson,* p. ix.

118. Louis Auchincloss, *Woodrow Wilson* (New York: Penguin, 2000), p. 95.

Chapter 4: Avoiding Nuclear Catastrophe

1. Woodrow Wilson, quoted in Frank Ninkovich, *The Wilsonian Century: American Foreign Policy Since 1900* (Chicago: University of Chicago Press, 1999), p. 72 (emphasis added).

2. Australian Ministry of Foreign Affairs, *Report of the Canberra Commission on the Elimination of Nuclear Weapons* (Canberra: Australian Government Printing Office, 1996), pp. 7, 9. (Emphasis added.)

3. The statement was first made at a historical conference in Moscow on the Cuban missile crisis, involving high-level former officials from the United States, the Soviet Union, and Cuba. See Bruce J. Allyn, James G. Blight, and David A. Welch, eds., *Back to the Brink: Proceedings of the Moscow Conference on the Cuban Missile Crisis, January 27–28, 1989* (Lanham, MD: University Press of America, 1992); and the Afterword to the second edition of James G. Blight and David A. Welch, *On the Brink: Americans and Soviets Reexamine the Cuban Missile Crisis* (New York: Hill and Wang/Noonday, 1990), pp. 325–350.

4. Dr. Hans Bethe, a Nobel Laureate in physics and a leader of the team of Los Alamos scientists who designed the first atomic bomb, reviewed a draft of this chapter and said that "it was the best that has ever been written on the subject [of nuclear danger]." However, he questions the wisdom of the declared nuclear powers completely eliminating nuclear weapons. He worries that there are "rogue" leaders who, in the face of complete elimination of nuclear weapons by the established nuclear powers, might attempt nuclear blackmail. To prevent this, he suggests that the nuclear powers might each retain "a few" nuclear weapons. His suggestion deserves full debate. But the issue need not be decided immediately. At least ten years will be required to reduce, in a verifiable way, the current global inventory of nuclear warheads from approximately 20,000 nuclear warheads to "a few."

5. See Ninkovich, *Wilsonian Century*, p. 49.

6. Woodrow Wilson, quoted in ibid., p. 72 (emphasis added).

7. Woodrow Wilson, quoted in ibid., pp. 64, 66. See also Stanley Hoffmann, *World Disorders: Troubled Peace in the Post–Cold War Era* (Lanham, MD: Rowman & Littlefield, 1998), pp. 67–68, on Judith Shklar's "liberalism of fear."

8. Ninkovich, *Wilsonian Century*, p. 77.

9. Bernard Brodie, *The Absolute Weapon* (New York: Harcourt, Brace, 1946), p. 76.

10. On the Baruch Plan, see Albert Carnesale, Paul Doty, Stanley Hoffmann, Samuel P. Huntington, Joseph S. Nye, Jr., and Scott D. Sagan, *Living with Nuclear Weapons* (New York: Bantam, 1983) pp. 80–81.

11. The number 100,000 is used by Nobel Peace Prize–winner Josef Rotblat, a cofounder of the Pugwash Conferences, who worked for a time as a physicist on the Manhattan Project. Jonathan Schell uses this number as well, indicating that 100,000 was reached sometime in the mid–1980s. See Jonathan Schell, *The Gift of Time: The Case for Abolishing Nuclear Weapons Now* (New York: Metropolitan Books, 1998), pp. 53–54, 68–69.

12. Dwight D. Eisenhower, quoted in Robert Jervis, *The Meaning of the Nuclear Revolution: Statecraft and the Prospect of Armageddon* (Ithaca, NY: Cornell University Press, 1989), pp. 4–5.

13. Charles de Gaulle, quoted in ibid., p. 1.

14. Nikita S. Khrushchev, quoted in ibid., p. 20.

15. Khrushchev, quoted in ibid.

16. These figures are cited in John D. Steinbruner, *Principles of Global Security* (Washington, DC: Brookings, 2000), pp. 26–34, and derived from several databases, especially William M. Arkin, Robert S. Norris, and Joshua Handler, *Taking Stock: Worldwide Nuclear Deployments 1998* (Washington, DC: National Resources Defense Council Nuclear Program, March 1998).

17. Steinbruner, *Principles of Global Security,* p. 24.
18. Australian Ministry of Foreign Affairs, *Report of the Canberra Commission,* p. 9.
19. International Physicians for the Prevention of Nuclear War (IPPNW), *Briefing Book on Nuclear War, 1992.* Quoted in Charles J. Moxley, Jr., *Nuclear Weapons and International Law in the Post Cold War World* (Lanham, MD: Austin & Winfield, 2000), p. 423.
20. IPPNW, *Briefing Book on Nuclear War, 1992.* In Moxley, *Nuclear Weapons and International Law in the Post Cold War World,* pp. 421–423.
21. Testimony of Mr. Iccho Itoh, Mayor of Nagasaki, November 7, 1995, to the International Court of Justice. Quoted in Moxley, *Nuclear Weapons and International Law in the Post Cold War World,* p. 432.
22. Personal communication to the authors from a former senior U.S. military officer.
23. Personal communications to the authors from individuals familiar with plans for U.S. nuclear forces.
24. Bruce G. Blair, "America Doesn't Need All These Warheads," *International Herald Tribune,* June 14, 2000, p. 6.
25. Ibid., p. 6. See also Blair, *The Logic of Accidental Nuclear War* (Washington, DC: Brookings, 1993); and Harold A. Feiveson, ed., *The Nuclear Turning Point: A Blueprint for Deep Cuts and De-alerting of Nuclear Weapons* (Washington, DC: Brookings, 1999), especially Chapter 6 ("De-alerting Strategic Nuclear Forces"), written by Blair.
26. See Herman Kahn, *On Escalation* (Baltimore: Penguin, 1968).
27. Steinbruner, *Principles of Global Security,* p. 25.
28. Jonathan Schell, "The Folly of Arms Control," *Foreign Affairs,* Vol. 79, No. 5 (September/October 2000), pp. 22–46, p. 27.
29. On the "loose nukes" issue, see Graham Allison, Owen Cote, Jr., Richard Falkenrath, and Steven Miller, *Avoiding Nuclear Anarchy: Containing the Threat of Loose Russian Nuclear Weapons and Fissile Material* (Cambridge, MA: MIT Press, 1996).
30. Ashton B. Carter and William J. Perry, *Preventive Defense: A New Security Strategy for America* (Washington, DC: Brookings, 1999), pp. 89–90.
31. The case is presented in Moxley, *Nuclear Weapons and International Law in the Post Cold War World,* pp. 155–250.
32. Nuclear Weapons Advisory Opinion of the International Court of Justice (1996), dissenting opinion of Judge Shahabuddeen of Guyana. Quoted in ibid., p. 186.
33. J. Robert Oppenheimer, quoted in James G. Blight, *The Shattered Crystal Ball: Fear and Learning in the Cuban Missile Crisis* (Lanham, MD: Rowman & Littlefield, 1990), p. xix.
34. Bernard Brodie, *Strategy in the Missile Age* (Princeton, NJ: Princeton University Press, 1959).
35. U.S. National Conference of Catholic Bishops, *The Challenge of Peace: God's Promise and Our Response* (Washington, DC: U.S. Catholic Conference, 1983), p. vii (emphasis added).
36. Technically, the Reverend Hehir is called the Chairman of the Executive Committee of Harvard Divinity School. Although he occupies the office of the dean and carries out the dean's duties, the term "Chairman" is preferred by the Roman Catholic Diocese of Boston, and the special nomenclature has been accepted by Harvard.
37. J. Bryan Hehir, "Moral Issues in Deterrence Policy." In Douglass MacLean, ed., *The Security Gamble: Deterrence Dilemmas in the Nuclear Age* (Totowa, NJ: Rowman & Allanheld, 1984), pp. 53–71, p. 58.

38. Ibid., p. 48.

39. See, for example, Wohlstetter, "Bishops, Statesmen, and Other Strategists on the Bombing of Innocents."

40. Ibid., pp. iii–iv.

41. Ibid., p. 43.

42. Ibid., p. 63.

43. U.S. Catholic Bishops, *Challenge of Peace*, p. 55.

44. Hehir, "Moral Issues in Deterrence Policy," p. 69.

45. The transcripts of the audiotaped deliberations of the Executive Committee during the crisis are now available, thanks to the Herculean efforts of Ernest R. May and Philip D. Zelikow, the editors of *The Kennedy Tapes: Inside the White House During the Cuban Missile Crisis* (Cambridge, MA: Harvard University Press, 1997).

46. James G. Blight, Bruce J. Allyn, and David A. Welch, *Cuba on the Brink: Castro, the Missile Crisis and the Soviet Collapse* (New York: Pantheon, 1993), pp. 56–63, and *passim*.

47. General Anatoly Gribkov elaborated on these points in a meeting at the Woodrow Wilson Center, Washington, D.C., on April 5, 1994.

48. The evidence from all sides is presented and evaluated in Aleksandr Fursenko and Timothy Naftali, *"One Hell of a Gamble": Khrushchev, Castro & Kennedy, 1958–1964—The Secret History of the Cuban Missile Crisis* (New York: Norton, 1997). On why the three sides' intelligence services were so mistaken, see James G. Blight and David A. Welch, eds., *Intelligence and the Cuban Missile Crisis* (London: Cass, 1998).

49. See Anatoly Dokochaev, "Afterword to Sensational 100 Day Nuclear Cruise," *Krasnaya Zvezda*, November 6, 1992, p. 2; and V. Badurikin interview with Dimitri Volkogonov in "Operation Anadyr," *Trud*, October 27, 1993, p. 3.

50. Blight et al. *Cuba on the Brink*, pp. 250–251.

51. Fidel Castro, in ibid., p. 251.

52. Fidel Castro, in ibid., p. 252.

53. Identical conclusions were reached by the Canberra Commission, *op. cit* and the Carnegie Commission, *Preventing Deadly Conflict* (Washington, DC: Carnegie Commission on Preventing Deadly Conflict, 1997).

54. Deuteronomy 30:19–20. Quoted in U.S. Catholic Bishops, *Challenge of Peace*, pp. 91–92.

55. Frances FitzGerald, *Way Out There in the Blue: Reagan, Star Wars and the End of the Cold War* (New York: Simon & Schuster, 2000). The title comes from playwright Arthur Miller's epitaph for Willy Loman in *Death of a Salesman*: "He's a man way out there in the blue, riding on a smile and a shoeshine."

56. Ronald Reagan, quoted in ibid., p. 20.

57. Ronald Reagan, quoted in ibid., p. 207.

58. Ronald Reagan, quoted in ibid., p. 208.

59. See, for example, George N. Lewis, Theodore A. Postal, and John Pike, "Why National Missile Defense Won't Work," *Scientific American*, August 1999, pp. 36–41.

60. Joseph S. Nye, Jr., *Nuclear Ethics* (New York: Free Press, 1986), pp. 125–126.

61. Edward Teller, quoted in John Newhouse, *War and Peace in the Nuclear Age* (New York: Knopf, 1988), p. 204.

62. I have refreshed my memory of the Glassboro summit by consulting the following: McGeorge Bundy, *Danger and Survival: Choices About the Bomb in the First Fifty Years*

(New York: Random House, 1988), pp. 549–550; Anatoly Dobrynin, *In Confidence: Moscow's Ambassador to America's Six Cold War Presidents* (New York: Times Books, 1995), pp. 162–167; and Newhouse, *War and Peace in the Nuclear Age,* pp. 203–206.

63. Newhouse, *War and Peace in the Nuclear Age,* p. 233.

64. Personal communications to the authors from Gen. Viktor Staradubov and Gen. Nikolai Detinov, members of the Soviet delegation to the talks leading to the ABM Treaty.

65. See FitzGerald, *Way Out There in the Blue,* pp. 494–496.

66. George W. Bush, quoted in Peter Boyer, "When Missiles Collide," *New Yorker,* September 11, 2000, pp. 42–48, pp. 47–48.

67. "A Missile Defense Pause," *International Herald Tribune,* September 4, 2000, p. 12.

68. Igor Ivanov, "The Missile-Defense Mistake: Undermining Strategic Stability and the ABM Treaty," *Foreign Affairs,* Vol. 79, No. 5 (September/October 2000), pp. 15–20, p. 15.

69. Ibid., p. 16 (emphasis added).

70. General Igor Sergeyev, quoted in David Hoffmann, "Russia Assails U.S. on Missile Plan," *International Herald Tribune,* July 1–2, 2000, p. 2.

71. General Leonid Ivashov, quoted in ibid.

72. On Theater Missile Defense (TMD), see John Deutch, Harold Brown, and John P. White, "National Missile Defense: Is There Another Way? In *Foreign Policy,* Summer 2000, pp. 91–100.

73. See John C. Polanyi, "Collaboration, Not a Missile Shield, Is the Best Defense Solution," *International Herald Tribune,* August 18, 2000, p. 4. Polanyi is a member of a committee of the American Academy of Arts and Sciences that is studying the Joint Data Exchange Center.

74. John Pomfret, "Beijing Issues Warning on U.S. Missile System," *International Herald Tribune,* July 14, 2000, p. 5.

75. Lloyd Axworthy, quoted in Doug Struck, "Allies Signal Opposition to a U.S. Missile Shield," *International Herald Tribune,* July 14, 2000, p. 1.

76. Hubert Védrine, quoted in ibid.

77. William J. Perry, "Lessons of the Cold War," *Carnegie Reporter,* Summer 2000, pp. 30–41, p. 41.

78. Ibid., p. 41 (emphasis added).

79. Sigmund Freud, *The Future of an Illusion,* trans. and ed. by James Strachey, Vol. 21 of *The Complete Psychological Works of Sigmund Freud* (London: Hogarth, 1928), pp. 3–56, especially pp. 30–33.

80. FitzGerald, *Way Out There in the Blue,* pp. 24–25.

81. Robert S. McNamara, "The Military Role of Nuclear Weapons: Perceptions and Misperceptions," was published in *Foreign Affairs* in the Fall 1983 issue. It is reprinted in full in William P. Bundy, ed., *The Nuclear Controversy: A Foreign Affairs Reader* (New York: Meridian, 1985), pp. 77–98. The quotation in the text is from pp. 97–98 in the Bundy, ed., anthology.

82. General G. Lee Butler, quoted in Schell, *Gift of Time,* p. 199–208.

83. McGeorge Bundy, William J. Crowe, Jr., and Sidney Drell, *Reducing Nuclear Danger: The Road Away From the Brink* (New York: Council on Foreign Relations, 1993), p. 100.

84. General Andrew Goodpaster, Chair, *An Evolving Nuclear Posture* (Washington, DC: The Stimson Center, December 1995).

85. Australian Ministry of Foreign Affairs, *Report of the Canberra Commission,* August 1996, p. 7.

86. Committee on International Security and Arms Control, *The Future of U.S. Nuclear Weapons Policy* (Washington, DC: National Academy of Sciences Press, 1997), p. 59.

87. Ibid., p. 80.

88. Lord Louis Mountbatten, quoted in Solly Zuckerman, *Nuclear Illusion and Reality* (New York: Viking, 1982), p. 70.

89. Lord Michael Carver, quoted in the *London Sunday Times,* February 21, 1982.

90. Henry Kissinger, "NATO Defense and the Soviet Threat, *Survival,* November–December 1979, p. 266.

91. Melvin Laird, quoted in the *Washington Post,* April 12, 1982.

92. Helmut Schmidt, statement made in a BBC Radio interview with Stuart Simon, July 16, 1987.

93. Admiral Noel Gayler, "The Way Out: A General Nuclear Settlement." In Gwin Prins, ed., *The Nuclear Crisis Reader* (New York: Vintage, 1984), pp. 234–243, p. 234.

94. General Larry Welch to Adam Scheinman, March 21, 1994.

95. General Charles Horner, quoted in *The Boston Globe,* July 16, 1994.

96. See Jonathan Schell, *The Gift of Time,* pp. 183–186.

97. This is the preferred formulation of both the Canberra Commission (see its *Report on the Elimination of Nuclear Weapons)* and the Committee on International Security and Arms Control, (see *The Future of U.S. Nuclear Weapons Policy.)*

98. John P. Holdren, "Getting to Zero: Too Difficult? Too Dangerous? Too Distracting?" In Maxwell Bruce and Tom Milne, eds., *Ending War: The Force of Reason* (New York: St. Martin's, 1999), pp. 33–56, pp. 52–53.

99. See, for example, the "Special Report" of George Rathjens, the secretary general of the Pugwash group, concerning two meetings on the nuclear threat held in early 2000: one in La Jolla, California, January 15–16; and one in London, March 3–4. In *Pugwash Newsletter,* June 2000, pp. 2–7, especially p. 4, in which Rathjens criticizes the Canberra Commission on the issue of whether or not nuclear weapons have been sufficiently delegitimized to warrant movement toward zero nuclear weapons among the major powers.

100. See Holdren, "Getting to Zero," p. 54.

101. Lord Michael Carver, quoted in Schell, *Gift of Time,* p. 131.

102. Steinbruner, *Principles of Global Security,* p. 67.

103. Australian Ministry of Foreign Affairs, *Report of the Canberra Commission,* pp. 50–51.

104. See Barbara Crossette, "Five Atom Powers Agree to Scrap Arms," *International Herald Tribune,* May 22, 2000, p. 6.

105. Australian Ministry of Foreign Affairs, *Report of the Canberra Commission,* pp. 52–63.

106. Ibid., pp. 64–65.

107. Ibid., p. 66.

108. This point is made by Steinbruner, in *Principles of Global Security,* p. 84.

109. Paul Ramsey, quoted in Walzer, *Just and Unjust Wars,* p. 270.

110. Walzer, ibid., p. 271.

111. Ibid.

112. On the Vietnam war as a "crisis in slow motion," see Robert S. McNamara, James G.

Blight, and Robert K. Brigham, with contributions by Thomas Biersteker and Col. Herbert Schandler, *Argument Without End: In Search of Answers to the Vietnam Tragedy* (New York: PublicAffairs, 1999), pp. 396–397.

113. See Herman Kahn, *On Escalation: Metaphors and Scenarios* (Baltimore: Penguin, 1968), and Brodie, *Absolute Weapon.*

114. Ninkovich, *Wilsonian Century,* p. 72.

Chapter 5: Reducing Human Carnage

1. Woodrow Wilson, speech in St. Louis, Missouri, September 1919. Quoted in Louis Auchincloss, *Woodrow Wilson* (New York: Penguin, 2000), p. 116.

2. Frank Ninkovich, *The Wilsonian Century: U.S. Foreign Policy Since 1900* (Chicago: University of Chicago Press, 1999), p. 48.

3. Carnegie Commission on Preventing Deadly Conflict, *Preventing Deadly Conflict: Final Report with Executive Summary* (Washington, DC: Carnegie Commission, 1997), p. xii.

4. Samuel P. Huntington, "The Lonely Superpower," *Foreign Affairs,* Vol. 78, No. 2 (March/April 1999).

5. John Steinbruner, *Principles of Global Security* (Washington, DC: Brookings, 2000), p. 212.

6. Isaiah Berlin, "The Bent Twig: On the Rise of Nationalism." In *The Crooked Timber of Humanity: Chapters in the History of Ideas* (New York: Knopf, 1991), pp. 238–261, p. 261.

7. Thomas Nagel, *Mortal Questions* (New York, Oxford University Press, 1979), pp. 53–74.

8. Reinhold Niebuhr, quoted in Richard Fox, *Reinhold Niebuhr: A Biography* (New York: Pantheon, 1986), p. 225.

9. Michael Ignatieff, "The Seductiveness of Moral Disgust." In *The Warrior's Honor: Ethnic War and the Modern Conscience* (New York: Metropolitan Books, 1997), pp. 72–108.

10. Australian Ministry of Foreign Affairs, *Report of the Canberra Commission,* (Canberra: Australian Government Printing Office, 1996).

Epilogue: Listening to Wilson's Ghost

1. Woodrow Wilson, September 8, 1919. Quoted in Herbert Hoover, *The Ordeal of Woodrow Wilson* (Washington, DC: Woodrow Wilson Center for Scholars, 1992), p. ix (first published in 1958).

2. Ronald Steel, "Mr. Fix-It," *New York Review of Books,* October 5, 2000, pp. 19–21, p. 21.

3. R. G. Collingwood, quoted in Jonathan Glover, *Humanity: A Moral History of the Twentieth Century* (New Haven: Yale University Press, 2000), p. 411.

4. See, for example, James G. Blight, Bruce J. Allyn, and David A. Welch, *Cuba on the Brink: Castro, the Missile Crisis and the Soviet Collapse* (New York: Pantheon, 1993); and Robert McNamara, James G. Blight, and Robert K. Brigham, with contributions by

Thomas Biersteker and Col. Herbert Schandler, *Argument Without End: In Search of Answers to the Vietnam Tragedy* (New York: PublicAffairs, 1999).

5. Steel, "Mr. Fix-it," p. 21.

6. Archibald MacLeish, "The Young Dead Soldiers." Quoted in Gloria Emerson, *Winners and Losers: Battles, Retreats, Gains, Losses, and Ruins from the Vietnam War* (New York: Penguin, 1976), p. 365.

ACKNOWLEDGMENTS

S OME OF THE POSITIONS developed in *Wilson's Ghost* have been evolving for many years, chiefly in dozens of public lectures given around the globe by Robert McNamara. He thanks the administration of those universities and institutions at which he has lectured on the issues taken up in *Wilson's Ghost*. These include the University of Edinburgh, Ben-Gurion University, the University of California, Berkeley, Harvard University's John F. Kennedy School of Government, and especially Brown University's Thomas J. Watson Jr. Institute for International Studies. Still other ideas in the book have germinated during our nearly 15 years of joint research on the lessons of the Cold War for the future.

All of them began to combust into this book as we traveled with our colleague, Professor Robert K. Brigham of Vassar College, discussing our 1999 book, *Argument Without End: In Search of Answers to the Vietnam Tragedy*. At each of the several dozen lectures, seminars, and colloquia in which we have participated together, a good deal of attention has been given to the lessons of that war—and of the tragic history of the 20th century generally—for the 21st century. We thank Bob Brigham for working with us in many settings to craft the argument underlying this book.

It took a decisive conversation with our publisher, Peter Osnos, to embolden us to draft a book as wide-ranging as this one. And it was Peter who first insisted that the book be a manifesto, a call to action, and that it be written so as to engage the general reader while, at the same time, it should be challenging to specialists in international affairs and public policy.

We are particularly indebted to Dr. Svetlana Savranskaya, of the National Security Archive at George Washington University in Washington, D.C. She worked for several months at the outset of the process as our full-time research assistant and did a marvelous job of supplying us everything we asked for, and more. She also translated many articles for us from Russian into English.

We are also deeply grateful to the American Academy of Arts and Sciences in Cambridge, Massachusetts, for hosting a two-day critique of the first draft of the manuscript of *Wilson's Ghost*. In particular, thanks are due to Carl Kaysen, co-director of the Academy's Committee on International Security, and to George Rathjens, secretary general of the Pugwash Conferences on Science and World Affairs, for co-sponsoring and co-chairing the two days of discussions. Other participants in the manuscript review conference were: Francis Bator, professor of economics emeritus, Harvard University; Jeffrey Boutwell, executive director of Pugwash; James Der Derian, professor of international relations (research), Brown University; Mark Garrison, former director of the Center for Foreign Policy Development, Brown University; Raymond L. Garthoff, retired State Department and CIA official; Paul Golob, executive editor, PublicAffairs; Harry Harding, dean of the Elliott School of International Affairs, George Washington University; J. Bryan Hehir, dean of the Harvard Divinity School; P. Terrence Hopmann, professor of political science, Brown University; Michael Ignatieff, Carr visiting professor of human rights, John F. Kennedy School of Government, Harvard University; janet M. Lang, senior research associate, Watson Institute for International Studies, Brown University; Martin Malin, executive director, Committee on International Security, American Academy of Arts and Sciences; Steven E. Miller, director of studies, Belfer Center for Science and International Affairs, Harvard University; Peter Osnos, publisher and chief executive officer, PublicAffairs; John C. Polanyi, professor of chemistry, University of Toronto; Barry Posen, professor of political science, Massachusetts Institute of Technology; Stephen Van Evera, associate professor of political science, Massachusetts Institute of Technology; and David A. Welch, professor of political science, University of Toronto. We are indebted to all the participants for taking the time to read and constructively criticize the manuscript. We also benefitted from very helpful written critiques of the manuscript from three scholars who, as usual, did not let their close ties to both authors prevent the dispensation of tough, wide-ranging, and very helpful criticism: Mark Garrison, Robert A. Pastor, and David A. Welch.

We also extend our gratitude to Prof. Thomas J. Biersteker, director of the Watson Institute for International Studies at Brown University, for his support for this project over the past two years. The Watson Institute provided not only a home base for it, but a seminar at which we first tried out some of our ideas publicly, with the associate director and professor of history Abbott (Tom) Gleason in the chair. We also thank the members of the Watson Institute staff who facilitated this project in various ways: Susan Costa, Sheila Fournier, Rebecca Garner, Cynthia Gurdjian, Jean Lawlor, Margareta Levitsky, and Nancy Soukup.

Paul Golob, our editor at PublicAffairs, has done a superb job of helping us pull together into a coherent package the disparate ideas and issues dealt with in the book. His hands-on approach has been much appreciated by both of us.

Finally, janet M. Lang helped us as always to see our way through or around many otherwise difficult obstacles on the road to publication. janet's clarity of vision and purpose over the past year, especially, provided a living example of the wisdom of a famous line from the American poet Theodore Roethke: "In a dark time, the eye begins to see."

While we are delighted to acknowledge the assistance of all these people, we alone remain responsible for errors of fact or interpretation in the book.

ROBERT S. MCNAMARA
JAMES G. BLIGHT

ABOUT THE AUTHORS

ROBERT S. McNAMARA was Secretary of Defense to Presidents John F. Kennedy and Lyndon B. Johnson from 1961 to 1968. He came to the Defense Department from the Ford Motor Company, where he was president. From 1968 to 1981, he was president of the World Bank. Among his books are *The Essence of Security*; *One Hundred Countries, Two Billion People: The McNamara Years at the World Bank*; *Blundering into Disaster*; and *Out of the Cold*. He is the author most recently of *In Retrospect: The Tragedy and Lessons of Vietnam* (1995) and *Argument Without End: In Search of Lessons to the Vietnam Tragedy* (1999), written with James G. Blight and Robert K. Brigham, with contributions by Thomas J. Biersteker and Col. Herbert Schandler. He was a member of the Canberra Commission on the Elimination of Nuclear Weapons (1996). He resides in Washington, D.C.

JAMES G. BLIGHT is Professor of International Relations (Research) at Brown University's Thomas J. Watson Jr. Institute for International Studies. He came to the Watson Institute from Harvard's John F. Kennedy School of Government, where he was a research fellow from 1984 to 1990. Among his books are *Cuba on the Brink: Castro, the Missile Crisis and the Soviet Collapse* (1993), written with Bruce J. Allyn and David A. Welch, *Politics of Illusion: The Bay of Pigs Invasion Reexamined* (1998), written with Peter Kornbluh, and *Argument Without End: In Search of Answers to the Vietnam Tragedy*.

INDEX

PUBLICAFFAIRS is a new nonfiction publishing house and a tribute to the standards, values, and flair of three persons who have served as mentors to countless reporters, writers, editors, and book people of all kinds, including me.

I.F. STONE, proprietor of *I. F. Stone's Weekly*, combined a commitment to the First Amendment with entrepreneurial zeal and reporting skill and became one of the great independent journalists in American history. At the age of eighty, Izzy published *The Trial of Socrates*, which was a national bestseller. He wrote the book after he taught himself ancient Greek.

BENJAMIN C. BRADLEE was for nearly thirty years the charismatic editorial leader of *The Washington Post*. It was Ben who gave the *Post* the range and courage to pursue such historic issues as Watergate. He supported his reporters with a tenacity that made them fearless, and it is no accident that so many became authors of influential, best-selling books.

ROBERT L. BERNSTEIN, the chief executive of Random House for more than a quarter century, guided one of the nation's premier publishing houses. Bob was personally responsible for many books of political dissent and argument that challenged tyranny around the globe. He is also the founder and was the longtime chair of Human Rights Watch, one of the most respected human rights organizations in the world.

·   ·   ·

For fifty years, the banner of Public Affairs Press was carried by its owner Morris B. Schnapper, who published Gandhi, Nasser, Toynbee, Truman, and about 1,500 other authors. In 1983 Schnapper was described by *The Washington Post* as "a redoubtable gadfly." His legacy will endure in the books to come.

Peter Osnos, *Publisher*